Russian America:
The Forgotten Frontier

ENGRAVING from a drawing by Gavriil Sarychev of a temporary camp on Chugach Bay, 1790.
From Sarychev Atlas. Alaska and Polar Regions Deptartment, Elmer E. Rasmuson Library, University of Alaska, Fairbanks.

Edited by Barbara Sweetland Smith and Redmond J. Barnett

Published in conjunction with the exhibition, "Russian America: The Forgotten Frontier."
Jointly produced by the Washington State Historical Society and
the Anchorage Museum of History and Art.

Published by the Washington State Historical Society, Tacoma, Washington
1990

Production Coordinator and Photo Editor: *Richard Frederick*
Designer: *Amy Hines*
Printer: *Publishers Press*
Typographer: *Christina Orange*
Copy Editor: *Judith C. Gouldthorpe*
© Copyright 1990 by The Washington State Historical Society

The production of this book has been made possible by generous grants from the National Endowment for the Humanities and Puget Sound Bank. It was prepared in conjunction with the traveling exhibition "Russian America: The Forgotten Frontier," a joint project of the Washington State Historical Society and the Anchorage Museum of History and Art. The exhibition was curated by Barbara Sweetland Smith and supported by a major grant from the National Endowment for the Humanities and additional grants from foundations, corporations and individuals.

Front Cover: *Kotleian - Toien of Sitka Island with His Wife*, by Mikhail T. Tikhanov, 1818. Paper, watercolor, lead pencil. Kotleian was a member of the Kiksa'di moiety and a leader of the Tlingits who destroyed the Russian fortress at Old Sitka in 1802. He wears an imperial Russian medal, given to him as a peace offering by his old adversary Baranov. His wife, shown both in profile and full-face, sits near the *toien*. In the background is the Russian fortress at New Archangel (Sitka) and the sloop *Kamchatka*, on which the artist traveled around the world. (Collection of the Scientific Research Museum of the Academy of Arts, USSR; photograph courtesy of the Shur Collection, Elmer E. Rasmuson Library, University of Alaska, Fairbanks.)
Back Cover: *Pribiloff Island View*, a watercolor by Louis Choris, ca. 1818. Choris was expedition artist with the Otto von Kotzebue round-the-world expedition of 1815-1818. The ship in the background is the *Riurik*. (Alaska State Library, Juneau.)

Library of Congress Cataloging in Publication Data
Russian-America: The Forgotten Frontier
  256 p.
  Includes bibliographical references.

  ISBN 0-917048-65-2
  1. Russians—Alaska—History—Exhibitions.
  2. Alaska—History—Exhibitions.
  3. Russians—North America—History—Exhibitions.
I. Washington State Historical Society.
F907.R963 1990
979.8'0049171073—dc20
90-38339 CIP

Table *of* Contents

RUSSIANS AND NATIVE AMERICANS

RUSSIA'S LEGACY IN NORTH AMERICA

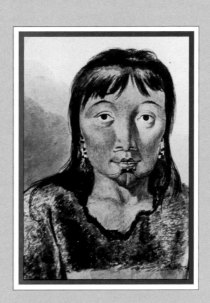

Acknowledgments

This book accompanies a major exhibition, "Russian America: The Forgotten Frontier." The organization of this ambitious project and its companion volume could not have been accomplished without the support and resourcefulness of many individuals and organizations.

Curators and registrars of museums and libraries that contributed artifacts, artwork, and photographs frequently extended themselves to be of assistance. Too numerous to mention, they gave help and support that made the exhibit possible.

We would also like to acknowledge the tireless support of Betty Berry, volunteer assistant to the curator. In addition, the National Park Service, Alaska Region, provided a curatorial management database as well as professional services that were invaluable to the project. Special thanks to Garry Davies, Connie Estep and Pat McKnight. The Alaska State Office of History and Archaeology was of assistance to the curator in the search for artifacts. Most especially, Patricia B. Wolf, director of the Anchorage Museum of History and Art, and David L. Nicandri, director of the Washington State Historical Society, and their staffs, provided invaluable aid at all stages of the project.

Bradford L. Miller and others of Promotion Products Inc. are responsible for translating the curator's vision into a three-dimensional exhibit. Numerous people assisted in vital ways with assembling artifacts and photographs, or provided essential skills and information. Assistance with special photography was provided by Chris Ahrend, Jon Isaacs, Archpriest Joseph Kreta, Archpriest Paul Merculief, Darcy Richards, Mike Rogstad, Al Sanders, and Myron Wright. For their contributions of services, ideas and/or leads we thank Joan M. Antonson, Katherine Arndt, Lynn Birdsall, Professor Lydia T. Black, Dr. Donald Clark, Timothy (Ty) Dilliplane, Dr. William Fitzhugh, Ralph Godwin, Bishop Gregory (Afonsky), George Hall, Professor Stephen Haycox, Mina A. Jacobs, Professor William S. Laughlin, John Magee, Steven M. Peterson, Archpriest E. Nicholas Molodyko-Harris, Ray Hudson, Professor Richard Pierce, Bill and Diane Pritchard, Donna Redding-Gubitosa, Dr. Bert Rhoads, Margaret Shannon, David Shayt, John Thelenius, Professor Douglas Veltre, Dr. Don Wilson (archivist of the United States), the Weyerhaeuser Design Group, and United States Representative Norm Dicks and his staff.

In particular, we would like to acknowledge the exceptional effort of the Cultural Resources Department of the Kodiak Area Native Association in organizing and financing production of an authentic, traditionally crafted bidarka, bailer, and paddle for the exhibit. The school children of Akhiok, Kodiak Island, deserve special praise. In addition, we thank their teachers, Steve and Diane Rounsaville, and the elders who guided the children's work: Larry Matfay,

Alfred Naumoff, Nick Peterson, Jr., and Arthur Peterson. Rick Knecht, director of cultural resources for KANA and Joe Kelly, director of education, organized the project and raised the necessary funds.

Donors of services and financial support were essential to the exhibit's existence. A grant from the National Endowment for the Humanities provided major funding for the exhibit and for this book. Additional support for this volume came from Puget Sound Bank.

Further funds and special services were provided by Alaska Airlines, the Ben B. Cheney Foundation, the Forest Foundation, Grantmaker Consultants Inc., the Municipality of Anchorage, the Tacoma Arts Commission and the City of Tacoma, the State of Washington, Alaska Cleaners, ARCO Alaska, the Frank Russell Company, Totem Ocean Trailer Express, the Goodwill Arts Festival™, *The Morning News Tribune*, Brown & Haley, the Greater Tacoma Community Foundation, Concrete Technology Corporation, the Florence B. Kilworth Foundation, the Port of Tacoma, Sea-Land Service, Stone McLaren, MarkAIR, Scalamandré, Spenard Builders' Supply, Alpac, the Anchorage Hilton, Holland-America Westours, and Weyerhaeuser Foundation.

The curator also would like to thank the Institute of Ethnography of the Academy of Sciences and the institute's director, V. A. Tishkov, for extending hospitality and assistance during her research in the Soviet Union. S. Ia. Serov, also of the institute, was an invaluable guide and resource.

And to Floyd V. Smith and Suzanne W. Barnett, who unselfishly shared ideas and put up with much, our thanks is understood, but nonetheless gratefully extended.

—*Barbara Sweetland Smith,*
Redmond J. Barnett

Introduction

"There are Russians on all the principal islands between this [Unalaska] and Kamchatka for the sole purpose of furing and the first and great object is the Sea Beaver or Otter or the fur seal."
—*Captain James O. Cook, 1778*

The arrival of the Russian Empire as a contender for the spoils of the North Pacific took many nations by surprise. The Russians had not been seafarers, their empire having been built on conquest of neighboring tribes and nations. Indeed, the Russians had pushed their dominion all the way across Siberia to the shores of the Pacific as early as 1639, but remained landlocked, poised but unable or unwilling to move for nearly one hundred years. It was Tsar Peter, aptly named "the Great," who realized the potential for Russia in the islands and lands to the east beyond the shore. Dismayed by the decline of Siberian furs that fed the lucrative China trade and eager to lay claim to whatever lay to the east, if it could be had without a fight, Peter in 1725 initiated a series of moves that led Russia into the great land battle for North America.

The story of Imperial Russia's challenge to the British, Spanish, French, and the Americans for hegemony in northwestern North America is not well known to most Americans, nor to most Soviets. As tourists visit Alaska to revel in its natural beauty, they are invariably surprised and delighted to discover tiny Orthodox churches tucked away in little villages inhabited almost entirely by Native Americans—Aleuts, Eskimos, or Tlingits. They try to pronounce the unfamiliar Russian names of these villagers and of the mountains, inlets, and towns of the land. They have discovered Russian America.

Through the legacy of language, culture, and most particularly people, Russian America is a lively part of contemporary American society. But to most Americans it is a forgotten legacy....

Russian America: The Forgotten Frontier

The museum exhibit "Russian America: The Forgotten Frontier" is the first comprehensive display of the rich history of Russia's involvement in the life and times of North America. It brings together well over six hundred artifacts, documents, and original art of the explorations and, equally important, evidence of the enduring legacy of Russian America. Fifty-two individuals, organizations, and institutions in the United States have contributed objects, as have Soviet museums and the National Museum of Finland.

The exhibit has three principal themes, which are well borne-out by the articles in this volume:

1) Russian America offers a variation on the colonial pattern familiar elsewhere in North America. Initially exploitative of the Native population and natural resources of the region, the Russians eventually developed policies that encouraged Native language and custom, supported widespread education and employment of Natives in responsible positions, and advanced conservation of the marine resources of the North Pacific.

2) The relations of the United States with Russian America are of long standing, dating from the first Boston trader's foray into Russian waters in the 1790s. Involvement for both parties was marked by hostility as well as economic interdependence, resulting in such unusual practices as American-Russian joint ventures to acquire sea otter pelts within four years of American connivance with the Tlingits in the destruction of Sitka in 1802.

3) Russian America developed a surprisingly rich cultural base, which endures to the

A 1754 MAP of the two voyages of Captain Vitus Bering, prepared by Gerhard F. Müller to accompany the only eighteenth-century "official" history of the voyages. Although Müller did not accompany Bering on either voyage, he drew his information for the map and his history from personal knowledge of the participants and their diaries, logs, and charts.

Alaska and Polar Regions Dept., Elmer E. Rasmuson Library, University of Alaska, Fairbanks.

present day, primarily through the continuing vitality of the Orthodox church.

The first theme is elaborated in the articles by Fortuine, Dauenhauer, Oleksa, and Black. The second is most fully developed by Haycox and Shannon, while the third is treated in detail by Krauss, Fienup-Riordan, Lidfors and Peterson, and Smith. The balance of the articles provide fresh insights into important aspects of how and why Russia came to America, its relations with important contenders for domination, how the Russian-American Company functioned, and how the Aleuts, in particular, responded to Russian overlordship.

Overview: Russian America

The Russians arrived in America slowly at first, led by those intrepid hunters interested only in "furing," as Cook put it. Peter the Great's vision led Vitus Bering in 1728 to explore the ocean between Russia and America. Failing in his first effort (although traversing the straits that today bear his name), Bering set out again in 1741, with his companion of the earlier journey, Lt. Alexeii Chirikov, in a sister vessel. The two spotted land independently in July 1741, made separate landfalls, and turned toward home. Chirikov reached Siberia first, and news of the furbearers among the islands of the ocean inspired a rush to find the precious "soft gold." Organized into temporary enterprises that lasted as long as the voyage, adventurous trappers, or *promyshlenniki*, explored and exploited the islands closest to the Siberian mainland, then moved eastward, forming more elaborate business arrangements and settling on the more distant islands such as Unalaska and

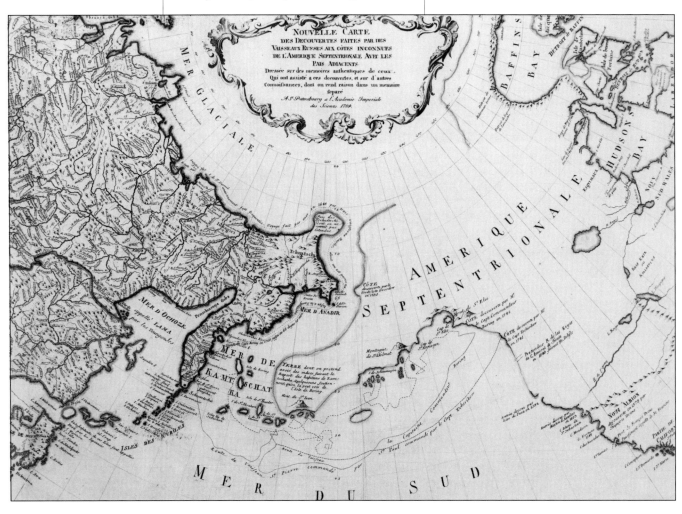

Kodiak. For thirty years they were undisturbed, except by occasional visits from Spanish, French, and English ships. In 1762, Catherine II, also aptly known as "the Great," came to the throne. She wanted to gain control over this haphazard and motley extension of empire, and in 1764 initiated the first of a number of official mapping expeditions designed to chart and document the reach of her dominion. The Russians were soon launched on round-the-world expeditions, which gained them new prestige as well as provisions for the burgeoning colony now settled along the most northern of the coasts of Northwest America.

Two names are most often identified with this early period in the history of Russian America: Grigorii Shelikhov and Alexander Baranov. Shelikhov was a Siberian merchant who unsuccessfully importuned Catherine in 1788 to give his fur-trading company monopoly rights in the North Pacific trade. A believer in free trade, Catherine scathingly denied the request while at the same time rewarding Shelikhov and his partner I. Golikov for their exceptional enterprise in extending Russian domination as far as Kodiak Island. Shelikhov's company eventually received those monopoly rights under Catherine's son Paul in 1799, but by then Shelikhov himself had died.

Shelikhov's exceptional energy and vision laid the foundation for Russian rule in these new lands. He established the first permanent Russian settlement on Kodiak Island and directed the first agricultural colony at Slava Rossii (Glory of Russia), near present-day Yakutat. His town plans called for ordered streets, public facilities such as schools and libraries, and gardens. He has left us a design for forts at Afognak and Kenai that reflects a keen knowledge of geometry. But for all of this, Shelikhov was not a government official. He was a

ALEXANDER BARANOV served the Shelikhov Trading Company and its successor, the Russian-American Company, from 1790 to 1818. Thanks to his vigorous leadership as chief manager and governor, Russian influence expanded in a vast arc from the Aleutian Chain to northern California and included Hawaii for a brief time. This image is an engraving after an oil by Mikhail T. Tikhanov, painted in 1818, just before Baranov's retirement at the age of seventy-one.

Oregon Historical Society, Portland.

businessman, carrying out a business venture with the approval of the throne.

While the formation of the trading company and the establishment of permanent settlements in North America must be among Shelikhov's great contributions, perhaps his most astute action was to hire a failed merchant from Kargopol as his chief manager for the Kodiak Island station. Alexander A. Baranov was forty-three and near bankruptcy when he was hired by Shelikhov in Siberia. Shelikhov, nonetheless, recognized exceptional qualities of enterprise, determination, and hardiness in the small fair-haired man. His judgment proved good. Baranov served Shelikhov's company, and later the Russian-American Company, from 1790 to 1818, when he retired at age seventy-one. In his lifetime, Baranov became the subject of legend, for he commanded respect, awe, and fear among various populations. Government inquiries into his activities left even the most critical inspectors impressed by his decisiveness, dedication, energy, and self-deprivation.

Baranov's tenure as chief manager

GRIGORII SHELIKHOV'S own account of his voyage of 1783-86, which led to the first permanent European settlement in the North Pacific, at Kodiak Island. Published first in 1791, this edition shows a fanciful Shelikhov, the merchant, trading with the equally fantastic Aleuts.

Alaska and Polar Regions Dept., Elmer E. Rasmuson Library, University of Alaska, Fairbanks.

coincided with the rapid expansion of Russian America to the south and east. When he arrived in 1790 there were only three Shelikhov Company outposts east of the Aleutians—on Kodiak and Afognak islands, and at Fort Alexandrovsk (present-day English Bay), on the Kenai Peninsula. When he left in 1818, the Russian-American Company reached into Prince William Sound, the Alexander Archipelago, and even into northern California, where he had established a post called Fort Ross. In a vast arc from the Kamchatka peninsula along the chain of the Aleutian Islands and down the coast of North America, embracing even for a short time the Hawaiian Islands, Baranov was known as Lord of Russian America.

In the course of twenty-eight years, Baranov moved the headquarters of the company first to St. Paul Harbor (present-day Kodiak), a better site on Kodiak Island, and then in 1808 to his new capital in the heart of Tlingit country, at New Archangel, today's Sitka. He saw to the development of support industries for the fur trade, such as shipbuilding, blacksmithing, woodworking, and brickmaking. He implemented the policy that continued throughout the Russian era of training young Creoles (persons with Russian fathers and Native mothers) for service with the company, first by providing elementary schooling and then technical courses or training on the company ships; a number of Creole men and women were sent to Irkutsk and St. Petersburg for advanced education.

Baranov's administration of the colonies for the Russian-American Company was innovative, energetic, and often harsh, particularly toward Natives. Because of the bravura nature of his administration, he was the subject of a number of complaints that led eventually to government investigation. In 1818 his pleas to be replaced were heeded and he was rather unceremoniously "retired."

Baranov's style was not the style of the new order that took over in Russian America. Shelikhov had laid the visionary plan and Baranov had been the builder. During the forty-nine years that were left to Russian rule in Alaska, management fell to the Russian Imperial Navy. From 1818 all the chief managers of the Russian-American Company were also naval officers. The company was still a business enterprise, but it had always had a quasi-governmental role. The imperial bureaucracy did not appreciate government by businessmen, however, and from the early 1800s gradually filled the board of directors with state officials.

The naval era in Russian America is generally considered an enlightened one. The harsh measures of discovery, seizure, and settlement were replaced by cool administration. Cautious and careful husbanding of resources replaced the bold ventures and catastrophic exploitation of the Baranov years. The new naval leadership advanced education and religious missions. Public health became company policy. Exploration and the placement of strategic trading posts opened new prospects in interior Alaska, while new industries offered hope of an alternative to a dwindling fur resource. Contracts with both Boston merchants and Hudson's Bay Company factors resolved the provisioning crisis, which had plagued the colony from its outset. Russia's outpost in California became obsolete and was sold in 1841.

In 1867 a combination of pressures led to Russia's decision to sell her North American possession and to the United States' decision to buy. Interestingly enough, it was not economics that was the determining factor for Russia. After a serious falling-off of the fur trade, the Russian colony had struggled back into the black by diversifying its operations and gaining a monopoly on the sale of Chinese tea to Russia. But how different North America appeared in 1867 from 1799 or even 1821. The Northwest was no longer open for the taking. The United States had taken everything south of the 49th parallel. Great Britain's Hudson's Bay Company was dominant to the east, and Russia also had lost a foolhardy war to the British in the Crimea only a few years earlier. Those at the court in

CATHERINE II, empress of Russia from 1762 to 1796, resisted Shelikhov's requests for a monopoly for his trading company, but she did honor the merchant with a set of jeweled swords and medals in recognition of his service to the empire in expanding Russian influence to the lands of the North Pacific.

Alexander F. Dolgopolov Collection, Alaska State Library, Juneau.

St. Petersburg who promoted the colony's sale also pointed to the change in Russia's relations with China. In a series of battles and treaties, Russia had gained important land concessions on her southeastern border in the rich Amur River region. All of these factors convinced Tsar Alexander II that the colony based at Sitka had become superfluous to Russia's interests in the last half of the nineteenth century. And so Russian America became just "America."

Russia's Colonial Style

The Russian outreach to North America was unique among the colonizing powers that overran the continent in the fifteenth to eighteenth centuries. Spain and Great Britain exerted governmental control at the outset of their incursions. France did likewise. The Russian enterprise was initially a commercial advance into a vacuum. The imperial government took an oversight interest in its colony in North America, but organized neither settlement nor military control, and most importantly, it did not expend great resources on its development, unlike Britain and Spain. At no time did the number of Russians exceed 823 in Russian America, while the more stable Russian population was from 300 to 500. This was clustered in Kodiak, Sitka, and a few "retirement communities" established by the colonial administration.

This being said, Russian administration of its colony was markedly more humane than that of its neighbors in North America. From 1741 to 1867, a succession of cartographers, linguists, ethnographers, botanists, teachers, priests, and officials lived with and worked with the Native population of Aleuts, Eskimos, and Tlingits (and the Athabaskans to a lesser degree). Over the course of this century and a quarter, Russian interaction with the Native population changed dramatically. Initially, the encounters were bloody and catastrophic for the Aleuts, some experts estimating the loss of four-fifths of the population from 1743 to 1800. Despite this sorry start, the Russians left a legacy of affection and support that their American successors found hard to understand.

The reason for this legacy can be found in the official policy enunciated in the company charters from 1821, which forbade exploitation of the Natives and supported this by frequent inspection trips. In addition, Native Alaskans received education and advancement through the Russian system. A man of Aleut-Russian parentage, A. F. Kashevarov, retired in Russia's service as a brigadier general. Scores of others were shipwrights, carpenters, teachers, feldshers (paramedics), metal smiths, iconographers, explorers—all educated at Russian expense, and often in both Russian and their Native language. The Orthodox church developed devout adherents and dedicated missionaries, including a number who were of Native parentage. This heritage continues to the

VIEW OF Shelikhov's Establishment on the Island of Kadiak, *engraving by W. Alexander from a drawing by Martin Sauer, 1790-92. This scene includes a traveling church, astronomical tent, and a ship (galleon) hauled ashore for repair. Sauer, an Englishman in the employ of Imperial Russia, was secretary to Joseph Billings on Russia's second official exploration of the North Pacific, 1785-95.*

From Sauer, An Account of a Geographical and Astronomical Expedition to the Northern Parts of Russia (London, 1802).

present day in the policies of the heirs of this mission, Bishop Gregory and his thirty-five Orthodox clergy, half of whom are of Aleut, Eskimo, or Tlingit origin. Villages throughout Alaska today observe ancient Russian customs in church and community. Their residents speak Yup'ik and Aleut, with many words borrowed from those Russians of two hundred years ago. The villagers bear such names as Merculief, Nikolai, and Shaiashnikov—and many hundreds of other Russian forebears.

A New Frontier

Through the legacy of language, culture, and most particularly people, Russian America is a lively part of contemporary American society. But to most Americans it is a forgotten legacy, neglected during the days of the old, cold war. The frontier we have shared receded across the icy Bering Strait in 1867, and Russia's many contributions to American science, education, culture, and cartography were easily forgotten even by many Alaskans. But today a new bond is being forged that spans the North Pacific. Alaskans in increasing numbers are reaching across the Bering Strait to set up joint economic ventures, cultural exchanges, and family visits in the Soviet Far East. Once again we are able to meet, not as strangers, but as old friends.

—*Barbara Sweetland Smith,*
Redmond J. Barnett

Barbara Sweetland Smith owns Alaska Historical Resources, an Anchorage consulting firm, and is curator of the exhibit "Russian America: The Forgotten Frontier."

Redmond J. Barnett is a historian at the Washington State Historical Society.

A Note on Transliteration

Standardizing transliteration of Russian names and terms among so many authors is a daunting task, but we have attempted to follow the Library of Congress system in the main. Where names have become current in English, such as Sts. Herman and Innocent and the town of Kodiak, we have preferred that usage to "German," "Innokentii," and "Kad'iak." For general readers we have given the Russian name of such places as New Archangel, but coupled it with Sitka for easy comprehension. A number of Russian terms appear frequently throughout the text, such as *promyshlennik* (the ubiquitous fur-trader, trapper, wily entrepreneur), and we have chosen to italicize them. The same is true for measurements (examples are *pud* and *sazhen*).

MATERIALS FROM the life of a nineteenth-century Siberian promyshlennik: *A simple wooden backpack for carrying furs rests on top of an iron-banded wooden chest used for carrying documents and personal effects; a powder kit with powder horn, tamper and measure; a pistol, knife, and personal icon (worn around the neck).*

State Unified Museum of Irkutsk, Siberia.

EXPLORATION AND DISCOVERY

Finding America

by Raymond H. Fisher

The purpose of the expedition was...to lay the foundation for an empire...and for the exploitation of its natural resources.

F inding America"—that was the intention behind the two voyages of Vitus Bering, often referred to as the First and Second Kamchatka expeditions. The first voyage, in the summer of 1728, carried Bering, captain in the Russian Imperial Navy, through the strait later named after him, but he did not find America. The second voyage, of two vessels commanded by Bering and cocaptained by Alexeii Chirikov in the summer of 1741, resulted in the sighting of the coast of southeastern Alaska, portions of its southern coast, and some of the Aleutian Islands. Chirikov and his crew made it back to Kamchatka that same summer. Bering and his crew were forced to winter on Bering Island, where he and half of his crew perished from scurvy. The survivors returned to Kamchatka the next summer. With one minor exception, these voyages mark the beginning of the Russian discovery of America. America had been found, but not explored.[1]

The search for America was initiated by Peter the Great. Just when he became interested in finding America is not known. Several individuals in the course of his reign urged him to arrange a search for a northeast passage to the Pacific, but to look for America was another matter. There is evidence from the report of a conversation he had in Amsterdam in 1697 with Nicolaas Witsen, a Dutch visitor to and student of Russia, that the latter thought there existed a close connection between Kamchatka and America in the form of a large island or American peninsula called Juan de Gama Land. Until Bering's second voyage it would seem that the Russians underestimated the distance between America and Kamchatka in the middle latitudes. By 1719 Peter was sufficiently interested to direct Ivan Evreinov and Fedor Luzhin to describe the local areas around Kamchatka and ascertain whether America was joined with Asia, making a search in the south and north, east and west. They reached Kamchatka by sea from the west, and visited the east coast in the winter of 1720-21, and the northern Kurile Islands to the south in the summer of 1721. The land to the north was already known to the Russians. They found no connection with America, and Evreinov reported this to Peter in 1722 in Kazan, where he was pausing on his way to the campaign against Persia. A further hint that Peter had been thinking of a search for America is seen in a conversation reported by Fedor Soimonov, naval officer, cartographer, and future governor of eastern Siberia. In an exchange with Peter in 1722 during the Persian campaign, Soimonov pointed out the advantages enjoyed by the Russians in searching for the Japanese and Philippine archipelagoes and the areas from Kamchatka to America itself along the west coast of the island of California compared to the western European maritime countries. Peter replied: "Listen, I know all this, but not now, in the future."[2]

Bering's First Voyage

The future came rather soon. In January 1725, just before his death, Peter drafted the instructions for Bering's first voyage. Although for more than two hundred years it has been believed that Peter sent Bering into the North Pacific to determine whether Asia and

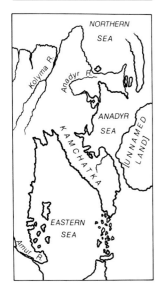

Map 1:
MAP OF KAMCHATKA by Johann Homann, 1725. This map was familiar to Peter I and showed the state of knowledge of the North Pacific at the time. It depicts North America as being close to but not connected to Kamchatka.

From A. V. Efimov, ed., Atlas of Geographical Discoveries in Siberia and in Northwest America XVII-XVIII Centuries, *No. 58 (Moscow, 1964).* University of Washington Press.

America were joined at their northeastern and northwestern extremities, one searches Peter's instructions in vain for any reference to that question as the reason for the voyage. To be sure, he ordered Bering to sail "along the land which goes to the north and according to expectations (because its end is not known) that land appears to be part of America." But then, in paragraph three, he goes on to order Bering to search for the place where this land is joined with America, to seek a European settlement or vessel, find out what the coast is called, explore and map it, and return to Kamchatka. The most likely identification of "the land which goes to the north" is the unnamed land to the east of Kamchatka depicted on a map of Kamchatka in Johann B. Homann's *Grosser Atlas*, published in 1725 in Nuremberg, a map printed in 1722 from one prepared in Russia and sent to Homann for publication (Map 1). The eastern part of the land was "not known" because it was cut off by the right border of the map. It is believed that Bering carried a copy of this map with him on his voyage. This northward-going land reflected the belief in the existence of the mythical Juan de Gama Land between Asia and America. If I am right in my reading of Peter's instructions, what he had in mind was that Bering should sail east along the southern coast of this land until he reached America and there look for a European settlement, which not only would serve to ascertain the northern limit of European settlement on the west coast of America, but also would reinforce any future claim Russia might make to unclaimed land there. It is significant that Bering's vessel, the *St. Gabriel*, was built and equipped only for coastal sailing, not for open-sea navigation.

Why Peter was interested in America is not known with any certainty. No statement by him has turned up telling his reasons for sending Bering to America.

Any answer has to be conjectural. But it is quite plausible that he wanted to find a new Siberia rich in fur-bearing animals to replenish a treasury hard hit by his reforms, the long Great Northern War with Sweden, and a decline in fur revenue from Siberia. Perhaps, too, he had in mind America's wealth in precious metals. Furs, gold, and silver clearly motivated the planners of Bering's second voyage, men who had been associated with Peter.

But somewhere en route across Siberia to Kamchatka, Bering came to the conclusion that there was no such "Unnamed Land" as shown on the map. That meant for him and his two lieutenants, Chirikov and Martin Spanberg, that the land going north was the coast north of Kamchatka, and if it was joined to America, it would have to be in the north that Bering would look for a land connection, one that if followed far enough would take him in an arching curve to America and a European settlement—a roundabout route certainly, but how else interpret Peter's instructions in the absence of Juan de Gama Land? This belief in and search for a land connection emerges clearly, though not explicitly, from a careful reading of statements by Chirikov and Bering in the last few days of the outbound voyage.

Having followed the coast from the lower Kamchatka River northward and northeastward to the face of the Chukotskii Peninsula, on August 13 (nautical dating), 1728, at 65°30' north latitude the voyagers found themselves out of sight of land as they approached and passed through the strait.[3] Heavy fog concealed the land on both sides. Chukchi Natives previously interviewed by the Russians had reported that the coast would turn west farther up the line. This led Bering to consult with his two lieutenants as to what should be done next: continue on or turn around and go back to

Kamchatka. Chirikov's advice is revealing. In a written statement he remarks that the land they had been following, they thought to be joined with America. That being so, he argued that by virtue of Peter's instructions they had to proceed along that land to a European settlement—that is, to return to the coast and follow it, unless, he wrote, further advance was blocked by ice or *"unless the coast led away to the Kolyma River"* (emphasis added). If it turned north, by the twenty-fifth of the month they should look for a winter haven, preferably on the land reported to lie east of the Chukotskii Peninsula. In other words, disbelief in a land connection with America had not yet set in; and he rejected sailing westward to the Kolyma. Bering chose to continue north, possibly on the theory that, by following the chord of the arc formed by the land connection, he would find America.

The climax of the voyage occurred during the next three days. It has long been believed that during those three days Bering continued sailing north until he reached 67°18' north latitude in the Chukchi Sea. Concluding that the land no longer went north, he decided to turn around and head back to Kamchatka. But a recent study by the Soviet scholar Arkadii Sopotsko reveals a different picture. In 1973 he uncovered in the naval archives the official logbook of the *St. Gabriel,* long thought to have been lost. From its navigational data he has traced the course of the voyage in detail, day by day, often hour by hour. According to his reconstruction of the voyage, Bering reached 67°18' north latitude at midnight August 14, and until four o'clock August 16 he followed a back-and-forth course east and west that took him as far north as 67°24' north latitude and east to longitude 167°50' west. Here, fearful of being trapped in a hostile environment by adverse winds, he turned around and sailed back to Kamchatka on a more-or-less straight course, passing through the strait near Cape Dezhnev, the easternmost tip of Asia (Map 2). Cape Prince of Wales on the American side was not seen because it was shrouded in fog. Sopotsko believes that this back-and-forth sailing constituted an effort by Bering to find America. He finds his explanation in two earlier episodes, when Bering followed a back-and-forth course that enabled him to find Cape Chukotsk, at the southeast corner of the Chukotskii Peninsula, and St. Lawrence Island to the south, where taking a straight course had failed. But his third use of this technique failed to produce the desired result, since at 68° north latitude the coast of America is one

DRAWING OF A fur seal, sea lion, and a sea cow, on the chart of Bering's second expedition, 1741. The illustrations, probably by Sven Waxell, show animals first described by the naturalist Georg W. Steller. The drawing of the sea cow is the only known illustration of this marine mammal, driven to extinction by Russian traders who depended on its savory flesh to sustain them as they moved eastward.

From Frank B. Golder's Bering's Voyages (1922). Anchorage Museum of History and Art.

hundred miles to the east, for the Seward Peninsula recedes markedly to the northeast from Cape Prince of Wales.

Subsequently, after returning to St. Petersburg on March 1, 1730, Bering explained why he turned back in the "Short

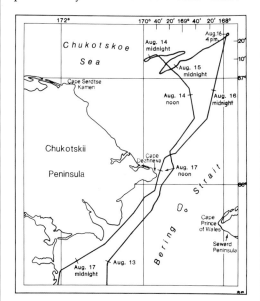

Map 2:
VOYAGE OF the **St. Gabriel,** *1728, simplified.*

From A. Sopotsko, History of the Voyage of Bering on the Ship St. Gabriel in the Northern Arctic Ocean *(Moscow, 1983).*

Account" of his expedition, which he presented to the empress Anna the following month:

> On August 15 [civil time] we arrived at 67°18' N. lat. I judged that according to everything that had been seen and to the instructions given by his Imperial Majesty... there had been fulfillment because the land no longer extended to the north and no land of any kind approached the Chukotsk or eastern corner, and I turned back.[4]

He said nothing about sailing west. He also expressed his concern over the safety of his vessel and crew because of the lateness of the navigation season (August 15 was August 26 by the Western calendar). He had sailed along the land that went north, seeking its juncture with America, but now it was evident that there was no such juncture. He had done as much as time permitted, and in that sense he had carried out Peter's order,

though obviously he had not fulfilled that part of the assignment contained in the third paragraph of Peter's instructions, to reach a European settlement in America.

This latter failure may explain the entry in the logbook for August 16, repeated in the journal of Petr Chaplin, a junior officer, which seems to contradict Bering's claim of fulfillment of his instructions. It reads: "At 3:00 p.m. the *gospodin* [captain] declared that contrary to the *ukaz* [Peter's instructions] in [its] execution he must return, and turning the boat around, ordered keeping to the SW."[5] The instructions in the second paragraph of Peter's order he had carried out; those in the third paragraph he had not.

Bering returned to the lower Kamchatka River, and thereafter his efforts to find America were directed to the east, as Peter originally had in mind. Noting signs that he took to indicate land east of Kamchatka, in June 1729 Bering made a short excursion to the east. He sailed some 130 miles before, frustrated by fog, he turned around and sailed southwest around Kamchatka to Okhotsk and traveled thence across Siberia to St. Petersburg. After his arrival he presented to the Admiralty College a proposal for a second voyage to find America. Still believing that America lay not too far east of Kamchatka, he thought that it would "be possible to search for this route *directly* [emphasis added] if a vessel [were to be] built of a size, for example, of 40 or 50 lasts [80 or 100 tons]."[6]

I must confess that until recently I have missed the significance of Bering's use of the word "directly," as have all the previous investigators of his voyages. If one assumes that Peter sent Bering to the Pacific to determine the union or separation of Asia and America, as scholars until recently have, then his proposal for a second voyage that would go east appears irrelevant. But if Peter sent Bering to find

ARTIST'S CONCEPTION of
the voyage of Semen Dezhnev
and his companions as they
passed through the straits
that separate Russia and
North America in 1648. Six
companion vessels were lost
and Dezhnev's wrecked, but
his journey was the first
successful passage through
the straits, proving that
North America and Asia were
not joined. Official news of
his feat did not reach St.
Petersburg for almost eighty
years, after the departure of
Bering's first expedition.

Central Naval Museum, Leningrad.

the route to America, the word "directly"
becomes relevant, for it tells us that Bering
recognized that by sailing east he might
well achieve that objective as he had not
been able to do by sailing the roundabout
route to the north of the first voyage.
There would be no coastal sailing to
America this time, but open-sea navigation, for which a bigger vessel would be
needed.

Land Connection Disproved

At the outset of Bering's 1728 voyage he
appears to have believed in a land connection between Asia and America. However, the purpose of the voyage was not to
demonstrate that connection, but to find
America in light of that belief. Nevertheless, demonstrating the actuality or
absence of that land connection came to be
generally understood as the purpose of
the voyage, and, ironically, it was Bering's
conversations with Gerhard F. Müller of
the Academy of Sciences that gave rise to

that understanding, a thesis I plan to
develop elsewhere at a future date.
Meanwhile, the fact remains that the
disconnection between Asia and America
had been demonstrated eighty years
before. In 1648 a merchant's agent, Fedot
Alekseev Popov, organized at
Srednekolymsk a party of ninety members, mostly *promyshlenniki* (fur hunters),
with several cossack interlopers, to search
for the Anadyr' River, reported to be rich
in sables and have a considerable Native
population. At the last hour, one Semen
Dezhnev, a cossack in government
employ, was assigned to represent the
state's interests (i.e., collect tribute in furs).
In June 1648 the party departed from the
Kolyma River in seven boats called *koches*
and headed east along the Siberian coast.
Four of the boats and their occupants were
lost before reaching the end of the
Chukotskii Peninsula. A fifth was

wrecked on the peninsula and its occupants taken by Alekseev into his boat. The two remaining boats rounded the peninsula only to be thrown ashore south of the Anadyr' River in a storm. Alekseev and his companions were later killed by Natives. Dezhnev and his twenty-four companions survived the wreck, but half of them subsequently disappeared in a snowstorm. Dezhnev and the survivors reached the Anadyr' overland and moved upstream to the forest line, where they founded the Anadyrsk outpost and imposed tribute on the Natives. Seven years later he sent in two reports to the commandant at Iakutsk in which he mentioned the voyage and described "the great rocky cape," the Chukotskii Peninsula, around which he had sailed. He lived to tell about the voyage; Alekseev did not, so the voyage has come down in history under Dezhnev's name. A hazy knowledge of the voyage, of the fact of such a voyage, without dates or names of the participants, seems to have filtered through northern Siberia and northern Russia, but there is no evidence that either Peter I or Bering knew about it. Nevertheless, eighty years before Bering's voyage, Semen Dezhnev, an illiterate cossack, and his party of Russian fur hunters demonstrated the separation of Asia and America by sailing around the northeastern corner of Siberia. They were the first Europeans to do so.

The *St. Gabriel*'s Second Exploratory Mission

Two years after Bering's first voyage and nine years before his second, another expedition, sailing in his vessel, did find a bit of America, Cape Prince of Wales, the westernmost tip of the American mainland. This voyage, though authorized by the Governing Senate and with some personnel assigned by the Admiralty College in St. Petersburg, was largely the outgrowth of Siberian initiative. An Iakutsk cossack, Afanasii Shestakov, went to St. Petersburg in 1724, where he proposed an ambitious expedition including a move against the recalcitrant Chukchi and Koriaks in northeastern Siberia and an investigation of the "Big Land" reported by the Chukchi to lie across the water from the Chukotskii Peninsula. In 1727 he was given command of fifteen hundred men to be recruited in Siberia and assembled in Iakutsk, then the main administrative center of northeastern Siberia.

RUSSIANS WERE fascinated by Aleut prowess in their one- or two-hatch bidarkas (kayaks), but proved unable to master the hunters' skills themselves. Engraving by Luka Vornonin, expedition artist with the Billings-Sarychev expedition of 1790-92.

From Sarychev's Atlas (St. Petersburg, 1826). Alaska and Polar Regions Dept., Elmer E. Rasmuson Library, University of Alaska, Fairbanks.

However, once in Siberia he had to share command with Dmitrii Pavlutskii, captain of dragoons, selected by the governor of Siberia in Tobol'sk and assigned four hundred of the fifteen hundred men. Pavlutskii's task was to subdue the Chukchi in their homeland, the Chukotskii Peninsula.

In July 1729, Shestakov arrived in Okhotsk, where he made his base, taking over the supplies and vessels, including the *St. Gabriel*, that Bering had left there. His first move was against the Chukchi, who had invaded Koriak territory north of Kamchatka. In a fight with them in March 1730 he was killed and his force destroyed. This left Pavlutskii in command of what remained of the expedition. He proceeded to order navigator Iakov Gens, assistant navigator Ivan Fedorov, and geodesist (or surveyor) Mikhail Gvozdev, then in Okhotsk and Tauisk—all appointees of the Admiralty College—to take the *St. Gabriel* to the Anadyr' River, whence they were to sail east and investigate the "Big Land" and any islands en route. Pavlutskii relieved Gens of command because of the latter's blindness and an ulcerated leg, and placed Gvozdev in charge. Fedorov, also suffering from a badly ulcerated leg, tried to beg off, but was forcefully carried aboard the *St. Gabriel*. Leaving the Anadyr' on July 23, 1732, the expedition, which consisted of the two top commanders, Gvozdev and Fedorov, a junior officer, four sailors, thirty-two service men (to collect tribute?), and an interpreter, reached Big Diomede Island on August 17, where the Russians landed, and Little Diomede Island on the twentieth. They found no forests on either island, and the Natives refused to pay tribute. On the twenty-first the Russians sighted the "Big Land" at Cape Prince of Wales. Seeing no habitations ashore, they moved southward to where habitations were seen, but were prevented from landing by shallow water and adverse winds. Continuing southward, they discovered King Island, but

could not land, again because of contrary winds. Lateness of the navigation season (September 8 by the Western calendar), low food supply, and a leaking vessel prompted return to Kamchatka, where they arrived on September 27.

This voyage was an extension of the pattern of conquest of Siberia: the search for and subjugation of Natives, who could be made to

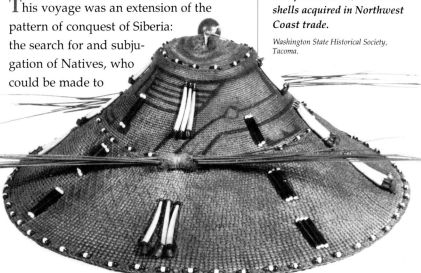

pay tribute in furs, in the course of which geographical information was obtained. This was why Gvozdev was added to the expedition by the Admiralty College. Provision for one was not a part of Shestakov's original proposal. Even so, there was a lack of direction and control of the Shestakov-Pavlutskii expedition from St. Petersburg, which was also a part of the pattern. Admittedly, the Governing Senate authorized the expedition, and the Admiralty College provided personnel and instruments for an accurate survey of far eastern Siberia, but thereafter they seem to have lost contact with the development of the expedition as it took form in Siberia. There the two leaders quarreled and each acted increasingly as a law unto himself. The authorities in Tobol'sk and Iakutsk failed to maintain a firm control over the two men. There was little communication between the two leaders or between them and Tobol'sk, and less between Tobol'sk and St. Petersburg. It was Shestakov, and after Shestakov's death, Pavlutskii, who gave the search for the Bering Strait islands and the "Big

Land" a high priority. And after taking over full command, it was Pavlutskii who replaced Gens with Gvozdev without consulting higher authority. It is striking that the Admiralty College, which oversaw naval operations, did not learn of Gvozdev's and Fedorov's voyage and discoveries until 1738, presumably from one of the sailors who had been sent to St. Petersburg on criminal charges.

This tenuous relation between center and field, as well as between the officers in the field, is noticeable in the reporting of the voyage and its findings. Upon returning to Kamchatka, Gvozdev wrote a detailed report of the voyage and sent it to Pavlutskii along with the official logbook, incomplete because Fedorov, a sick man, had not always made the entries required of the navigator. Both logbook and report disappeared after reaching Iakutsk, Pavlutskii not being there. No map of the voyage was made since Fedorov, in the last stages of his illness, rejected Gvozdev's request to add the missing entries in the logbook, essential to the drafting of a map. Thereafter, Fedorov's death in June 1733 and Gvozdev's assignment to other activities unrelated to the voyage removed the two principals on the voyage from further involvement in it.

Nearly a decade passed before the

voyage again received attention, this time from the local officials at Okhotsk. First to show interest was Anton Devier, the new commandant at Okhotsk. In 1743, Spanberg, who had taken over command of the Second Kamchatka Expedition after Bering's death, visited Okhotsk. There Gvozdev had petitioned for promotion to naval rank (he was a geodesist). As a condition for approval, Spanberg required him to write a detailed account of the 1732 voyage and submit the logbook and map of the voyage. The logbook he had long since sent to Iakutsk, and the map had never been made. At this juncture there appeared—how is unknown—an unsuspected primary document, the personal journal kept on the journey by Fedorov for his own information, a journal with more entries than he had made in the official logbook. In September 1743 Spanberg turned the journal over to Gvozdev and ordered him, with the assistance of two subpilots, to prepare a map of coastal Siberia from the Kamchatka River to the Chukotskii Peninsula. This they did. The map showed part of the route of the voyage, from the Diomede Islands to Cape Prince of Wales (Cape Gvozdev to the Russians) and along its southern coast (Map 3). Neither map, journal, nor logbook identified the "Big Land" as America, though others later made the connection. The new information led Spanberg to promise the Okhotsk authorities that he would send another expedition to the strait, but this was before he learned that the Second Kamchatka Expedition had been officially terminated.

Thus did the Russians discover and record a tiny bit of northwestern America. Even so, it is not clear that the discoverers understood the significance of their discovery, that the "Big Land" was America. But perhaps more to the point, it was a discovery without important consequences such as followed the

Map 3:
BERING STRAIT, showing part of the voyage of Gvozdev and Fedorov (1732).

From A. V. Efimov, ed., Atlas of Geographical Discoveries in Siberia and in Northwest America XVII-XVIII Centuries, No. 69 (Moscow, 1964). University of Washington Press.

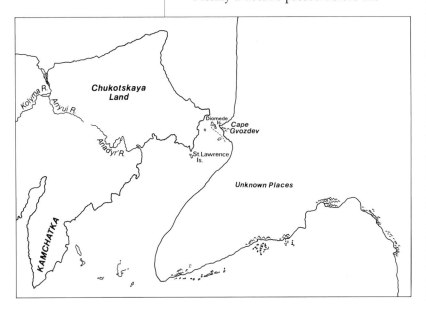

discovery of northwestern America by Bering and Chirikov in 1741. There was no follow-up; there were no attempts to subjugate the Natives, probably because the areas seen promised no profit for the sovereign. Only a bit of geographical knowledge, little disseminated, had been obtained. Bering no doubt knew of the discovery while preparing for his second expedition; but the effect of this knowledge on the planning of that expedition appears to have been negligible. The planning of the voyage to America focused on the area south of the Aleutian Islands.

The Second Kamchatka Expedition

Bering's proposal to the Admiralty College for a second voyage to find America also contained proposals for voyages to Japan and along the Siberian Arctic coast from the Ob' to the Lena River. In 1732 the Governing Senate acted on these proposals and expanded them into the most extensive program of exploration undertaken by a European state up to that time, if not beyond. Placed under the supreme command of Bering, it became known as the Second Kamchatka Expedition and later by other names. Our interest, however, is confined to the component expedition sent to find America, which was the last of the Second Kamchatka Expedition to be mounted. It will be referred to as the American expedition.

Bering was named the supreme expeditionary commander of the two vessels that made up the American expedition. He captained the *St. Peter*, and Chirikov, the *St. Paul*. The purpose of the expedition has long been thought to have been scientific, but though its leaders did record much information of scientific interest, it was not planned or organized as a scientific enterprise with a contingent of

scientists aboard, as was Captain James Cook's first voyage into the South Pacific in 1768-71—the first truly scientific maritime expedition. To be sure, Georg Wilhelm Steller, the German naturalist and member of the Imperial Academy of Sciences, accompanied Bering on the *St. Peter,* but was employed as a mineralogist and assayer, not as a scientist. Louis

Delisle de la Croyère, an astronomer and also a member of the Academy of Sciences, accompanied Chirikov on the *St. Paul.* He was to assist in choosing the route to America and in making celestial observations. Given to drink, he was increasingly ignored by Chirikov.

Rather, the purpose of the expedition was political and economic—that is, to lay the foundation for an empire in that part of North America not yet claimed by other European powers and for the exploitation of its natural resources: fur-bearing animals and precious metals. This purpose was clearly expressed by two of the expedition's major proponents. In October 1732 Vice Admiral Nikolai Golovin, vice president of the Admiralty College, proposed sending two frigates and a transport to Kamchatka to assist Bering in his preparations for the American expedition. Russian naval presence in the North Pacific, Golovin wrote, would enable the Russians "to go everywhere without danger and to look for lands and islands...passages, harbors, straits, and the like." Further, he wrote:

RUSSIAN possession plaque #12, found on Sitka Island in 1936. Like other colonial powers, Russia left evidence of its intent to dominate the islands it occupied. A number of these plaques were buried in Russian America, but only this one has been found. Made of thin sheet copper, it was found at the site of Old Sitka, the first Russian fort in southeast Alaska.

Sitka National Historical Park.

In exploring America there may be the following great gains for the state: very rich mines, of both gold and silver, are there which are still unknown, [and it is known] what profits the Spanish, English, and Portuguese kingdoms receive and how important commerce and navigation to the regions are for these kingdoms now.[7]

Sometime in 1733 or 1734 Ivan Kirilov, senior secretary of the Governing Senate and a prime mover in organizing the Second Kamchatka Expedition, presented a memorandum to the empress Anna regarding the expedition. He stated that the American expedition was to search for new lands and islands not yet conquered, to bring them under Russian dominion, and to search for minerals and precious metals. He explained the thinking behind the enterprise as follows:

The benefit to be expected is that from the eastern side Russia will extend its posses- sions as far as California and Mexico, although it will not receive immediately the rich metals the Spanish have there. How- ever, without preparing for war we can in

time acquire them through kindness.... [T]he local people are greatly embittered against the Spanish and for that reason have to escape to unknown places farther away (and it appears that there are no other places except closer to us). Here on our side it is firmly established not to embitter such people....[8]

However unrealistic this analysis, it does express the ambitions in America of the Russian leadership.

Late in December 1732 instructions were issued by the Governing Senate to the Admiralty College regarding the Second Kamchatka Expedition, including the American component. They reflect the Russian technique in the conquest of Siberia. Bering was to investigate a "Big Land" reported to be situated opposite the Chukotskii Peninsula and to have many fur-bearing animals and forests.[9] The Natives in the land discovered were to be invited to pay tribute and to give hostages. Gifts were to be given to the Native chiefs to induce submission. The members of the expedition were to look for islands en route to America and for landing places, harbors, and forests. They were to go ashore and undertake a search for mineral ores and metals, samples being provided to help in identifying them. A mineralo- gist was to accompany the expedition to assist in the search.

For the most part, the expedition failed to accomplish its official tasks. The two vessels left Petropavlovsk (Avacha Bay) in Kamchatka on June 4, 1741. After search- ing in vain as far south as 46° north latitude (that of Astoria, Oregon) for Juan de Gama Land, the alleged land en route to America, the two vessels became sepa- rated in a storm on June 20 and thereafter went their individual ways. Chirikov made his American landfall at the southern end of the present-day Alaska

PETER I (THE GREAT) set in motion Russia's dominance of the North Pacific in 1725 when he ordered Vitus Bering to explore Russia's Pacific coast and to make contact with America, if possible.

Engraving from Alexander F. Dolgopolov Collection, Alaska State Library, Juneau.

Panhandle on July 15 (July 26 by the Western calendar), and Bering made his the next day at the northern end. Two weeks later Chirikov lost both of his shore boats and fifteen men in a disappearance that to this day remains unsolved. Unable to go ashore to investigate and obtain fresh water, he had no choice but to start back to Kamchatka. Bering found himself in strange waters late in the navigation season—precious time had been spent looking for Juan de Gama Land—and, fearful of being locked in by adverse winds, he turned back.

On their return trips both captains sighted sections of the Alaska mainland and some of the Aleutian Islands. Chirikov made it back to Kamchatka. Bering did not. On November 6 his vessel was thrown into a lagoon on Bering Island, where he and half of his crew died of scurvy over the winter. The rest survived to rebuild the vessel in smaller form and reached Petropavlovsk in August 1742 (Map 4). Thus ended the American expedition. It had found northwestern America, and stretches of its coast and islands had been sighted and placed on a map. But beyond that, few of the objectives set forth in the instructions to Bering had been achieved. Only two visits ashore were made, to replenish the water supply of the *St. Peter*. No Natives were brought under submission, no tribute collected, no hostages taken. On top of that, Chirikov had lost his two shore boats and fifteen members of his crew, making it impossible for him to carry out the instructions. The state's efforts to extend Russian dominion into North America had failed.

Yet, the expedition had its successes, unplanned and unintended. They were the work mainly of one man, the physician and naturalist Steller. Though his official role was only that of mineralogist, he made it clear from the beginning that he would "make various observations on the voyage concerning the natural history, peoples, conditions of the land, etc." "Ever in a hurry, circling half the globe, and never in a position to prepare his manuscripts for publication, Steller had too much to do in too little time. He explored, collected, described, speculated, and moved on to do more of the same. Others after him gained reputation from the use of his information...." So writes O. W. Frost in his excellent introduction to

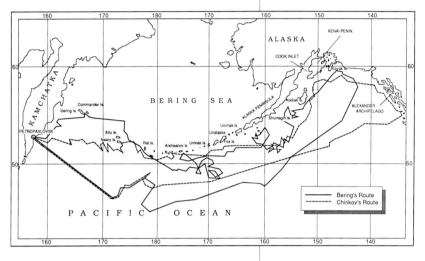

Map 4:
VOYAGES OF the **St. Peter** *and the* **St. Paul, 1741-42** *(translated and simplified).*

From V. A. Divin's The Great Russian Navigator A. I. Chirikov *(Moscow, 1953).*

a new translation of the journal Steller kept on the voyage.[10] Given a few hours on Kayak Island, against Bering's initial resistance, and permitted ashore during the water stop at the Shumagin Islands, Steller gathered and recorded an amazing amount of information and specimens. The eight-month sojourn on Bering Island provided much more time and opportunity to examine the environment. His interests embraced medicine, botany, zoology, and ethnology. He discovered a cure for scurvy made of local herbs and roots, and applied it to Bering's crew. He described the Arctic fox, the sea otter, the now-extinct sea cow, and their behavior, as well as other animals. His knowledge and conduct were probably the main reason why as many as did survived the severe winter on barren Bering Island. It is clear that such scientific character as the American expedition acquired was due to the extracurricular activity of this remarkable man.

America, or more precisely northwestern America, had been found by Russians from the west, not by Spanish or English from the south or east. But Bering and Chirikov had seen only a small part of northwestern America—some stretches of coast, some offshore islands, several of the Aleutian Islands, and Bering Island. The distance from America to Siberia was now known, as were the latitudes at which it could be found; but the sightings left some questions unanswered, particularly the question of whether the land seen was continental or insular, or a combination of both. Two maps made later on the basis of the data gathered on the two voyages depicted the land bordering the Gulf of Alaska on the north as a large sausage-shaped peninsula extending far to the southwest, its northern side running northeast to north to the cape seen by Gvozdev in 1732. One map, not published until the mid-twentieth century, was made in 1746 in the Naval Academy under the supervision of Chirikov. The other was made in the Academy of Sciences under the direction of Gerhard Müller, author of the first published account of Bering's voyages, and published in 1758. Only where the coast had

been seen was a solid line used; where it had not been seen and was speculative, a broken line appeared. It does show some of the islands (Map 5). Thus, the task remained to find the rest of coastal and insular America.

The Fur Rush

This task was carried out by private individuals, entrepreneurs who invested their own capital, built their own boats, and hired their own crews with only modest aid from local government officials. Their objective, however, was finding not America, but two sea mammals, the sea otter (or sea beaver, as the Russians called it) and the fur seal. The survivors of Bering's crew, upon returning to Kamchatka after the winter on Bering Island, brought with them some nine hundred pelts of the sea otter, fur seal, and blue Arctic fox, killed for food and body covering. The Russians were not unfamiliar with the sea otter, having caught it in the waters off Kamchatka; but they were ignorant of its habitat. It is a playful animal with luxuriant fur, more luxuriant and more valuable even than that of the Siberian sable, which had drawn the Russians across Siberia to the Pacific. The fur seal pelt was not particularly luxuriant, but it commanded a good price. The best market for these pelts was Kiakhta, on the Siberian-Mongolian border south of Lake Baikal, visited by Chinese merchants.

The news about the whereabouts of the sea otter set off a fur rush to the east that resulted in finding more of northwestern America. The move was financed by merchants and traders from European Russia and Siberia. The manpower was furnished by *promyshlenniki*—fur hunters and trappers—petty entrepreneurs, peasants, and Kamchadals in Siberia. In locally constructed vessels, some eighty voyages were made between 1743 and 1790. The voyages were carried out by

Map 5:
BERING'S VOYAGE of 1728, simplified from the map of 1758 by Gerhard F. Müller.

From Müller's Voyages from Asia to America (London, 1764).

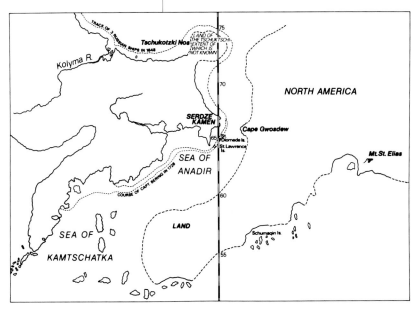

independent companies, typically organized on the basis of a single voyage. Merchants or traders, even *promyshlenniki* or state servitors with some capital to invest, individually or as a group, would organize a so-called company. Shares in the company would be assigned to investors, skipper, and crew, usually *promyshlenniki.* A boat would be built by them and equipment and supplies laid in. After a cargo of furs had been acquired and the boat returned to Kamchatka, assuming that disaster at sea or at the hands of Natives had not occurred, a ten-percent tax was paid to the state, and the proceeds from the venture were distributed according to the shares assigned at the outset. The company then went out of existence. Investors were free to organize other such companies concurrently or subsequently, and did.

The boats used for these voyages have traditionally been described as crudely built, lasting scarcely one trip, and their crews as landlubbers unskilled in navigation, with a high casualty rate at sea. Though this was true often enough to provide a basis for this characterization, it is an overdrawn picture. Lydia Black points out that several boats, *shitiki,* constructed without nails in the absence or scarcity of metal, their planks and joints

lashed together with thongs, are known to have made five or six trips. The average was three. Many *promyshlenniki* were landlubbers to begin with; others were experienced navigators of the Siberian rivers. Those who survived the perils of the sea became proficient mariners. Many spent a lifetime sailing the Aleutian waters, learning the currents, winds, and vagaries of the weather. They could sail these waters better than many navy men who came later in imperial ships and felt only contempt for these men, who were rough and hardy and not gentlemen. The naval officers' prejudiced appraisal has prevailed. Nonetheless, official naval expeditions had several of these experienced fur hunters aboard their vessels when they sailed from Kamchatka to the American coast.

The fur rush got underway in 1743 with the voyage of Emel'ian Basov to Bering Island. For the next thirteen years the Russians went no farther east than the Near Islands, the group closest to Kamchatka. Then, between 1756 and 1780, some forty-eight voyages were made, in the course of which the rest of the Aleutian chain was found, as well as the southwesternmost part of Alaska and the Alaska Peninsula. The order of discovery

THE SETTLEMENT of Illiliuk, on the island of Unalaska, as recorded by Kotzebue expedition artist Louis Choris, ca. 1818. Unalaska was first discovered in 1759 by Russian traders who settled there as early as 1778.

Anchorage Museum of History and Art.

NATIVES OF OONALASKA and Their Habitations, *engraving by John Webber, with the James Cook expedition, 1776-79. The British began exploring the North Pacific twenty-five years after the Russians. Cook reported finding as many as five hundred Russians occupying the Aleutian Islands.*

Anchorage Museum of History and Art.

was not a progressive eastward succession; it had a hit-or-miss character.

Many skippers on these fur-gathering voyages made maps, often crude ones in the absence or scarcity of navigation instruments; or they provided information used by local authorities to have maps made. But not all skippers provided cartographic data. Some, to protect their hunting grounds, withheld information or deliberately distorted their maps. Enough reasonably accurate information was assembled, however, so that more and more of America became known. This information, on the other hand, was confined to official circles and not disseminated abroad.

The heavy hunting among the islands nearer Kamchatka depleted the supply of fur-bearing animals and forced the Russians farther east. This necessitated longer voyages, which tied up capital for a longer time. In turn it became necessary to gather larger cargoes, which meant larger vessels and larger crews. This development gave the advantage to merchants with larger amounts of capital. By 1780 the smaller venture was becoming obsolete. Thereafter the fur hunting and America-finding activity of the Russians fell into the hands of five big merchant-capitalists. Most notable was the first permanent company in the North Pacific fur trade, organized by the Irkutsk merchants Grigorii Shelikhov and Ivan Golikov in 1781. By 1799 it had absorbed,

driven off, or combined with its competitors to form the Russian-American Company, upon which Tsar Paul conferred a state-ordained monopoly of the Russian North Pacific fur trade. It was the employees of these companies who, during the last two decades of the eighteenth century, explored or surveyed the Alaska Peninsula, Cook Inlet, the Kenai Peninsula, the shores of Prince William Sound, the Pribilof Islands in the Bering Sea, the breeding grounds of the fur seal, and the islands of the Alexander Archipelago, along which Chirikov had sailed after his landfall in July 1741. By the end of the eighteenth century most of southern and southeastern coastal and insular Alaska had been found.

Late Eighteenth-Century Explorations

In the post-Bering period until the end of the century, the role of the state in searching for hitherto unknown or unseen parts of America was minimal. Only Catherine II showed some interest. In 1764 she dispatched a supposedly secret expedition to the North Pacific under Captain Petr Krenitsyn and Lieutenant Mikhail Levashev to obtain more information about the islands already discovered, to annex them formally, and to impose some control over the *promyshlenniki*. The expedition's efforts focused mainly on Unimak and Unalaska islands, providing more accurate information about them, but discovering no new areas. Later Captain Cook, who sailed into the Chukchi Sea in 1778-79 and surveyed the American coast from Bristol Bay to Icy Cape, stirred Catherine into commissioning the Joseph Billings expedition of 1785-92 into the Arctic Ocean and Bering Sea. It brought back accurate charts of the areas it surveyed, of value to the navy in particular; but, again, no new parts of America were found. By the end of the eighteenth century most of Russian America had been found. The vast interior of Alaska, however, remained mostly unexplored until the next century.

As we review in our minds the finding of America in the three-quarters of a century after 1720, we see that it was the state's effort, a transoceanic leap, that first found northwestern America. The state chose not to follow up on that discovery, but Bering's voyage opened the way to island-hopping by private entrepreneurs in pursuit of the valuable sea otter, and these men by incremental steps revealed the land and islands not seen by Vitus Bering and Alexeii Chirikov on their epoch-making voyages of 1741. It was a two-phase process that put Russia in America.

Conclusion

"Russian America" was the term used by the Russians to refer to their colonies in America, and it is so used in the title of the exhibit of which this volume is a part. By Americans at least it has been an oft-forgotten frontier, but what has also been little appreciated is that it became an American as well as a Russian frontier. To be sure, the Russians were the first to find the path to northwestern America, to Alaska, as its new owners called it, in pursuit of fur-bearing animals. But the Americans found a path there, too, in pursuit of fur-bearing animals. Both paths were encumbered by the same disadvantage, separation from the center by a continent and an ocean or oceans, making Russian America a distant frontier for each. It became the area of convergence of Russia's overextended imperial expansion and of the United States' commercial imperialism. After its acquisition by the United States, it became for a long time "Alaska: The Forgotten Frontier."

Raymond H. Fisher is Professor of History, Emeritus, University of California, Los Angeles.

For Further Reading

Barratt, Glynn. *Russia in Pacific Waters, 1715-1825: A Survey of the Origins of Russia's Naval Presence in the North and South Pacific.* Vancouver and London: University of British Columbia Press, 1981.

Fisher, Raymond H. *Bering's Voyages: Whither and Why.* Seattle and London: University of Washington Press, 1977.

Makarova, Raisa V. *Russians on the Pacific, 1743-1799.* Ed. and trans. R. A. Pierce and A. S. Donnelly. Kingston, Ontario: Limestone Press, 1975.

Pierce, Richard A. "Russian Exploration in North America." *Exploration in Alaska: Captain Cook Commemorative Lectures, June-November, 1978.* Ed. Antoinette Shalkop. Anchorage: Cook Inlet Historical Society, 1980.

Russian Penetration of the North Pacific Ocean: A Documentary Record, 1700-1797. Ed. and trans. B. Dmytryshyn, E. A. P. Crownhart-Vaughan, and T. Vaughan. Portland: Oregon Historical Society, 1988.

Wheeler, Mary E. *The Origins and Formation of the Russian-American Company.* Ph.D. dissertation, University of North Carolina, Chapel Hill, 1965. Ann Arbor: University Microfilms.

Notes

1. This voyage is the subject of a study I made several years ago: *The Voyage of Semen Dezhnev in 1648: Bering's Precursor* (London: The Hakluyt Society, 1981). See esp. chapters 7-9.
2. Raymond H. Fisher, *Bering's Voyages: Whither and Why.* (Seattle and London: University of Washington Press, 1977), p. 160.
3. The nautical day began at noon and was half a day ahead of the civil day.
4. Quoted in Fisher, *Bering's Voyages*, p. 94.
5. Arkadii A. Sopotsko, *Istoriia plavaniia V. Beringa na bote, "Sv. Gavriil" v Severnyi ledovityi okean* [History of the voyage of V. Bering in the boat *St. Gabriel* to the Arctic Ocean] (Moscow, 1983), p. 129; Vasilii V. Vakhtin, *Russkie truzheniki moria. Pervaia morskaia ekspeditsiia Beringa dlia resheniia voprosa, soediniaetsia li Aziia s Amerikoi* [Russian toilers of the sea. Bering's maritime expedition to decide whether Asia is joined to America] (St. Petersburg, 1890), p. 57.
6. Quoted in Fisher, *Bering's Voyages*, p. 112.
7. Ibid., p. 131.
8. Ibid., p. 186.
9. This instruction was discarded the next year in favor of a more southerly route south of the yet-to-be-discovered Aleutian Islands.
10. Fisher, *Bering's Voyages*, p. 128; O. W. Frost in Georg W. Steller, *Journal of a Voyage with Bering, 1741-1742* (Stanford: Stanford University Press, 1988), p. 18.

M. T. Tikhanov (1789-1862), Artist-Traveler

by Diliara Safaralieva

The name of the Russian artist Mikhail Tikhonovich Tikhanov, forgotten in the last century, has become much more prominent in this century. His work originally attracted the attention of historians; later, researchers in other fields found it valuable. During the past twenty-five years an unusual interest in his work has developed, mainly among American scholars. Only recently has an adequate assessment of his contribution been possible, either by Russian or world culture.

Tikhanov's work is associated with the circumnavigation of the globe by the sloop *Kamchatka* under the command of Captain-Commander V. M. Golovnin in 1817-19. In his pictures, as in the ship's journal, the route of the expedition is revealed: Kronstadt, Copenhagen, Portsmouth, Rio de Janeiro, Kal'iao, Petropavlovsk at Kamchatka, Kodiak Island, New Archangel (Sitka), Monterey, Bodega (Gulf of Rumiantsev), Hawaiian Islands, Island of Guam, Manila (Philippine Islands), Island of St. Helena, Ascension Island, Faial Island (the Azores Islands), Portsmouth, Copenhagen, Kronstadt.

The expedition had vast and diverse goals. Among them was the inspection of the Russian-American Company, founded in 1799. The company unified the separate Russian commercial and industrial companies that carried on their activities by economically integrating the northwest coasts of America and their offshore islands. The company also organized exploration and promoted commerce on the Pacific Ocean, particularly in its northeastern areas, and existed until 1867, when Russian ownership in America was sold to the United States. Apart from examining the work of the company, members of the crew were to correct the charts, compile descriptions of the shores of America, and study the lives of the people with whom they made contact. Playing a significant role was Tikhanov, the artist of the expedition—a man with an unusually short creative life and a painfully tragic fate. His works are unique artistic-ethnographic sources for the history and culture of the people encountered on the voyage.

An Obscure Beginning

Information about the life and work of M. T. Tikhanov is exceptionally poor. Nothing is known of his origins, the place or exact date of his birth, whether he had previously studied, and, if so, where and with whom. The first mention of Tikhanov in archival documents is found in 1806, when Prince D. N. Golitsyn turned to the Academy of Arts with a petition to take his serf boy, Mikhail Tikhanov, for training.

Few facts have been preserved about the academic period in Tikhanov's life. We know only that he studied in a class for historical painting with the well-known professors G. I. Ugriumov and V. K. Shebuev. In the collection of the State Tretiakov Gallery there is a work by Tikhanov that was done for the completion of his academic course. This picture, painted in 1813 on a theme concerning the Patriotic War of 1812, is entitled, *The Return to God and State of Russian Citizens Shot in Moscow, Who Went to Their Deaths With Firm and Pious Souls, Refusing to Obey Napoleon.* On his canvas the young painter graphically

Tikhanov— artist/realist— was one of those masters who raised naturalistic drawing to the level of great art.

Translated by Mina A. Jacobs

PANNIOIAK—A Woman from Kad'iak Island, Baptized Pelageia, *by Mikhail T. Tikhanov, 1818. Paper, watercolor. Tikhanov was instructed by the Academy of Arts to render each of his subjects in both profile and full-face.*

Collection of the Scientific Research Museum of the Academy of Arts, USSR; photograph courtesy of Shur Collection, Elmer E. Rasmuson Library, University of Alaska, Fairbanks.

portrayed the heroes of the Russian people. The strong patriotic feelings that committed them to great deeds in the name of their homeland are clearly visible. Tikhanov's work was recognized with a small gold medal, but the artist's lack of freedom prevented him from receiving it.

Turning Points

In 1815 Tikhanov celebrated two important events in his life: on the fifth of June he was freed from serfdom, and on September 1 he completed the academy course and received a first degree certificate and the rank of class artist. Following the successful completion of his education, Tikhanov was retained for two years at the academy to perfect his craft. When the two years were up, the artist was not sent abroad, as was the normal practice, because the academy was short of money.

With no real means of earning his own living, Tikhanov received help from the president of the Academy of Arts, A. N. Olenin, at a critical time. Olenin was a patron of artists, writers, and masters in the fine arts. Being on friendly terms with Golovnin, and knowing that the captain would undertake the command of the around-the-world voyage, Olenin seized the opportunity to suggest that Golovnin include, as the expedition's artist, Tikhanov, whom he considered particularly well suited for the assignment.

The Around-the-World Expedition

Olenin supplied Tikhanov with detailed instructions regarding the purpose of the mission and the nature of the staff artist's work. He emphasized the necessity of precision and the exact rendering of nature. The artist must notice all the subtleties pertaining to the features of faces, shapes of figures, the cut and decoration of dress, head wear, hairstyles, weapons, and so on. To obtain maximum accuracy, Olenin ordered that portraits be drawn in two positions, face on and in profile.

In this manner Tikhanov would provide memorable descriptions of the ethnographical and anthropological features of the various races of people. To achieve the expedition's objectives, of course, the work of the artist would have to undergo a fundamental reorientation. The job demanded from him a representation of reality, unadorned and as close to nature as possible, a move away from the canons of classical art that had been the foundation of artistic vision at the academy. At that distant time, when it was not possible to use either camera or cinema, the artist fulfilled the function of painstakingly recording the vital information of the journey.

The album of works by Tikhanov consists of forty-three watercolors. The plates are not dated, nor do all of them have detailed inscriptions. The archival documents of the expedition's participants that have been preserved include: the travel journal of F. F. Matiushkin, a Lyceum friend of A. S. Pushkin's; a diary of F. P. Litke, Russian navigator and geographer; and V. M. Golovnin's book,

Around the World on the Kamchatka, 1817-1819. They provide an opportunity to estimate the year, month, and occasionally even the day when work was begun on any particular watercolor. Unfortunately, it is not known where the entire series of pictures is located that was intended to illustrate a planned supplement to V. M. Golovnin's book. (The supplement was never published.) Along with them, numerous other sketches and scenic studies that Tikhanov mentioned in his only letter to Olenin, on June 11, 1818, have never reached us.

It might be assumed that the artist painted several plates from nature at once, but it appears that he did preliminary rough drafts, which he reworked and completed during the time he was sailing. It was then that the intense work set in for

AN ALEUT *Toien* **from the Fox Islands, Baptized "Kondratii," by Mikhail T. Tikhanov, 1818. Paper, watercolor, lead pencil. The subject, in two profiles and full-face, is holding an inflated bladder.**

Collection of the Scientific Research Museum of the Academy of Arts, USSR; photograph courtesy of Shur Collection, Elmer E. Rasmuson Library, University of Alaska, Fairbanks.

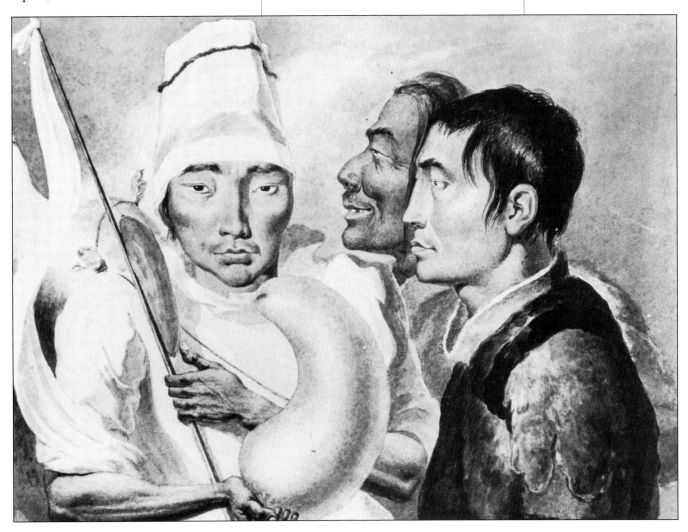

the master, summarizing the factual material collected on the expedition. The compositions of all the watercolors corroborate this idea, as does evidence from the recollections of eyewitnesses. Among the pictures are landscapes, seascapes, scenes with people, and portraits. The watercolors have been accomplished with great precision. They offer a vivid representation of the sights in these diverse lands.

Tikhanov's Technique

Tikhanov's talent impressed his fellow travelers. He managed to reveal himself through the varied techniques of representational art. His use of detail in the portraits resulted in a series of original works. It is extremely important to recognize his iconographic precision. His portraits of individuals seem to form part

of a narration, suggesting former times, lands, and social systems. In addition, the portraits are individual stories of a people and their spiritual world. In his heroes, Tikhanov portrays a wise, searching look. Attention to detail provides a rational foundation to his portraits, but he by no means deprives his subjects of their warm feelings.

Working with nature, the artist must solve the problems of capturing the light and airy perspectives of the landscapes. Tikhanov's art represents a significant step forward in the development of realistic landscape painting during the first quarter of the nineteenth century. His ability to find beauty in the simple and commonplace is his historic contribution to this type of painting. In his works, the people are always occupied with daily, unsophisticated business. Their circle of activity

AN INHABITANT of the Copper River in North America, *by Mikhail T. Tikhanov, 1818. Paper and watercolor. With eagle down in his hair, the subject, in profile and full-face, holds a large piece of copper. His cloak, in brilliant red, further emphasizes the Copper River setting.*

Collection of the Scientific Research Museum of the Academy of Arts, USSR; photograph courtesy of Shur Collection, Elmer E. Rasmuson Library, University of Alaska, Fairbanks.

TOIEN FROM Ngatsk Bay, Kad'iak Island, *by Mikhail T. Tikhanov, 1818. Paper, watercolor, lead pencil, and India ink. The* toien, *in profile and full-face, wears a medal bearing the date 1807 and the initials "PAK" for the Russian-American Company.*

Collection of the Scientific Research Museum of the Academy of Arts, USSR; photograph courtesy of Shur Collection, Elmer E. Rasmuson Library, University of Alaska, Fairbanks.

does not exceed the limits of their simplest, most fundamental interests. (He also enthusiastically studied the many beautiful examples of decorative art that he came across.)

Equally as important as the works done of nature are those painted spontaneously of specific people. In these, particularly noticeable are the anthropological characteristics of the models: the size and structure of the facial skeleton, the hair, pigmentation, form of the nose, size and color of the eyes, and so on. How faithfully the artist fulfilled his responsibility to

A KOLOSH WARRIOR from Baranov Island, *by Mikhail T. Tikhanov, 1818. The Russians referred to Tlingits as Kolosh. This warrior is wearing painted hide armor and carries a dagger and a flintlock rifle.*

Collection of the Scientific Research Museum of the Academy of Arts, USSR; photograph courtesy of Shur Collection, Elmer E. Rasmuson Library, University of Alaska, Fairbanks.

Olenin! In his richly ornamented work, hunters, fishermen, and gatherers reflect a certain vigilance. Their faces personify their own mythology. The ethnographic material depicted in the watercolors illustrates Tikhanov's ability to handle diverse styles of composition and form, an ability typically displayed by great artistic talents.

A Tragic Ending

From the time he left Russia in 1817, right up to June 1819, Tikhanov worked fruitfully. In the Azores Islands, his work suddenly came to an end. He fell seriously ill, became melancholic, then within several days fell into a morbid depression and finally went out of his mind. In this state he was sent to Kronstadt, then quickly on to the infirmary at the Academy of Arts. Toward the end of

October, after his condition improved, he was discharged and began to work on putting his pictures in order.

Apparently, by May 1, 1820, Tikhanov's illness again worsened, for he was sent to a boardinghouse and given a generous imperial pension of six hundred rubles a year for his part in the around-the-world expedition. In December 1820 he was transferred to the psychiatric section of Obukhovskaia Hospital. In February 1822 Tikhanov was taken in by I. V. Luchaninov, a former colleague from the Academy of Arts. Not long after, Luchaninov died, and his wife continued to care for Tikhanov. The artist lived to the age of seventy-three, but never returned to a full existence or creative activity.

Tikhanov's Legacy

In 1819, on the return to his homeland, Golovnin handed over Tikhanov's drawings to Olenin, who should have had the watercolors made into engravings for the publications of the captain. Ultimately, however, Golovnin's book was published without the illustrations. In 1831 the academician engraver A. G. Ukhtomskii was entrusted with the works. He completed twenty-two plates, but by 1841 only two impressions of each plate had been made. In September 1842 Olenin finally transferred the watercolors to the Academy of Arts library. The works were still there in 1907 when the historian and writer A. S. Korotkov corresponded with the library as part of his research on Tikhanov.

In 1941 the album of forty-three watercolors was transferred to the Academy of Arts Museum. During the past few years it has attracted more and more scholars from around the world.

Tikhanov was one of the first Russian artists to paint on the American continent and its islands. Unfortunately, only a part of his important work has reached us.

These watercolors are invaluable testimony to Tikhanov's art and to the lives of people in distant lands.

Tikhanov—artist/realist—was a master who raised naturalistic drawing to the level of great art. His work is an integral part of Russian culture in the first quarter of the nineteenth century. In our time his legacy plays a particularly important role in the enrichment of cultural ties between people.

Diliara Xanym Safaralieva is head of the Graphics Department of the Scientific-Research Museum of the Academy of Arts in Leningrad.

Mina A. Jacobs is Assistant Archivist, Anchorage Museum of History and Art.

American ships caused problems for the Russians. Whenever they made deliveries to New Archangel, or Sitka, they seemed to poach sea otters and smuggle to the Tlingits. Moreover, the American supplies were mostly traded for Russian fur seal skins, which fetched from fifteen to twenty-five rubles each in St. Petersburg or Moscow but only eight rubles at Sitka; the Russians would have preferred to market the skins themselves, of course, but they lacked anything else (such as specie) that the Yankees would accept in return, and even skins had to be replaced by bills of exchange after 1829 because of the depletion of fur seals. As overhunting depleted the sea otters, the New England shipmasters took from the Natives more and more land furs, primarily beaver, which came from the interior via the Skeena, Nass, and Stikine river valleys through Native middlemen. In the early 1820s, American coasters were getting three to five thousand beaver pelts annually; a decade later they were taking double this number. In so doing, they offered the Indians more than the Bay men, who consequently had to follow suit and pay more for fewer pelts. Thanks to this competition, which the Indians naturally welcomed, the price of beaver (and hence the terms of trade) rose fivefold on the coast during the 1820s.

The Hudson's Bay Company Challenges American Traders

The Russian-American Company could do nothing about the encroachment of American traders, other than protest unsuccessfully to Washington, because it was so dependent upon them for supplies; but the Hudson's Bay Company lay under no such restraint and, particularly under George Simpson, governor of the HBC's Northern Department, was determined to counter the "American opposition." Following his inspection of the Columbia Department (Oregon Country) in 1824-25,

Governor Simpson began making the company leaner and meaner by restructuring and rationalizing its operations and eliminating its competitors. The merger of 1821 had disposed of the Canadian competitor, and the Russian-American Company was normally an insignificant rival because it was preoccupied with sea furs and neglected the interior. The main threat, though, was what Simpson called the American "birds of passage," that is, transient traders without permanent bases. To thwart them, the governor decided to employ both trading vessels and trading posts. Fort Vancouver was built in 1825 on the right (and presumably eventually British) bank of the lowermost Columbia River at the mouth of the Willamette (and became departmental headquarters and entrepôt), Fort Langley in 1827 on the Fraser River just above its delta, Fort Simpson in 1831 near the mouth of the Nass River, and Fort McLoughlin in 1833 on Queen Charlotte Sound. The *Dryad,* or Stikine, affair in 1834 was exceptional: The Russians prevented a Hudson's Bay Company coaster from ascending the Stikine River to establish a post that would have intercepted the flow of furs downriver to the Russian redoubt of St. Dionysius at its mouth.

This strategy of the Hudson's Bay Company entailed several other essential elements: trustworthy information, suitable vessels, competent seamen, and tradeable goods. The information was provided by Lieutenant Aemelius Simpson, who was made head of the company's "naval department" in 1827, and who in the following years reconnoitered the northern coast and submitted a detailed report on the coast trade. Several ships were built on the coast or brought from England, but they proved too small or too slow, and at first the captains, too, proved unseaworthy, knowing too little and drinking too much. Shipping did not become satisfactory until the company

THE FUR SEAL also was prized by the Russians as an element in their trade with China and Europe. The Russians first discovered the Pribilof Islands in 1786-87, drawn by the noise of the North Pacific's prime breeding grounds. They forcibly resettled Aleuts on these uninhabited islands to harvest the seals, a practice that continued under American ownership. This is an 1872 scene of the drive to the killing grounds.

From Henry W. Elliott's History and Present Condition of the Fishery Industries: The Seal Islands of Alaska (Washington, D.C., 1881). Washington State Historical Society, Tacoma.

on June 1, 184
The Hudson's
deliver annua
(payable in bi
burg) 8,400 bu
salted beef, 8
wheat flour, c
Oregon, plus
tures as well a
otters, and to
(135,000 silve
Dryad, or Stik
Russian-Ame
lease the *lisièr*
mile-wide coa
Panhandle be
between Cape
Fairweather) a
north latitude
Company for
thousand land
Dionysius Re
American coa
America's po
emergencies.
remain in forc
hostilities bet
a remote poss
worsening rel
government c
can Company
because it wa
favor in matte
Turkey).[1]

The accord v
For the Russia
line had been
sever the trou
tion. The last
in 1839 and r
supply line w
rubles per tor
goods on Hu
versus 194 to
Russian-Ame
180 rubles pe
moreover, on

decided in 1828 to deploy three vessels on the coast—two to make the yearly voyages from London to Fort Vancouver and return, and one to stay on the coast—and in 1831 hired four American officers, all veterans of the coast trade, and bought a newish American brig, the *Lama*. Trade goods proved more problematical owing to damage to cargo on the "London ship," its late arrival at the Columbia River, and even shipwreck. It was not until 1835 that the company's supply of goods for the coast trade became sufficient.

Thus, by the mid 1830s, the Hudson's Bay Company was in a position to oust the "American adventurers," even offering the Indians more for their furs than the Yankees and incurring short-term losses in order to gain sole control of the trade and recoup in the long run. Some American traders, however, persisted, mainly because they enjoyed an additional source of coastal profit: Sitka's demand for provisions. So Governor Simpson had to usurp that market as well as the Indian market. And by now he was in a position to do just that, thanks to the success of company farming at several posts, principally Fort Vancouver. As part of his economy drive of the mid 1820s, the governor

had directed the factors of the posts to become as self-sufficient as possible and replace costly imports with "country produce"—locally produced commodities, including provisions (fish, game, crops, and livestock). Some posts soon developed productive farms; Fort Vancouver was meeting its own food needs by 1828, and by 1835 it was provisioning the London ship instead of vice versa. And from the mid 1830s the Willamette settlers, mostly retired company servants (until 1843, when they were overwhelmed by American migrants), were growing excess wheat, which they exchanged for goods at Fort Vancouver. These agricultural surpluses enabled Simpson to approach the Russian-American Company as early as 1829 and offer to supply Russian America with Columbia provisions and English manufactures in return for furs, specie, or even promissory notes. This offer was repeated in 1832 and again in 1836.

Initially, the Russians hesitated, not wanting to have to rely upon a competitor for something as vital as food. But by the mid 1830s they were more receptive to Simpson's proposal, thanks to two circumstances. One was the withdrawal of

*NEW ARCHAN
1829. In 1804 a
took the Tlingi
near the site of
Sitka, and erec
own. The settl
the capital of t
1808, when adn
was moved fro
From this vant
Governor Bara
to establish ad
relations with
and Hudson's l
traders, who si
provisions tha
to arrive from .*

Published by permissi
Bay Company.

Pacific slope by Great Britain and the United States, and in 1841 Russian California was sold for 30,000 piasters (silver dollars), or 42,857 rubles, to John Sutter, who was to pay mostly in wheat. Its sale, as well as the abandonment of St. Dionysius Redoubt in 1840, saved both money and labor for the Russian-American Company. St. Dionysius Redoubt had cost twelve thousand rubles yearly in upkeep, and Russian California had been losing fourteen to fifteen thousand rubles annually in the late 1830s.

The redundant manpower (even though most of Ross's was infirm) was sorely needed, for from 1838 through 1842, for example, 101 company employees re-turned to Russia and 80 died in the colony, while only 67 recruits arrived, for a net loss of 114. In addition, the leasing of the *lisière* to the Hudson's Bay Company incurred political as well as financial benefits in that, by clearly demarcating an international boundary, it served to mute American territorial pretensions and silence American protests over the non-renewal of the 1824 conven-tion; it also eliminated the basis of territo-rial conflict with the British in the "Kolosh [Tlingit] Straits" (the myriad of straits, sounds, "canals," and passages dividing the Alexander Archipelago and the adjacent mainland). The *lisière* was now off-limits to Russian-American Company operations, of course, but the company had not been able to compete with its British rival in the coast trade anyway because the latter offered the Indians higher prices and better goods. The Russians still sent a trading vessel into the Kolosh Straits every summer, but from 1851 through 1859 the Tlingits virtually ceased trading with the Russian-American Company, channeling nearly all of their traffic to the Hudson's Bay Company. That organization strengthened its coastal

position with the new post of Fort Victoria (1845), which replaced Fort Vancouver as the company's Columbian headquarters with the extension of the American-British boundary along the 49th parallel from the Rockies to the Pacific in 1846 (a Russian steamer began plying the Kolosh Straits again in 1860 for furs and provisions, chiefly potatoes). Owing to intense competition among American, British, and Russian traffickers for more than half a century, the coast trade no longer offered very much to the Russian-American Company (it considered the *lisière* "very poor" in sea otters, for example), so it turned to Kodiak Island, the Alaska Peninsula, the Aleutians, and the Kuriles, where the absence of keen competition and the implementation of conservation measures had sustained furbearers. In contrast, sea otters became extinct on the Northwest coast. At the same time, the company began to spread its economic risk by diversifying into the Shanghai tea trade, the Kamchatka retail trade, the California ice trade, and other ventures.

The chief benefit of the 1839 agreement to the Russian-American Company was the reliable supply of abundant and economi-cal provisions, whereas the main advan-tage to the Hudson's Bay Company was domination—near monopolization—of the coast trade, one of Simpson's long-standing goals. Deprived of their Sitkan market for supplies, the American traders withdrew, leaving the traffic of the entire Northwest coast (including the *lisière* but excluding the Alexander Archipelago) in the hands of the British, who were conse-quently able to lower fur prices in the absence of competition. They were also able to eliminate "Indian rum," which they had traded on the assumption that if they did not sell it, the Americans or Russians would, and get more furs. Fewer posts were likewise needed now, so Forts McLoughlin and Taku, or Durham, were abandoned in 1843 as was Fort Stikine, or

Highfield (which had replaced St. Diony-sius Redoubt) in 1849.

The coast trade was now, in Simpson's language, "tranquil."[2] It was also substantial and profitable. In the early 1840s, the company's coast trade yielded up to 10,000 beaver and land otter (plus small furs) annually; nearly all of these returns came from the *lisière*, which in 1843, for instance, furnished 12,343 pelts worth some eight thousand pounds.[3] These collections were particularly valuable in that they offset the decline in returns from the lower Columbia basin (the southern half of the Columbia Department, or Oregon Country). The *lisière's* 1843 returns, for example, were equal to one-half of those of the lower Columbia and between one-sixth and one-fifth of those of the entire Columbia Department.[4]

The Hudson's Bay Company gained, too, from the delivery and sale of supplies to Sitka. It did have to go to the trouble and expense of creating a subsidiary, the Puget's Sound Agricultural Company, with farms at Nisqually and Cowlitz that produced more wool and hides than wheat and beef, but the former found a profitable market in Britain, and sufficient of the latter was obtained from Fort Vancouver's farm and bartered from the Willamette Valley's settlers to meet the terms of the "Russian contract." The Hudson's Bay Company paid the Willamette settlers in goods at three shillings per bushel of wheat, which it then sold to the Russians for about six shillings (including freight costs to Sitka); the resulting profit amounted to some £750 yearly. For British (mostly) and Russian manufactures, the company charged the Russians thirteen pounds per ton for delivery to Sitka on chartered vessels, which in turn charged the company only about one-third that freight rate; this profit equaled almost four thousand pounds in 1844.[5] Altogether, the Hudson's Bay Company netted £1,805 in 1841 and £1,461 in 1842 on the 1839 agreement.[6]

FORT NISQUALLY in 1845, a watercolor by Henry J. Ware. This Hudson's Bay Company post and its neighbor, Cowlitz Farm, supplied food-stuffs to the Russians at Sitka during the 1840s and 1850s.

Royal Ontario Museum, Toronto.

Contract Renewal

Both the Russian-American Company and the Hudson's Bay Company benefited from the terms of the 1839 accord, but when it was renewed for another ten-year term, from June 1, 1849, until mid 1859 (when the charters of both companies were due to expire), those terms were altered, thanks to the rapidly changing productive farm, at Fort Vancouver, and both farms of the Puget's Sound Agricultural Company, as well as the Columbia routeway to its New Caledonia posts. The Honorable Company was left with sizable farms at Forts Victoria and Langley only, and, in fact, they alone largely met the provisionment clause of the 1839 agreement in 1848 and 1849.

SEA OTTER, *an engraving by John Webber, artist with the British expedition led by James Cook, 1776-79.*

Anchorage Museum of History and Art.

political and economic geography of the Far West. For one thing, the provisionment clause was dropped because the British were no longer able to fulfill it. This inability stemmed from two new realities: the completion of the international boundary between British North America and the United States, and the California gold rush. In 1846 the Treaty of Washington put an end to the "joint occupation" of the Oregon Country by extending the international frontier along the 49th parallel from the Rockies to the Pacific via the Strait of Juan de Fuca, thereby impeding (by means of squatters and revenuers) the Hudson's Bay Company's use of most of its Columbian agricultural property, including its most

In addition, in 1848 gold was discovered at the mill of John Sutter, the same man who had bought Russian California seven years earlier (and who did not make his final payment until 1852, seven years overdue). The gold fever was caught by thousands, including Hudson's Bay Company servants and Willamette Valley settlers, who rushed to Sutter's Mill to make their fortune, leaving their Columbian farms to languish. Chief Factor James Douglas wrote to Governor Mikhail Teben'kov in 1849 that it would be "very difficult" for his company to provision Sitka at any price, since some two-thirds of the white settlers of the Oregon Country had abandoned their farmlands for California's gold fields.

"Everything has been abandoned in the Columbia and Oregon, where they formerly cultivated wheat," reported Teben'kov to his company's St. Petersburg headquarters; "everyone has gone to look for gold in California, where grain is now imported from Chile and sold for up to 20 silver rubles per *pud* [36 pounds] of ordinary wheat flour!"[7]

The impact of the 1846 boundary settlement was felt first, in fact, in that very year, when the Russian-American Company, content with the price but not the amount of the British provisions, began sending its own on chartered Finnish freighters out of Åbo (Turku). From 1850, it used its own ships, too, seven of which it bought in Britain, Germany, and the United States between 1850 and 1853. With the same ships the company likewise provisioned Kamchatka. And it began to ship not only grain from Baltic ports to Sitka, but also beef from Ayan, which it had begun to develop in the early 1840s as a safer port than Okhotsk (with a faster and cheaper Iakutsk link, over which the Yakut cattle were driven). The company shifted its Okhotsk factory to Ayan in 1843-48, and from 1846 it transported all of its Siberian freight via Ayan rather than Okhotsk, which lost its official port status in 1849.

Furthermore, when in the middle 1850s Russia reacquired control of the Amur River by establishing a series of military outposts along its banks, the Russian-American Company, which took a direct part in the reconquest, began to ship provisions for Russian America down the river from Transbaikalia. This was an attempt to circumvent the long-standing bottleneck between the Lena River at Iakutsk and the Okhotsk Seaboard by taking advantage of the only major artery to flow from the Siberian interior to the Pacific. By the early 1860s, the company annually sent to its colony 27,500 *puds* of flour and 2,500 *puds* of groats and rice

(virtually half of which was consumed at Sitka) on its own ships from Europe (St. Petersburg and especially Hamburg, with a surcharge of 45 percent for insurance, packing, and loading), and 1,500 to 2,000 *puds* of beef from Ayan, Amuria, and California (nearly all of which was consumed at Sitka).

In the early 1850s, California experienced a rejuvenation of commercial agriculture, and from 1852 the Russian-American Company established a "vice consul"—in fact, a commercial agent—in San Francisco to facilitate trade, including provisions (as well as Alaskan ice). From 1861 the company bought provisions in California and Hawaii because they were cheaper. Occasionally, Russian America suffered shortages of provisions, as in 1852, when no supply ship reached Sitka from Europe, and during the Crimean War (1854-56), when Russian transports were loath to risk capture by the stronger allied fleet; but in general the colony was amply and reliably served by the new multivariate system of provisionment, thanks to the increasing settlement, development, and mercantile ties of the lands of the North Pacific rim.

The 1849 agreement renewal was different from the 1839 original in a couple of other respects, too. The freight rate of thirteen pounds per ton for the delivery of manufactures to Sitka on British ships, so profitable to the Hudson's Bay Company and expensive for the Russian-American Company, was lowered to ten pounds by virtue of the large volume of cargo. But even before this reduction, of course, the Russians, as early as 1846, had taken the remedial measure of chartering freighters on their own account for no more than six pounds per ton, and then (from 1850) of acquiring their very own transports. This measure reflects the degree to which the company's naval arm had improved by mid-century, with better officers and better crewmen. Also in 1850, the company began to buy goods in Hamburg directly from the manufacturers rather than in London from wholesalers because both prices and expenses were lower in Germany. The brokerage fee, for example, was half as much in Hamburg as in London, and the cost for loading and hauling was reduced by almost one-half. At the same time, the company tightened quality control by sending an agent, Adolf Etholen, a former governor of Russian America, to Hamburg to check the supplies bought there. Thus, during the term of the renewed agreement, there was no shipping of British provisions and manufactures on British ships to Sitka.

Additionally, the rental terms for the *lisière* were changed. The Hudson's Bay Company wanted to pay less rent because of lower fur returns, but the Russian-American Company refused at first, only to relent after having been persuaded by Governor Pelly's argument that the lease was the best way of avoiding conflicts between the two companies on the Northwest coast. The rent was reduced first to two thousand land otter skins, then to fifteen hundred skins, and finally (in 1854, 1855, or 1856) to fifteen hundred pounds, the demand for land otters on the Chinese market at Kiakhta having fallen, thereby making the skins paid by the British less desirable to the Russians.[8]

The "Russian contract"—the little that remained after the dropping of the provisionment and freight clauses and the lowering of the *lisière*'s rent—was renewed four more times. In 1859 it was extended until the end of 1861, when the Russian-American Company's charter expired, on the condition that the Hudson's Bay Company engage in the trading of the *lisière*'s furs only. Earlier, the Russians had granted exclusive rights to the trading of other products (principally ice) to San Francisco's American-Russian Commercial Company. That firm's competitor, the North West Ice Company, had in 1853 signed a six-year contract with the Hudson's Bay Company for the purchase of glacial ice from the *lisière* for $14,000 annually, which was nearly double the Honorable Company's yearly rent of $7,200 (£1,500). This

THE ALEUTS, *forced by the Russians, developed an efficient and productive way of killing thousands of seals to serve the fur markets of the world. The techniques continued under American jurisdiction, as shown in this scene from 1872.*

From Henry W. Elliott's History and Present Condition of the Fishery Industries: The Seal Islands of Alaska (Washington, D.C., 1881). Washington State Historical Society, Tacoma.

competition had lowered ice prices in California and consequently Russian profits on sales there.

When the Russian-American Company's charter was extended in June 1861 until June 1, 1863, so was the agreement with the Hudson's Bay Company; it was renewed again until June 1, 1865, and once again until June 1, 1867. When this last renewal was being discussed in 1865, the Russians offered to either lease the *lisière* again or even sell it to the Hudson's Bay Company, which chose to rent; if it had opted to buy, the length of British coastline would have almost doubled, and the Alaska boundary dispute at the end of the century would have been avoided.[9] The Honorable Company apparently saw little or no commercial value in the mainland panhandle, and its disinclination to purchase left only one feasible buyer for the colony—the United States.

Neutrality Pact

Meanwhile, the Russian-American and Hudson's Bay companies had signed another accord, strategic rather than commercial, that led indirectly to the Alaska cession. This was the neutrality pact at the time of the Crimean War between Russia and the allies Britain and France. This conflict represented the first serious military threat to Russia's sole overseas colony. Russia had been at odds with rival great powers earlier, of course, as at the rift with Britain in 1807 and the war with Napoleonic France in 1812, but at those times Russian America was not an attractive prize, being thinly colonized and weakly developed. By the middle of the century, however, it was a much riper plum, containing more Russians and enjoying considerable seaborne trade (tea from Shanghai, ice to California, provisions to Kamchatka, salt from Hawaii), as well as whaling and regular round-the-world voyages. Moreover, the Russian-American Company simply could not afford adequate naval defenses, and the Russian navy was no match for the combined British-French fleet. This glaring indefensibility of the colony (which was to remain a key argument of advocates of its disposal) prompted the two companies in early 1854 to agree to neutralization of the colonial territory and colonial shipping of both firms in the event of war, which erupted shortly thereafter with Britain and France (hostilities with Turkey had begun the previous year). France did not officially recognize the agreement, but did honor it. The pact did not exempt shipping on the high seas or preclude a blockade of colonial ports, but during the war no Russian ships were taken and no blockade was mounted in Russian-American waters. Sitka was intimidated when it was visited for two weeks in the summer of 1853 (that is, just before the formal declaration of war with Britain and France) by the thirty-six-gun British frigate *Trincomalee,* but secure two years later when an Anglo-French squadron dropped anchor in Sitka Sound. The company's only losses during the war were three vessels that were seized in 1854-55 on the nonneutral Asiatic coast of Siberia. During the war, Russian America was supplied from California and Chile by the ships of neutral nations, although at greater expense; also, at least two company ships (the *Alexander II* and the *Nakhimov*) were operated in colonial waters under the American flag and with American crewmen. In 1854, 1857, and 1858, the colony was supplied by ships from Europe, and when Governor Stepan Voievodsky left in 1858, there were enough supplies on hand for one year.

Russia, as the weaker party, obviously had more need of the neutrality pact. Britain nevertheless favored the agreement so that Russia would not feel compelled to sell Russian America to the

United States in order to preclude a British seizure; in other words, the Hudson's Bay Company in effect accepted the agreement in return for a continuation of the *lisière* lease. Russia's minister to Washington, Edouard de Stoeckl, noted that this British kindness, "this act of affability, which is so little in harmony with English egotism, had a secret reason behind it. A rumor was gaining currency at the time that we were preparing to sell our colonies to the United States; and it was in order to block such a sale that the British government gave its approval to the agreement between the two Companies."[10] This, then, was the first time that the prospect of American acquisition of Russian-American territory was officially acknowledged. Furthermore, the future price of the Alaska purchase was first mentioned at this time. While the neutrality pact was being negotiated, the governor of Russian America (through the company's agent in San Francisco, Peter Kostromitinov) arranged a fictitious sale of the colony to the American-Russian Commercial Company for three years (May 1, 1854- May 1, 1857) for seven million dollars in order to forestall a British seizure in case

of war. Stoeckl devised another plan to issue licenses to Russian privateers to enable them to operate out of San Francisco against British and French merchantmen in the Pacific in the event of hostilities. Both of these schemes were aborted by the signing of the neutrality pact, but they reflected the extent of American sympathy for Russia and raised the possibility of a sale of Russian America to the United States.

Thus, by the early 1850s Russian America was much more self-reliant and much less dependent upon neighboring and competing countries, colonies, and companies for its existence. It had come a very long way since the turn of the century, when the colonial capital itself had to be retaken from the Tlingit Indians, the tsar's imperial chamberlain had to rescue the colony from starvation by sailing to San Francisco to plead for Spanish provisions, and the *promyshlenniki* had to partner rather than contest rival American coasters. The Russian-American Company had achieved this feat by enlisting more and more government support in the form of able naval officers as colonial governors (e.g.,

SITKA IN 1860 gives all the appearance of a bustling seaport town. Aleut and Tlingit kayaks compete for space in the harbor with sailing ships from around the world.

Engraving from P. A. Tikhmenev, A History of the Russian-American Company (St. Petersburg, 1863).

Ferdinand P. von Wrangell, Adolf Etholen, and Mikhail Teben'kov) and ship captains and also by diversifying the colony's economy. Meanwhile, the Hudson's Bay Company was being impaired by political compromise and changing fashion. That Russian America, albeit remote and exposed, was able to weather the Crimean tempest attests its remarkably strengthened position. Its robust state serves to remind us that it was not ceded to the United States in 1867 because it was no longer economically viable; political and strategic factors motivated St. Petersburg to dispose of a quite healthy colony.

James R. Gibson is Professor of Geography, York University, Toronto.

For Further Reading

The End of Russian America: Captain P. N. Golovin's Last Report, 1862. Ed. and trans. Basil Dmytryshyn and E. A. P. Crownhart-Vaughan. Portland: Oregon Historical Society, 1979.

Gibson, James R. *Farming the Frontier: The Agricultural Opening of the Oregon Country, 1786-1846.* Vancouver: University of British Columbia Press, 1985.

_____. *Feeding the Russian Fur Trade: Provisionment of the Okhotsk Seaboard and the Kamchatka Peninsula, 1639-1856.* Madison: University of Wisconsin Press, 1989.

_____. *Imperial Russia in Frontier America: The Changing Geography of Supply of Russian America, 1784-1867.* New York: Oxford University Press, 1976.

_____. "Diversification on the Frontier: Russian America in the Middle of the Nineteenth Century." *Studies in Russian Historical Geography.* Ed. J. H. Bater and R. A. French. London: Academic Press, 1983, vol. 1, pp. 199-242.

Notes

1. The English text of the agreement has been published in E. H. Oliver, ed., *The Canadian North-West: Its Early Development and Legislative Records* (Ottawa: Government Printing Bureau, 1914), v. 2, pp. 791-796, and United States Congress, Senate, *Proceedings of the Alaskan Boundary Tribunal* (Washington, 1904), v. 1, pp. 150-152.

2. Hudson's Bay Company Archives (hereafter cited as HBCA), A.12/2; D.4/66.

3. HBCA, D.4/110; A.12/2, fo. 292; D.4/66, fo. 52v.

4. See James R. Gibson, *Farming the Frontier: The Agricultural Opening of the Oregon Country 1786-1846* (Vancouver: University of British Columbia Press, 1985), Table 30, p. 201.

5. HBCA, A.12/2, fo. 292v; D.4/66, fo. 53; D.5/8, fo. 153; P. A. Tikhmenev, *A History of the Russian-American Company,* trans. Richard A. Pierce and Alton S. Donnelly (Seattle: University of Washington Press, 1978), pp. 327, 355.

6. HBCA, D.5/8, fo. 161v. The Hudson's Bay Company may also have profited from a percentage of the cargo insurance it arranged in Britain for the Russian-American Company.

7. United States, National Archives and Records Service, File Microcopies of Records in the National Archives: No. 11. Records of the Russian-American Company 1802-1867: "Correspondence of Governors General," roll 55, fo. 146, fo. 150v.

8. Rossiisko-Amerikanskaia Kompaniia [Russian-American Company], Otchyot Rossiisko-Amerikanskoy Kompanii Glavnavo Pravleniya.... [Report of the Head Office of the Russian-American Company] (St. Petersburg, 1853), p. 4; Rossiia, Departmenta manufaktur i vnutrennei torgovli [Russia, Department of Manufactories and Domestic Trade], Doklad Komiteta ob ustroistve Russkikh Amerikanskikh koloni [Report of the Committee on the Organization of the Russian-American Colonies] (St. Petersburg, 1863), pt. 2, appendix X; Tikhmenev, *History*, p. 355.

9. Memorandum of A. Rutkovik to the Board of the Hudson's Bay Company, January 14/26, 1865, HBCA, F.29/2.

10. Quoted in S. B. Okun, *The Russian-American Company,* trans. Carl Ginsburg (Cambridge, Mass.: Harvard University Press, 1951), p. 241.

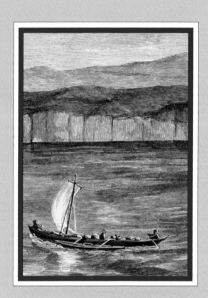

Merchants *and* Diplomats: Russian America *and the* United States

by Stephen W. Haycox

One merchant, though, was prepared to step in to help the Russians, and help himself at the same time.

T he relationship between the United States and Russian America involved two important issues: America's commercial growth and its expansion to the Pacific. During the early national and antebellum periods, the contest over sovereignty on the Northwest coast, the developing Pacific and Northwest trade, and the lucrative Bering Sea whale fishery drew Russia and the United States into significant diplomatic negotiations that were sometimes cooperative, sometimes competitive, but always of great importance and considerable consequence to both countries. The Russian decision to sell Russian America to the United States in 1867 came about because the imperial government had become convinced that it was but a matter of time before the United States, having expanded rapidly westward to the Pacific, would look north and set its sights on the modest Russian colony.

Trade

B efore the American Revolution, East Coast American entrepreneurs had established important trading relations with Russia. The firm of Boylston and Green of Boston shipped cargoes of sugar, indigo, rum, mahogany, and sassafras to St. Petersburg as early as 1763. American voyages were very small in number compared to the shipping to Russia from England proper, but such American trading to Russia as did exist before the Revolution introduced important American mercantile houses to Russian idiosyncrasies and, more importantly, helped familiarize the Americans with Russia's own trading capabilities.

Most American trade was suspended during the Revolutionary War, but very soon after Grigorii Shelikhov founded his first permanent Russian settlement in America on Kodiak Island in 1784, American merchants looking for new markets and products discovered the potential for trade in sea otter pelts from the Northwest coast. Following the treaty of American independence, Britain so severely restricted American trade to the West Indies that American merchants had to look for alternatives. In 1787 the American merchant ships *Washington* and *Columbia* sailed for the Northwest, the first American vessels to do so. Robert Gray in the *Columbia* completed America's first world circumnavigation and, in 1792, also discovered the mouth of the Columbia River. The discovery established an American claim to the Northwest coast, which the British also had claimed since the voyage of James Cook in 1778. During the voyage Gray collected 1,050 sea otter skins from Indians along the Northwest coast and sold them in Canton for $21,404. After that, an American rush to the Northwest was on. Merchants from Boston, Salem, New York, and Philadelphia hastened to invest in the expeditions. But since most of the traders were out of Boston, the Natives, and later the Russians, called them (and all Americans) Bostonians, Bostonmen, or, more simply, "Bostons."

The Spanish also claimed the Northwest, somewhat audaciously asserting sovereignty over all of the west coasts of South and North America. On the strength of that claim, Estaban Martinez in the *Princesa* and Lopez de Haro in the *San Carlos* had proclaimed Spanish dominion over Unalaska Island on a visit there in 1788. The next year they captured three British vessels that were trading with Indians at Nootka Sound, on Vancouver Island. Both the *Washington* and the *Columbia* had visited Nootka earlier, but had left by the time the Spanish arrived. Another American vessel, *Fair America*, captained by teenaged Thomas Humphrey Metcalfe, blundered into the sound while the Spanish were there, and also was captured. He and his vessel were released later without much fanfare, but the capture of the British ships led to an international incident. The Spanish soon recognized that they were overextended, however, and settled the affair in the Nootka Convention, by which they effectively vacated their claims on the Northwest coast from Nootka northward.

Before 1795, the British predominated in the Northwest trade, having discovered the Chinese market for sea otter pelts ten years earlier. But by 1795, American merchantmen had made fifteen separate voyages to the Northwest coast, most of them highly profitable. The Americans traded directly with the Indians of the coast, who sold them sea otter pelts they had hunted especially for the trade. The traders took the pelts to China, where they brought handsome prices paid in Chinese trade goods, including tea, silk, nankeen (buff-colored cotton cloth), and porcelain. The Americans paid the Indians six yards of cloth and a mirror, scissors and beads, or a gun plus powder and lead for one sea otter pelt. At this they outbid the British traders, who had been paying only a yard and a half of woolen cloth or one gun and some powder for five or six pelts. Over the next decade, the American prices nearly drove the British out of the trade altogether; between 1795 and 1804, sixty-eight American ships were on the coast trading for furs, compared to just nine British vessels. American traders were able to pay higher prices because the Chinese trade goods brought much higher prices in America than in England. In the

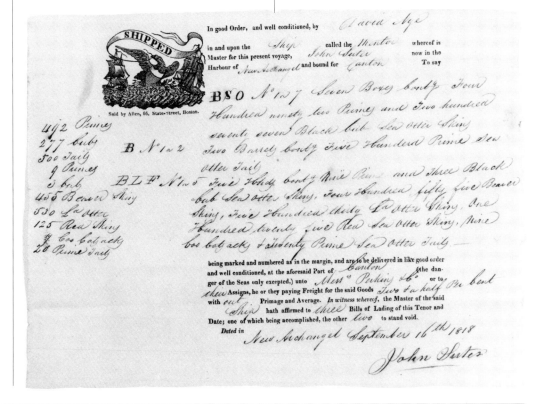

BILL OF LADING, *September 16, 1818, dated at New Archangel (Sitka), showing the number and types of furs loaded aboard the* **Mentor,** *out of Boston, destined for Canton, China.*

John Suter Papers, Massachusetts Historical Society, Boston.

United States, profits of two hundred thousand dollars and more for a two-year voyage to the Northwest and China were not extraordinary. Americans would continue to trade furs with the Indians along the coast until after the 1820s.

Russian-American Company

The Russians regarded the British and American trade as a threat to their northern posts and their territorial plans. By 1795 they were firmly established along the Alaska Peninsula, on Kodiak and neighboring islands, and in Cook Inlet (which they called Kenai Bay) and Prince William Sound (Chugach Bay), and had territorial designs on the whole of the Northwest coast as far south as Spanish San Francisco. They were also highly concerned about the peltry, which they hoped to control and profit from. When the government in St. Petersburg chartered the Russian-American Company in 1799 with a monopoly over all Russian fur-gathering and trading in America, orders were issued to Alexander Baranov, who held the offices of governor of the colony and manager of the Russian-American Company, to extend the dominion of the company, and Russia, as far southward as possible without bringing conflict with other powers. When, in 1802, the Tlingit Indians destroyed St. Archangel Michael's Redoubt, the post he had established in the Alexander Archipelago, Baranov immediately resolved to re-establish Russian presence there. The government approved this decision, and renewed Baranov's instructions to establish posts as far to the southward as possible without causing open conflict with foreign powers. The new post, New Archangel (Sitka), would become his permanent colonial headquarters. Among other considerations, in the colonial contests of the Western powers, possession still was a good portion of law.

This also applied to the Native populations. Like the other European powers that colonized America, Russia treated Natives as inferiors because of their generally less sophisticated technologies and their non-Christian ideologies. From a pragmatic standpoint, none of the Indian populations on the Northwest coast had developed firearms on their own, or ships that could sail across oceans. Moreover, they did not have a knowledge of global geography. The Europeans extended their assumption of superiority beyond the practical to include culture. Politically, they concluded that the Indians could not successfully defend the land, and therefore, the European powers should appropriate it and exercise their sovereignty over the Native populations. To some degree this was a fiction, for the Russian hold on their portion of the coast was always somewhat insecure. On the other hand, the Russians, English, Spanish, and Americans all were able to prevail technologically over the Natives, and the major historical question would become how they would treat Natives who had occupied the land and built cultures upon it before European contact, and especially to what degree they would acknowledge Native land and human rights.[1]

The Russian hold on the coast was tenuous for other reasons as well. Though company profits grew from increasing numbers of pelts taken each year, neither the government nor the company board of directors ever conceived of colonial America as an area for large-scale settlement. Russian America was a fur resource that the Russians sought to exploit as efficiently and cheaply as possible as long as it might last. They never committed vast resources to found a colonial enterprise on the scale of the British American colonies or even the Spanish colonies in America. Boston was a town of 20,000 souls in 1741 when Bering discovered North America from the west, but the largest number of Russians ever in Russian America was 823. Supply from St. Petersburg was never adequate, and ever-present shortages of basic necessities grew worse during the Napoleonic Wars. The supply situation was further complicated by the fact that the Chinese would allow foreigners to trade in only one port. The British and the Americans were able to trade at Canton, on the Pacific, but the Russians were restricted to Kiakhta, a village on the Russian-Chinese border in the mountains south of Irkutsk, in eastern Siberia.

After a few years of struggle with the problem of supply, Baranov attempted to deal with the shortages by forming joint ventures with American mercantile companies. In November 1803, an Irish-American, Joseph O'Cain, struck a bargain with Baranov: O'Cain would sell his cargo of basic goods to Baranov, and give him a share of the pelts collected. O'Cain and the other Americans needed the Aleuts because the Spanish, also annoyed

at American traders, had prohibited them from landing anywhere in Spanish possessions. O'Cain asserted that by anchoring outside the territorial limit, and sending the Aleuts ashore in boats, he could circumvent the Spanish restrictions. Baranov agreed to the proposal. At the conclusion of the voyage, Baranov's profit amounted to eighty thousand dollars.

Soon other American traders rushed to offer similar deals, and together they became middlemen in the brisk trade of Russian sea otter pelts to the Chinese at Canton. By the outbreak of the War of 1812, Baranov had supplied Aleut hunters on similar terms for twelve separate American hunting expeditions on the California coast. In May 1806, the *O'Cain*, this time captained by Jonathan Winship, Jr., probably landed Aleuts in Humboldt Bay, on the California coast. In 1811, one Russian and four American ships were anchored near San Francisco Bay while more than three hundred Aleut hunters harvested sea otters along the coast. Meanwhile, other ships continued to trade

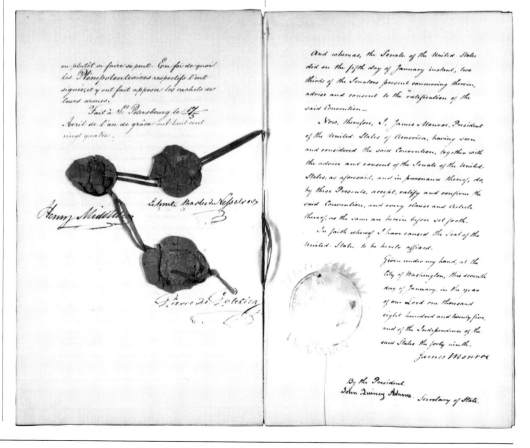

RUSSO-AMERICAN Treaty of 1824. This first treaty between the United States and Russia gave Americans the right to trade freely along the coasts occupied by Russia, and was a major victory for President James Monroe and Secretary of State John Quincy Adams. It also established that Russia would not attempt to extend its influence below 54°40' north latitude.

National Archives, Washington, D. C.

with the Indians along the coast north of Nootka Sound. Merchants and their companies engaged in the Northwest trade at this time included Abiel Winship, Benjamin Homer, Nathan Winship, John D'Wolf, Joseph Coolidge, Theodore Lyman, Samuel and Sylvanus Gray, J. and T. Lamb, J. and T. H. Perkins, Russel and William Sturgis, James Lloyd, A. C. Dorr, J. K. Jones, Andrew Cabot, James and Henry Lee, T. C. Amory, Oliver Keating, Boardman and Pope, John Jacob Astor, and others; in short, most of the major merchant families of Boston, Salem, Providence, Bristol, and the other New England shipping ports.[2]

In the fall of 1805, Nikolai Rezanov, grand chamberlain to the tsar and a former chief director of the company (he had married Shelikhov's daughter), arrived in the colony and spent the winter with Baranov at New Archangel reviewing policies and making plans for future expansion. Rezanov hoped to establish company posts in Hawaii, at the mouth of the Columbia River, and on the California coast. While there, the chamberlain got firsthand experience with shortages in the colony, for by winter supplies had dwindled dangerously low. In October he purchased the American vessel *Juno*, owned and captained by John D'Wolf of Bristol, which had arrived after collecting a full cargo of furs along the coast. In March, Rezanov took the vessel south to see if he could buy supplies from the Spanish at San Francisco. Along the way, the captain of the voyage, Lt. Kvostov, attempted unsuccessfully for two days, March 31 and April 1, to get across the Columbia River bar, nearly losing a boat and crew in the process. The vessel continued on to San Francisco, where Rezanov arranged for emergency purchases, and gained a useful impression of Spanish capabilities and intentions regarding the coast north of there.

As it happened, the *Juno*'s failure to get into the Columbia River was significant, for remarkably, unknown to Rezanov, the American explorers Lewis and Clark had camped all winter at the mouth of the river. The two American captains had broken camp just a few days earlier, on March 23. On the night of the thirty-first, as the Russian ship lay off Cape Disappointment, near the Columbia estuary, Lewis and Clark were camped near the present site of old Fort Vancouver, one hundred miles upriver from the coast. It is entirely conceivable that had Rezanov's ship made it across the Columbia River bar, Indian runners would have been sent after Lewis and Clark, who had delayed their departure from Fort Clatsop partly in hopes that they might make contact with American or English trading vessels sailing along the coast. Had Rezanov been able to found a post at the mouth of the river, the American claim to the Northwest coast would have been substantially weakened, and the Russian presence immeasurably strengthened. It would have been a difficult undertaking, however, as was manifested by the shipwreck of the Russian schooner *Sv. Nikolai* and the capture of its crew on the Oregon Country coast in 1808 by coast Indians. Nonetheless, in 1812, Baranov was successful in securing a lease to a small area on the California coast ninety miles north of San Francisco, where he established Fort Ross. The modest post was to supply grain to the Russian-American colony, and serve as a station from which to hunt sea otters along the California coast.

Despite Baranov's cooperation with some Boston traders taking furs along the coast, the Russians were not happy with the Americans' trading. The Americans disregarded both Russia's claimed sovereignty, and potential profits. In addition, over Russian protests, the Americans traded firearms to the Indians, which made them a major threat to the Russian hold on the Alexander Archipelago. It is likely that some of the guns the Tlingits used when they captured Baranov's first post in the islands in 1802 had been obtained from American traders. As early as 1808, the Russians made an official protest through the American consul-general in St. Petersburg, and over the next two years protests were made through the American ambassador to Russia, John Quincy Adams, and through Russian diplomats in Washington, D.C. Their complaints were ineffective, however, the American government taking the position that whatever the traders did was fair capitalism.

John Jacob Astor

One merchant, though, was prepared to step in to help the Russians, and help himself at the same time. Since the return of Lewis and Clark, New York fur merchant John Jacob Astor had sought to monopolize the western American fur trade, a trade principally in beavers. His plan included establishing a permanent post at the mouth of the Columbia. To help ensure his control of the area drained by the Columbia, Astor was prepared to make a long-term deal with Baranov.

By November 1809, Astor had persuaded the Russian consul-general to the United States, Andrei Dashkov, to write to Baranov urging him to purchase all his provisions from Astor. At the same time, Astor sent to Sitka one of his ships laden with trade goods, the *Enterprise*, commanded by John Ebbets, who had considerable experience in the China and the Northwest trade. The *Enterprise* cargo was typical of the goods the Russians were prepared to purchase at this time. It included, among other items, eighteen hogsheads of brown sugar, fifty-four of rice, ten of tobacco and thirty-four of molasses, seventeen barrels of vinegar, twenty-two of flour, and forty-three of turpentine; there was also soap, tea, rum, gin and brandy, cartridge paper, fishing nets, scissors, needles and sealing wax, twenty-three pairs of woolen stockings, and five pieces of white serge. Ebbets sold the whole cargo for twenty-six thousand dollars. He then agreed to take a cargo of Russian furs to Canton. He traded them there for Chinese goods, which he took back to Sitka. The furs were valued at seventy-four thousand dollars total in Canton; there were three thousand sea otter pelts, which brought $21.50 apiece, assorted sea otter tails for $2.215, sixty-six thousand fur seal pelts, dressed ones fetching $2.00 each and undressed, $1.00, and beaver pelts for $6.50 each, and one hundred *puds* of whalebone, as well as miscellaneous foxes, river otters, and walrus teeth. Ebbets charged Baranov eighteen thousand dollars in freight charges, and a five-percent commission.[3]

When he first arrived at Sitka, Ebbets had presented a number of papers to Baranov, including a letter from Dashkov, a letter from Astor, and a proposed contract regarding future trade relations with Astor. What Astor had in mind was a monopoly. In return for supplying all of Baranov's trade needs, Astor asked that Baranov prohibit any other American traders from operating on the coast. The letters and contract were written in English and French, but, through some oversight, no Russian copy had been included. Fortunately, a day or two later, the Russian sloop of war *Diana* appeared, commanded by Capt. Vasilii M. Golovnin, who, assisted by a subordinate, translated the letters and drew up the contract. However, though the negotiations were protracted, the governor and the ship captain could not reach an agreement, despite the supporting letter from

Dashkov. Astor had not included the prices he would charge, Baranov had not heard from the board of directors of the company in three years and did not know what other contracts they might have entered into, and Baranov doubted his own and Astor's capability to keep other American traders from the coast.

In the meantime, Astor had learned of the Russian concern over the sale of firearms to the Indians. In June 1810, he sent his son-in-law, A. B. Bentzon, to Washington to present his plan for a trading monopoly to the Russian minister to the United States, Count Fedor Palen. Astor sweetened his proposal by assuring that he would not provide the Natives with arms or ammunition. Palen communicated with St. Petersburg and was told that officials in the Russian government did not believe the United States had either the will or the power to limit its citizens' trade on the Northwest coast. However, officials were interested in the possibility of an agreement between the Russian-American Company and Astor's American Fur Company.

In 1811, Bentzon went to St. Petersburg to attempt to work out such an agreement. Negotiations were difficult, but in May 1812, a four-year convention between the two fur companies was signed by the Russians, and in December by Astor. By its terms, each company would refrain from trading with Natives in the vicinity of the other's posts, and would not sell firearms to the Natives. Astor had by now established his post, Astoria, at the mouth of the Columbia. Additionally, Astor would supply the Russian colony with the sort of goods Ebbets had delivered, and would transport Russian furs to Canton, and Chinese goods to Alaska. Each company agreed that it would not trade with merchants from other countries, meaning Britain, and would attempt to keep other American merchants from the Northwest coast.

This was a highly significant agreement, for it sought to bring Russia and the United States into full commercial control of the Northwest coast. Had it been implemented, it would have eliminated Britain from the coast, and probably would have further changed the development of the American West by eliminating much of Astor's competition there. However, the agreement was never put into force. In fact, when Astor signed it in December it was a forlorn hope, for on June 19, 1812, President Madison had declared war on Britain. With the United States in the War of 1812, the Northwest coast was not safe for American trading vessels. Already in 1812 a Canadian gunship, the *Racoon*, was fitted out for an attack on Astoria. Cutting his losses, Astor sold the post to his major competitor in the West, the Northwest Fur Company.

Monroe Doctrine

Following the war, circumstances on the Northwest coast soon approximated those before 1812. Yankee traders continued to operate with impunity along the coast, and the Russians continued to complain, but without effect. Between 1815 and 1821 more than one hundred American traders had reached the coast. The trade was dominated by the Boston firms of Bryant and Sturgis, J. and T. H. Perkins, Boardman and Pope, and Josiah Marshall. Astor also sent a number of ships.

James Monroe was reelected United States president in 1816, and he appointed as his secretary of state brilliant and aggressive John Quincy Adams. The Treaty of Ghent ending the War of 1812 provided that conditions were to return to *status quo ante bellum.* The United States had gone to war against Britain a second time in as many generations, and had emerged effectively unscathed. Adams and his countrymen chose to interpret this as a moral victory, and Adams sought to capitalize on that victory by clarifying America's boundaries in such a way as to provide for present and future economic development. One of his first steps was to press American claims in the Pacific Northwest. With Jefferson, Adams believed that the United States must acquire a land connection between the eastern cities and the Pacific Ocean in order to develop commerce with the Orient. There was still hope that an easy water connection might be found through the Rocky Mountains. But the closing of Astor's post had curtailed the development of the Northwest by American trappers, and the country was now occupied almost exclusively by Britons.

To help pursue American claims in the area, Adams added the Northwest to a treaty he negotiated with Britain in 1818 establishing the boundary below the St. Lawrence and along the northern reaches of the Louisiana Purchase. From the Lake of the Woods country to the continental divide, the boundary would run along

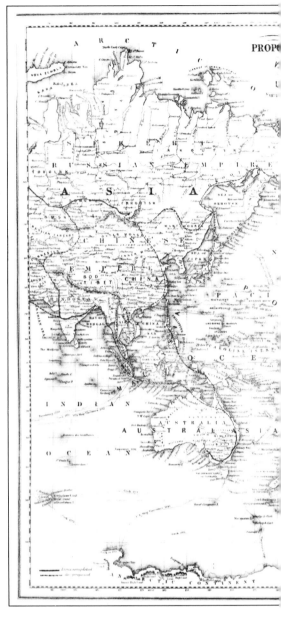

49° north latitude. The area west of the divide, called the Oregon Country, would be open to the "vessels, citizens and subjects" of both countries. Neither country could establish civil or military law or any other expression of sovereignty. The agreement was to hold for ten years, and be renewable. Not being able to agree how to divide the country, in other words, the two powers elected to postpone a decision for a decade, or longer if need be. The long-term significance of the agreement was the legitimization it brought to American claims in the Northwest, and its protection of the

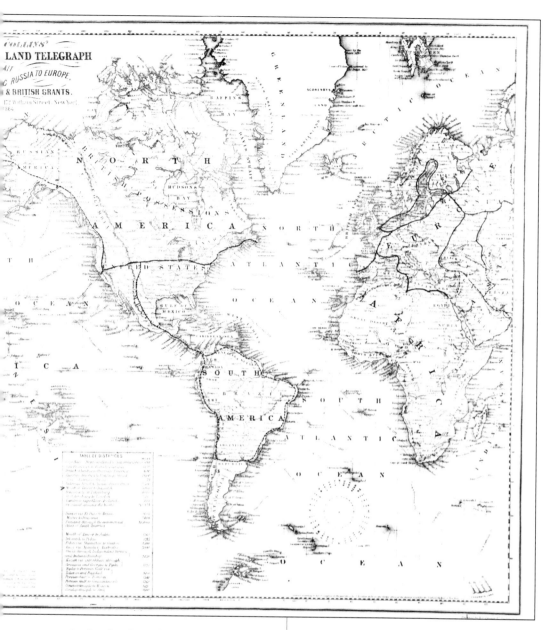

MAP OF THE proposed Collins Overland Telegraph Expedition, undertaken 1865-67. This effort to link the United States with Europe by telegraph through Siberia was never completed, but the scientists who accompanied the U.S. Signal Service on its work in Alaska provided much of the basic information that guided Congress in its debate over the purchase of the territory from Russia.

Alaska and Polar Regions Dept., Elmer E. Rasmuson Library, University of Alaska, Fairbanks.

opportunity for American economic expansion into the Oregon Country, and beyond. Within a generation, Americans would pour into the region to exploit its potential.

But where were the southern and northern boundaries of the Oregon Country? Adams addressed that question the next year in a broad treaty with Spain covering the whole southern boundary of the United States. Spain, which was not in a position to contest much, relinquished the Floridas and any claim to New Orleans. She also gave up any claim to the Northwest above 42° north latitude. In return, the United States relinquished any claim to Texas, and fixed the southern boundary of the Louisiana Purchase. Thus, 42° north latitude became the boundary between Oregon and California, and remains so today. The significance of the treaty for the Northwest coast was that one of the four claimants to it had been eliminated forever.

As the United States was negotiating these treaties with Britain and Spain, in Russia the charter of the Russian-American Company came due for renewal. The board of directors finally had allowed Baranov to retire, and in the new charter, issued in 1821, they placed the management of the American colony on a much more systematic foundation. New policies were promulgated that, among other considerations, directed that the manager/governors henceforth would be naval officers, each of whose terms would be limited to five years.

At the same time the government determined to act decisively to end American trading on the Northwest coast, which so far the Russians had claimed southward to 55° north latitude, near Dixon Entrance, the sound separating the Alexander Archipelago from the Queen Charlotte Islands. On September 16, 1821, the government issued an imperial *ukaz* (decree) extending the Russian claim south to 51° north latitude, just north of Vancouver Island, and prohibiting all foreign vessels from approaching within one hundred Italian miles of any shores and islands subject to Russia. Nine days later in a second *ukaz*, the tsar authorized the Russian-American Company "to annex...newly discovered places" south of 51° north latitude.[4]

Adams reacted immediately. His notion of the extent of the Oregon Country was northward to 55° north latitude. Russian presence in the area south of there he interpreted as a definite threat to future American development. In addition, he had no intention of interfering with the American trade on that coast, which was so important to New England merchants. He sent notes to the Russians through Henry Middleton, the American ambassador in St. Petersburg, saying that the United States expected territorial claims to be treated in negotiation, not by fiat, and expressing surprise at Russia's extension of her coastal claim "beyond the ordinary distance." In fact, Adams wrote bombastically in another note, the United States denied the right of Russia to any claim at all in North America. In any case, the United States would neither abide by the *ukaz*, he said, nor impair the rights of American citizens. Of course, Adams was begging the question; Russia was contesting the right of the United States to provide its citizens with the right to trade on the coast. But what Adams really was doing was challenging the Russian government; he was daring Russia to stand behind its claim with more than an

BILL OF LADING, *January 27, 1819, at Canton, China, noting the cargo bound for Boston in exchange for the furs taken on board* **Mentor** *at New Archangel the previous September.*

John Suter Papers, Massachusetts Historical Society, Boston.

imperial *ukaz*. Perhaps recognizing Russia's inability to do so, the tsar gave orders that Russian commanders were to prevent contraband trade only "within the limits recognized by other powers" while talks with the United States continued. Most traders curtailed their activities somewhat anyway, not wishing to risk confiscation of their ships and cargoes.[5]

In the meantime the *ukaz* generated a storm of protest in American newspapers, and in the halls of Congress. The negotiations dragged on for two years. Finally, in December 1823, in response to developments in Latin America, President Monroe issued his famous hemispheric doctrine proclaiming that the United States would not tolerate any further colonial settlement or development in South or North America. The Russian fulminations about 51° north latitude were definitely a consideration in the declaration of the Monroe Doctrine. Before Monroe's speech, the Russians had been informed of its contents. Adams told them the United States would meet any attempted expansion with force if necessary.

The Russian *ukaz* had perhaps been a bluff from the beginning, intended as an attempt to secure American cooperation on the matter of trading firearms and alcohol to the Indians. Or it may have been an attempt to goad the United States into negotiating a boundary between the coastal claims of the two countries. Whatever the motive, it generated a severe crisis in the Russian-American colony, for the colonists had become dependent on the supplies brought by the American trading vessels. Not understanding the situation, the board of directors did not send additional supplies from Russia, which led to near-starvation in some colonial posts, and great hardship in all. Moreover, without the Americans selling their furs for them in Canton, the company began to lose money. Instead of paying a dividend for the years during which the *ukaz* was effective, the company lost three hundred thousand rubles annually.

Russo-American Treaty

In the face of these circumstances, the Russians abandoned the position taken in the 1821 *ukaz*. In February 1824, diplomats from the two powers began formal negotiations on a treaty to clarify the status and future of the Northwest coast. Discussions now proceeded swiftly, and on April 17, 1824, Middleton signed the Russo-American Treaty. The agreement provided that citizens of both nations could navigate or fish without restraint at any point on the coast not already occupied, and that citizens of the United States were not to frequent any point on the coast where there was a Russian establishment without permission of the Russian governor; also, for ten years, the whole coast was to be open to the ships and citizens of both powers where there were no settlements. The most important clause was Russia's agreement not to establish any new posts or settlements south of 54°40' north latitude (bisecting Dixon Entrance more accurately than 55° north latitude). The United States agreed to establish no settlements north of that line.

Not only did the Russo-American Treaty throw open the coast again to American traders, but it also effectively established the northern limit of the Oregon Country. The United States had renounced any claim north of 54°40' north latitude. Britain followed suit the next year, in the Anglo-Russian Treaty of 1825, which established the formal boundary between British Canada and Russian America—that is, the boundary of Alaska. In the Alexander Archipelago, in order to protect the area where the Russians already were well established, it ran along the crest of the Coast Mountains approximately thirty miles inland from the coastal waters. In the northern interior, it ran along longitude 141° west, through a wilderness far enough away from where either the Russians or Hudson's Bay Company fur trappers operated in 1825 to prevent conflict when they might meet at some distant date when their normal expansion might take them into that wilderness.

After 1824 the sea otter population along the coast declined very rapidly, and over the next ten years most American traders gave up the trade voluntarily. By 1830 only the Boston firms of Bryant and Sturgis and Josiah Marshall were still very active. They continued to supply food-stuffs and manufactured goods to the colony, but after 1829 were paid in letters

of credit rather than peltry. In the 1830s the firms of William H. Boardman and Company and Perkins and Company became the major suppliers. In 1835 Boardman and Company found the trade so successful that they secured permission to extend their voyages to Kamchatka. Their cargoes routinely included tobacco, rum, sugar, molasses, hardtack, cotton, dry goods, and sundries. In 1834 the company even sold the Russians a steam engine.

In that year, the access to the coast that was guaranteed by the 1824 treaty expired, and the Russians officially closed their coast, the area above 54°40' north latitude, to American traders. Not long after, in September 1836, a Russian-American Company vessel surprised an American ship, *Loriat,* which was about to take fur seals on Forrester's Island, just north of the 54°40' treaty line. The Russians forced the American ship out of Russian territory. The Americans protested, but the Russians refused to yield. Heated negotiations produced no satisfaction for either party, and President Van Buren called attention to the matter in his annual message in December 1838, arguing that the United States had the right to trade with Natives anywhere along the coast "at unoccupied points."

The Russians were quite angry at the continuing American violation of the sovereignty of Russian America. The next year they took advantage of negotiations with the Hudson's Bay Company to attempt to secure aid in keeping the Americans out. They granted the British company a ten-year lease to take furs by hunting and trading in the coastal *lisière,* the land between tidewater and the crest of the mountains beside the Alexander Archipelago. In return, the Hudson's Bay Company was to provide foodstuffs and manufactured goods to the Russian

"A MAN OF KADIAK," an engraving by W. Alexander from a sketch by Martin Sauer.

From Sauer's An Account of a Geographical and Astronomical Expedition to the Northern Parts of Russia *(London, 1802). Washington State Historical Society, Tacoma.*

colony. The Russian-American Company terminated its contracts with Boardman and with Perkins, and hoped the British presence north of 54°40' would keep the Americans out. But it didn't, for by then there was an entirely new American commercial enterprise that came to mean even more to New England and the American economy than the sea otter trade.

Whaling

In the mid 1830s, American companies began to exploit the very lucrative Northwest whaling grounds. From 1835 on, large numbers of American whaling ships began to hunt along the coast and as far north as the Bering Sea. As that fishery replaced the Greenland grounds, after 1835 the Northwest coast produced 60 percent of all the oil secured by the American whaling fleet. More than 55 percent of the fleet worked Alaskan waters between 1840 and 1845. In 1845, of 257 vessels in the trade, 200 went to North Pacific waters, 139 to the Russian coast. Although many of the ships fished the Bering Sea, a significant number also worked along the Pacific coast, including the Alexander Archipelago.[6]

Profits from the industry, which supported seventy thousand people in the United States, were huge, benefiting Massachusetts primarily, and the Yankee captains of the whaling generation were as careless of Russian sovereignty as their fur-trading predecessors had been. In the face of the significant economic impact of the industry on the American economy, particularly after the Panic of 1837, the United States government did little to restrain the whalers. In fact, new grounds were opened off Kodiak Island in the early 1840s, pushing profits even higher. Overwhelmed by the number of vessels in the trade, the Russians could do little to keep them from landing at will wherever they chose. Their presence on the coast was a constant irritant, and one company report referred to the whaling vessels as

"hell-ships." Company officials complained that the Yankees stole things from the Aleuts and Eskimos, including food and women, leaving in return bad liquor and syphilis.

In addition to economic and diplomatic concerns, scientific interests also had brought Russians and Americans into contact in regard to the Northwest coast and Russian America from the time of the establishment of the Russian-American Company. In 1816-18 the Russian government funded a major scientific expedition to gather information about the North American Pacific coast. While Otto von Kotzebue explored the Bering Sea coast in the north, several expedition members visited California, and one, Rydalev, surveyed and wrote sailing instructions for San Francisco Bay. Later, between 1842 and 1848, Il'ia Voznesenski conducted one of the most extensive and comprehensive scientific reconnaissances ever mounted in North America. Voznesenski made meticulous observations and collected specimens of flora and fauna all the way from California to the Arctic coast over this six-year period. Virtually single-handedly he raised the level of understanding of the botany, geology, natural history, and ethnology of northwestern North America from the primitive to the sophisticated.

Manifest Destiny

Along with the trade carried on by the "Bostons" on the Northwest coast and their exploitation of the whale fishery, American westward expansion also greatly alarmed the Russians, who considered their American Northwest colony vulnerable to a northward turn of American settlement once the Pacific had been reached. Even some Americans were astonished at how rapidly settlers moved west in the 1840s. As late as the 1830s the plains were thought to be a "great American desert," and the west was considered a hostile place. Yet in 1841-44, one thousand wagons crossed on the Oregon Trail, some adventurers settling in Mexican California. At the same time, realizing that Fort Ross would never produce sufficient agricultural supplies for the colony, the Russian-American Company sold its California post to John Sutter in 1841.

In 1844 James K. Polk, running on a platform of unabashed expansionism, won the United States presidency over Henry Clay. At issue were American annexation of Texas and expansion into the Oregon Country. The agreement over the Oregon Country that had been worked out in 1818 was still in force—neither country would exercise its sovereignty there, but the nationals of either were free to operate and settle in the territory. The agreement was outmoded, though, for the fur resources of the Columbia basin had long been exhausted and American immigration into the region had been substantial. One of Polk's campaign slogans had been "54-40 or Fight," a threat to the British that the United States would go to war to gain all of the Oregon Country clear to Dixon Entrance if Britain would not cede it peacefully. It is unlikely that Polk was serious in this threat, but coupled with his willingness to go to war with Mexico over Texas, it made for exciting campaign rhetoric.

Upon Polk's election, the United States Congress acted to annex Texas even before he could be inaugurated, and immediately upon assuming his office, Polk informed the English that he intended to resolve the Oregon question. There was considerable concern in New England financial circles that war in the Pacific Northwest would destroy the whale fishery in Russian America, and at one point Polk's secretary of state, James Buchanan, issued orders that American vessels were not to proceed north of 54°40'. In 1846, however, a successful treaty was negotiated with the British, extending the United States-Canadian border along 49° north latitude to the Pacific coast, and then negotiating the San Juan Islands to the Strait of Juan de Fuca and the ocean, leaving Vancouver Island intact as a British possession. That same year, however, war came in the southwest, and in 1848, by the Treaty of Guadalupe-Hidalgo, the United States annexed New Mexico and California. Two years later California became a state, and, in 1859, so did Oregon.

Now the Russians became even more anxious, and in 1853 a high Russian naval officer, Count Nikolai Murav'ev, a staunch supporter of Russian expansion in Siberia, wrote to Tsar Nicholas advising that the American colony be ceded to the United States. The ultimate rule of the United States over the whole of North America was so "natural," Murav'ev argued, that sooner or later Russia must "recede" from the Northwest coast. Certainly any analyst of American developments in the 1840s and 1850s could easily have agreed with that view.

At this very time, Russia's loss to Britain in the Crimean War between 1854 and 1856 brought with it an unanticipated opportunity for Russia in the Siberian Far East. During the war the Russians sent supplies through Chinese territory, down the great Amur River, which drained southeast Siberia. Russia's defeat in the Crimean War had demonstrated that Russian America, half a world away, could not be defended successfully if attacked. The opening of the Amur provided an alternative fur resource for Russia, cheaper than Russian America, and more easily defended and supplied. To consolidate its hold on the new region, Russia forced China to relinquish all territory north of the Amur by the Treaty of Aigun in 1858, and by a later treaty gained the right to trap furs south of the river. Russian America, which was becoming increasingly expensive to maintain, no longer was necessary to the Russian fur trade.

American expansionism did not end with the acquisition of California in 1848. Economic expansionists such as William Henry Seward dreamed of a worldwide American commercial empire. Seward was particularly interested in developing markets for American manufactured goods in China and the East. The development of West Coast ports served this design perfectly, and had been one of the motivations for American adventurism in California. Two important California politicians, William Gwinn and Cornelius Cole, also were interested in developing opportunities for Western business interests in the Far East, as well as whatever resources in Russian America might be exploited. In 1848, they helped persuade the Russians to cancel the agreement with the Hudson's Bay Company, and give a new American company, the American-Russian Commercial Company, the contract to supply the Russian-American colony with necessities. The American-Russian Commercial Company was based in San Francisco, and included among its principal stockholders many of the most important commercial families of the city. Investment in this and other Alaska ventures played a significant role in San Francisco's early economic development. Among other products, the company would import Alaskan ice to San Francisco in the late 1850s. San Francisco merchants would be heavily involved in Russian America from then until the Alaska purchase in 1867, when one group, Hutchinson, Kohl and Company, would purchase most of the American assets of the American-Russian Commercial Company.

Soon after the Crimean War, a visionary American investor named Perry McDonough Collins devoted his considerable energies to the furtherance of the dream of an American commercial empire

A VIEW OF Norton Sound, Alaska. This engraving is one of the many works of art and documentation that emerged from the ill-fated Collins Overland Telegraph Expedition, 1865-67.

From W. H. Dall's Alaska and Its Resources (Boston, 1870). Washington State Historical Society, Tacoma.

in the East. Collins traveled throughout the Amur basin and in China, and established a number of important commercial contacts. Shortly after his return to the United States, he and the California politicians began to petition the American state department to negotiate a commercial treaty with Russia that would permit export of American goods to the Amur.

Later, Collins was responsible for American-Russian cooperation in an attempt to build a round-the-world telegraph line. After investor Cyrus Field had failed in several attempts to lay a transatlantic telegraph cable, Collins decided to try to make the connection going westward. With Western Union president Hiram Sibley, Collins organized the Russian-American Western Union Overland Telegraph Expedition to construct the line northward through British Columbia and Alaska to a short crossing under the Bering Strait, and then around the Sea of Okhotsk, up the Amur and across Siberia to Europe. The American government supported the enterprise in the name of the public interest, contributing army troops for survey and construction work, and a "scientific corps" to carry out exploration and observation. Robert Kennecott, a young American scientist who had explored in northwestern Canada and interior Alaska in 1861-62, was made head of the scientific contingent.

The telegraph project was given up in 1865 after Field was successful in his transatlantic project. However, the experience gained working in Russian America, and the detailed and accurate information collected by the scientific corps concerning Alaska's resources, Native people, and weather, were materially significant in

confirming American officials in their view of the value of Russian America and its usefulness to the United States.

The Sale

By the early 1860s, Russian officials already had determined to sell Russian America. The constant problem of supplying the colony, its vulnerability to attack and to American expansion, as well as declining profits, had turned Russian America from an asset into a liability. At the same time, the furs of the Amur basin could be developed more economically and securely. Once the American Civil War was over, serious negotiations for a sale could begin with the United States, the only realistic prospective customer. Russia could not sell the colony to Britain, which it still considered an enemy.

William Seward, the United States secretary of state, was very willing to discuss the purchase of the colony, for he saw it as a major step in his plan of American commercial expansion to East Asia. Like most informed Americans, he well appreciated the worth of Russian America, for the many commercial, scientific, and diplomatic contacts between the United States and Russian America, which had by then spanned many decades, had provided much information on the colony. Perhaps that is one reason why the purchase treaty passed the United States Senate by more than the required two-thirds majority, 29–12, on the first vote in the summer of 1867. The final, formal vote was 37-2.

Today the shared American and Russian legacy in Russian America is all but forgotten by most Americans. Yet for nearly a century, Russian and American merchants and diplomats solved the immediate problems connected with their encounters in Russian America. Competitive and cooperative by turns, always creative, they set a standard to which later negotiators might aspire.

Stephen W. Haycox is Professor of History, University of Alaska, Anchorage.

For Further Reading

The End of Russian America: Captain P. N. Golovin's Last Report, 1862. Ed. and trans. Basil Dmytryshyn and E. A. P. Crownhart-Vaughan. Portland: Oregon Historical Society, 1979.

Fedorova, Svetlana G. *The Russian Population in Alaska and California, Late 18th Century - 1867.* Ed. and trans. Alton S. Donnelly. Kingston, Ontario: Limestone Press, 1973.

Gibson, James R. *Imperial Russia in Frontier America: The Changing Geography of Supply of Russian America, 1784-1867.* New York: Oxford University Press, 1976.

Jensen, Ronald. *The Alaska Purchase and Russian-American Relations.* Seattle: University of Washington Press, 1975, pp. 83-92.

Johansen, Dorothy O., and Charles M. Gates. *Empire of the Columbia: A History of the Pacific Northwest.* New York: Harper & Row, 1957.

Kushner, Howard I. *Conflict on the Northwest Coast: American-Russian Rivalry in the Pacific Northwest, 1790-1867.* Westport, Conn.: Greenwood Press, 1975.

Pethick, Derek. *The Nootka Connection: Europe and the Northwest Coast, 1790-1795.* Vancouver: Douglas & McIntyre, 1980.

Russia's American Colony. Ed. S. Frederick Starr. Durham: Duke University Press, 1987.

The Russian American Colonies, 1798-1867. Ed. and trans. Basil Dmytryshyn, E. A. P. Crownhart-Vaughan, and Thomas Vaughan. Portland: Oregon Historical Society, 1989.

The United States and Russia: The Beginning of Relations, 1765-1815. Ed. Bashina et al. Washington, D.C.: U.S. Government Printing Office, 1980.

Vivier, Charles. "The Collins Overland Line and American Continentalism." *Pacific Historical Review* 28 (August 1959), pp. 237-253.

Wheeler, Mary E. "Empires in Conflict and Cooperation: The 'Bostonians' and the Russian-American Company." *Pacific Historical Review* 40 (November 1971), pp. 419-441.

The Wreck of the Sv. Nikolai: *Two Narratives of the First Russian Expedition to the Oregon Country, 1808-1810.* Ed. Kenneth N. Owens, trans. Alton S. Donnelly. Portland: Western Imprints, 1985.

Notes

1. Robert F. Berkhofer, Jr., *The White Man's Indian: Images of the American Indian from Columbus to the Present* (New York: Random House, 1978), pp. 25-31.
2. F. W. Howay, *A List of Trading Vessels in the Maritime Fur Trade, 1785-1825* (Kingston, Ontario: The Limestone Press, 1973), pp. 55, 57, 66-92.
3. Mary E. Wheeler, "Empires in Conflict and Cooperation: The 'Bostonians' and the Russian-American Company," *Pacific Historical Review* 40 (November 1971), pp. 428-429; Howard I. Kushner, *Conflict on the Northwest Coast: American-Russian Rivalry in the Pacific Northwest, 1790-1867* (Westport, Conn.: Greenwood Press, 1975), p. 4.
4. *The Russian American Colonies, 1798-1867,* ed. and trans. Basil Dmytryshyn, E. A. P. Crownhart-Vaughan, and Thomas Vaughan (Portland: Oregon Historical Society, 1989), pp. 337-352.
5. Ibid., pp. 367-369; Wheeler, "Empires," p. 434.
6. Clarence L. Andrews, "Alaska Whaling," *Washington Historical Quarterly* 9 (January 1918), pp. 3-10; Kushner, *Conflict,* p. 82.

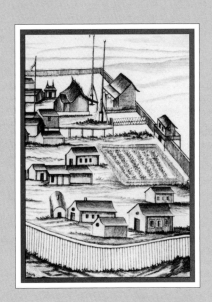

Russian America *and* China

by Richard A. Pierce

EXHIBITION · ВЫСТАВКА · ИНФОРМАЦИЯ · RUSSIAN AMERICA · INFORMATION

...Developments in Siberia, China, and Europe...exerted major influence on events in Russian America.

Russian America is often described in terms of operations carried on in present-day Alaska and on the coast of California. Much less is known of developments in Siberia, China, and Europe that exerted major influence on events in Russian America. The stormy period of exploration and fur-hunting in the Aleutians, Grigorii Shelikhov's establishment of the first permanent Russian settlement in North America (1784), and organization of the Russian-American Company, in charge of the region from 1799 to 1867, were as much the result of external political events and economic factors as of decisions in the field. The company organization and functioning in Russian America was linked closely with the main office, first in Irkutsk, and after 1798 in St. Petersburg, and a chain of suboffices and agencies across Siberia to Okhotsk and south to Kiakhta. These branches dispatched supplies from European Russia, provided housing, subsistence, and transportation to company personnel on their way to and from the colonies, and forwarded the all-important furs, the company's main commodity, to Moscow and St. Petersburg for the European market, or to Kiakhta for sale to the Chinese.

Kiakhta

The China trade, restricted to Kiakhta, was only a part of the company's total trade, just as the furs from Russian America were only a part of the transactions carried on at Kiakhta. However, in each case, for over a century, they were important parts of the whole.

Sino-Russian trade began in the seventeenth century and was given sanction by the Treaty of Nerchinsk in 1689. At first, trade was carried on by means of caravans to Peking, but with the Treaty of Kiakhta in 1727, this cumbersome and outmoded method was replaced by establishment of a trading center on the border between the two countries, at Kiakhta. Built on an arid, treeless plain nearly a thousand miles from Peking, the town provided Russia with an assured place for trade with the Celestial Empire, and gave China the benefits of trade while keeping the "foreign barbarians" from closer contact with its population. The Russian post of Kiakhta was built on the north side of the insignificant Kiakhta River, which formed the border, and the Chinese built their own settlement about two hundred yards southward. Each settlement had a large square, surrounded by the shops of the merchants, where trade was carried on and goods stored, and accommodations for the merchants and officials. An Orthodox church was built in Russian Kiakhta, and the Chinese erected an ornate pagoda in their settlement, known unofficially but generally as Maimaich'eng (the trading place). The Chinese government in detailed regulations permitted trade from approximately December until February, denied Chinese merchants the right to settle permanently and, in aid of that, prohibited the presence of women in the town. The Russian government, on the other hand, encouraged its merchants to settle in Kiakhta. Each government charged duties, and the restrictions and duties led in turn to evasions, bribery of officials, and smuggling.

In officially sanctioned trade, the Chinese merchants crossed the border to Kiakhta to

A PLATE FROM the service of Catherine II, Empress of Russia, ca. 1770-75. The Chinese catered to European taste by borrowing designs favored by royalty. This plate, made to order by Chinese artisans, bears a strong resemblance to work done at the Worcester (England) factory that was favored by Catherine in the 1770s. It bears the inventory mark of the Winter Palace, St. Petersburg, on the back.

Metropolitan Museum of Art, New York City.

examine the wares of their counterparts on the Russian side. Their selections were then removed and, in the purchasers' presence, sealed and placed in storage. After entertainment by the Russians, both parties then crossed to Maimaich'eng, where the Chinese goods to be offered in barter were examined, bargains were struck, and, after entertainment of the Russians by the Chinese, the goods were exchanged. The Chinese then took their purchases by caravan, by way of Urga and Kalgan, across nearly a thousand miles of desert to Peking, from where they were sent throughout the country.

The main item sold by the Russians in the eighteenth century was furs, for which China offered a constant demand. From 1768 to 1785, furs made up 85 percent of the Russian goods sold. Most of the furs were from Siberia, including quantities of cheaper varieties, particularly squirrel, which were intended for the mass market. Beginning in the 1740s, however, furs from the newly discovered Aleutian Islands, particularly sea otter pelts, were added to the supply of furs offered the Chinese. The remaining 15 percent of the wares offered by the Russian traders included leather goods, European textiles, glassware, and hardware. Cattle, horses, camels, and hunting dogs also were traded. In return, the Russians purchased Chinese goods—manufactured silk, cotton cloth (a number of varieties of the cheaper *daba* and the more choice *kitaika*, or

nankeen), tea, rhubarb root, tobacco, sugar, ginger, and handicraft items.

The Chinese merchants were well organized and regulated, whereas the Russians, following traditional patterns, operated informally. They had no joint stock companies, acting either as individuals or in temporary partnerships whose members, from the same family or locality, pooled their resources while at the border and then went their own way. Some of the well-to-do merchants engaged in the Aleutian trade formed companies, but rarely for more than one voyage. Most investors did not go to Kiakhta but conducted business there through agents. The companies represented at Kiakhta seem never to have acted together to control the market or to regulate prices.

Trade Difficulties

The almost total lack of joint action among the Russians gave the better-organized and -disciplined Chinese an advantage. The Russians had only the advantage of the cheapness of their furs at the source and the avidity of the Chinese merchants to purchase them.

Another difficulty facing the Russian traders stemmed from disputes between the two governments over defections, brigandage, border violations, and commercial questions in which the Chinese, trying to bring the Russians to terms, instituted frequent stoppage of trade. Most were for only a few days or weeks, but others were for much longer periods, from 1764 to 1768, from 1778 to 1780, and the longest and last, from 1785 to 1792. To avoid ruin, traders on both sides had to resort to smuggling or, in the case of the Russians, turn their attention to the less lucrative market in European Russia. It was during the latter period, in 1788, that Grigorii Shelikhov and his partner I. Golikov sought a substantial loan of two hundred thousand rubles, troops, and a ship from the government. Their request, however, was refused.

After 1792 there were no further stoppages; China was increasingly on the decline, whereas Russia was becoming more powerful and active, leaping ahead in political, economic, and military spheres. This change in relative power was reflected in the Kiakhta market. The volume of Russian furs continued to increase, but the relative proportion of furs to the total value of the goods offered now dropped steadily as Russian production of leather and fabrics increased. The most spectacular rise in Chinese exports was in tea, for which there was now an ever-greater demand in Russia. When the Napoleonic Wars cut off normal sources of tea for Europe, the Russians imported it via Kiakhta.

Also, in the eighteenth century Russian exports had been mainly natural and semi-processed products such as poultry, tanned hide, and leather, whereas the bulk of Chinese exports, the products of a more advanced industry, had been finished or manufactured products such as cotton and silk cloth. Now, in the nineteenth century, the situation began to reverse. Russian imports of Chinese cloth dwindled as Russia began to export its own woolen and cotton manufactures. There was also a shift from articles of costly consumption to those of more general use. Chinese silks, velvets, and finely processed cotton fabrics and precious stones were replaced by goods such as *kitaika*. Russian luxury items such as furs, hides, and fine leather gave way to commodities of woolen and cotton manufacture. Simultaneously, the demand for cheaper furs grew, while demand for more expensive sable, sea

CHINA, 1626. THIS map shows the extent of geographic and social detail known about the Chinese in the early seventeenth century, in contrast to North America, which had only received its first settlers and was truly terra incognita. Published by Bassett & Chiswell (London).

Alaska and Polar Regions Dept., Elmer E. Rasmuson Library, University of Alaska, Fairbanks.

otter, fox, land otter, and lynx declined.

In Russian America the harvest of sea otter pelts was simultaneously declining, as one area after another was hunted out, either by the Russians or by encroaching British and American vessels. The Russian-American Company complained repeatedly to the government of the foreigners poaching in territory regarded as the company's own preserve for furs that were sold at Canton, the Chinese port available to European and American merchants.

In 1803, in an effort to get a larger share of the maritime fur trade, the Russian government authorized the commanders of the first Russian round-the-world expedition, I. F. Kruzenshtern and Iurii F. Lisianskii, with the sloops *Nadezhda* and *Neva,* to dispose of cargoes of furs at Canton. However, although in decline, the Chinese government held firm to one principle—that privileges of foreigners were to be kept to a minimum and there was to be no drastic change in existing patterns of trade. Thus, in 1806, when the expedition called at Canton, the imperial government at Peking refused to grant them permission to trade, as Russia had

already been granted trade privileges in Kiakhta and existing regulations should not be violated. Kruzenshtern and Lisianskii bartered their cargoes with the help of local European merchants, and sailed just before a directive from Peking arrived ordering internment of the two vessels.

During the Napoleonic Wars, western European firms entered the Kiakhta trade, either independently or through Russian intermediaries. This caused the Russian government to take measures to set its China trade in order. Thus, in 1800, Russia issued a statute on trade in Kiakhta, followed by a new customs tariff lowering the export duties that had been in effect since 1761. The government set up control over Russian companies, and to reduce disputes between Russian and Chinese merchants, established strict price control in buying and selling. Measures were also taken to prevent foreigners from competing at Kiakhta; thereafter, they could only trade through Chinese citizens.

Declining China Trade

During the first quarter of the nineteenth century, continued decline caused Russia to lose interest in Kiakhta. By 1826, furs

"HARBOR OF ST. PAUL in the Island of Cadiack," an engraving after a drawing by Iurii F. Lisianskii, captain of Russia's first round-the-world voyage, 1803-06. Lisianskii was at Kodiak in 1804-05.

From Lisianskii's A Voyage Around the World in 1803-1806 *(St. Petersburg, 1809-12). Anchorage Museum of History and Art.*

comprised 47.5 percent of the transactions at Kiakhta, and tea was the main item among Chinese goods there. In 1825, tea represented 87.5 percent of the value of goods imported to Russia via Kiakhta.

Simultaneously, Russian interest in the Amur valley revived, and in the 1840s Governor-General N. N. Murav'iev and Captain-Lieutenant G. I. Nevel'skoi occupied the Amur mouth and established a Russian-American Company trading factory. In 1849, Russia occupied the region, reversing the cession of the region to China in 1689.

The continued decline of the fur trade and the lack of salable products from colonies other than seal skins from the

Pribilofs and ice from Kodiak and Sitka placed the Russian-American Company in an increasingly shaky position. Temporary relief was afforded by a removal of Russian tariffs on tea imports, which gave the company an opportunity to improve its situation by using larger vessels sailing directly to Europe. The *Atkha* arrived at Kronstadt on May 18, 1851, with 489 boxes of tea; the ship *Imperator Nikolai I* arrived at Kronstadt on May 18, 1852, with 2,052 boxes of tea. These and other vessels (except during the Crimean War) made similar voyages. However, the tea trade was not enough to justify retention of the Russian colonies in North America. The failure to find any other economic base and the vulnerability of the region to enemy attack shown by the Crimean War made disposal of the colonies inevitable.

Richard A. Pierce is Professor of History, University of Alaska, Fairbanks.

VIEW OF THE Chinese border town Maimaich'eng, which means "the buying/selling town". In the eighteenth and early nineteenth centuries, China closely guarded its contacts with foreigners. Russia was granted a window of trade only through this town created solely as a market. Across the river stood the Siberian town of Kiakhta, Russia's only legal port of entry into the exotic China market.

For Further Reading

Foust, Clifford M. *Muscovite and Mandarin: Russia's Trade with China and Its Setting, 1727-1805.* Chapel Hill: University of North Carolina Press, 1969.

Mancall, Mark. *Russia and China, Their Diplomatic Relations to 1728.* Cambridge: Harvard University Press, 1971.

Quested, R. K. I. *The Expansion of Russia in East Asia, 1857-1860.* Kuala Lumpur, Singapore: University of Malaya Press, 1968.

Sladkovskii, Mikhail Iosifovich. *Istoriia torgovo-ekonomicheskikh otnoshenii naradov Rossii s Kitaim (do 1917 g.)* [History of the Trade-Economical Relations of the Peoples of Russia with China (before 1917)]. Moscow: "Nauka," 1974.

to make ends meet and without incentive to pursue profit within the legal governmental framework.

Another equally unfortunate aspect of Spain's economic policy was prohibition of trade with other nations. At a time when Spain should have been encouraging economic independence in her California colony, when missions should have been allowed a market for their produce, when legal profits could have encouraged individual initiative and given impetus to a thriving culture, outside trade was illegal. Spanish citizens of Alta California understood very early that they must devise methods to bridge the chasm between laws of the crown and what they needed to survive on the frontier. This disparity between the theory of Spanish law and the reality of enforcing it also gave impetus to interaction between Russian and Spaniard. Alta California's economy clearly not only defined the parameters of Hispanic lifestyle, but also lay at the core of Russian-Hispanic relationships on the California frontier.

By the first decade of the nineteenth century, Alta Californians were experiencing the results of their fixed-price system with a vengeance. The military lacked supplies of every sort and frequently enough food as well. The padres were equally unhappy, for the military could buy only a small portion of their agricultural surpluses, leaving them with little profit for their efforts and large amounts of food they could not dispose of. Yankee traders, ever alert to opportunity, sailed into this economic void and a brisk smuggling trade flourished between the missions and American ships.

The Russian Arrival in California

As the Spanish were grappling with the realities of life in Alta California, the Russians were establishing fur-hunting and trading establishments in the Aleutian Islands and Alaska through the efforts of the Russian-American Company. Because both colonies lay on the farthest rims of their respective empires, it is hardly surprising that Russian colonists and fur hunters experienced food and supply difficulties similar to those that so plagued the Spanish. The answer to the problems of both Russian and Spaniard was found on the coast of Alta California.

The first meeting in California between these two nations occurred when Count Nikolai Rezanov visited the port of San Francisco in 1806. Rezanov, in the service of Tsar Alexander I and a high official of the Russian-American Company, arrived in the capital of Russian America, today's Sitka, in summer 1805 and was present during the calamitous winter of 1805-6. No Russian supply ships had arrived for several years, and by spring 1805 cupboards were nearly bare. Conditions worsened with the onset of winter. Starvation and death by scurvy loomed, as Sitka's residents were reduced to eating sea gulls and eagles. Dismayed, Rezanov decided to sail to California for supplies, and in April 1806 reached San Francisco with a shipload of goods he hoped to trade for food.

Rezanov's desire to trade for wheat surprised California authorities, and when they learned that he also hoped to negotiate a permanent formal trading agreement, they found themselves in a moral quandary. Although the prohibition against trade caused bitter dissatisfaction among needy Californians, Lt. Luis Arguello, acting *comandante* of the San Francisco presidio in his father's absence, and Governor Jose Joaquin de Arrillaga were unwilling to violate the ban openly as long as it was Spanish law.

The visitors found living conditions marginal at the presidio. Georg von Langsdorf, Rezanov's companion on the ship *Juno,* noted that most of the soldiers' families lived in small, low, one-room houses with leaky roofs and dirt floors. Even the Arguello home was small and uncomfortable. Although the main room of his residence boasted whitewashed walls and straw matting on the floors, the furniture was crude and inadequate. Rezanov did all in his power to make a good impression: he gave expensive gifts to presidio authorities, and worked diligently to allay long-held Spanish suspicions that the Russians wanted to occupy their territory. Yet despite his efforts, Governor Arrillaga maintained the position that he lacked authority to sanction general trade.

Despite official refusal of the Spanish to trade, Rezanov was hospitably received by Arguello and other presidio inhabitants, and became very friendly with Fathers Jose Ramon Abella and Martin Landaeta at Mission San Francisco. In common with the majority of Russians who followed him to California, Rezanov shrewdly brought samples of the trade goods on his ship to tantalize his hosts. Langsdorf wrote of the padres' reaction: "They were much pleased with some coarse and fine linen cloths, Russian ticking and English ticking we showed them. They inquired very much after iron and iron wares, particularly tools for mechanical trades and implements for husbandry, household utensils, shears for shearing and iron cooking vessels."[1]

As news of Rezanov's arrival spread throughout the region to Mission San Jose, Father Pedro de la Cuero agreed to provide 104 measures of the best wheat in return for four pieces of English blue cloth and seven pieces of linen—subject, of course, to Governor Arrillaga's consent. "It appeared," Langsdorf commented, "that this was by no means the first time of his being engaged in trade," a suggestion that the good father might have acquaintance with certain Yankee ship-masters who sailed California's coastline on moonless nights.[2] The needs of most missionaries exceeded their obedience to the law, and many openly advocated expanded trade with the Russians. The governor, in frequent communication with many fathers, was undoubtedly aware of their position—there were few secrets in Alta California.

However, despite such divine support, it was not until Rezanov proposed marriage to Concepcion Arguello, the *comandante's* daughter (his first wife had died), that he was actually allowed to barter his cargo for foodstuffs. In all, Rezanov received some two thousand bushels of grain and five tons of flour in exchange for 11,174 rubles' worth of Russian goods. Interestingly, most of the

NIKOLAI P. REZANOV was a stockholder in the Russian-American Company, as well as Grigorii Shelikhov's son-in-law. Arriving in Sitka in 1805 on an inspection trip, he found scurvy to be widespread. He immediately bought a ship from an American trader, John D'Wolf, and sailed south to California to seek supplies from the Spanish. He was a gifted planner and set out many reforms that guided the administration of the company for decades. He died en route home to St. Petersburg, at the age of 45.

Alaska State Library, Juneau.

grain was furnished by Concepcion Arguello's brothers and the rest by local missionaries.

It appeared, however, that by allowing barter between Rezanov and Spanish citizens, Governor Arrillaga had taken the first step toward bridging the gap between the law and the needs of his people. Following Arrillaga's precedent, in years to come all Spanish governors would use Russian trade as a means of sustaining their troops, despite the fact that they would be caught between the Scylla of illegal action and the Charybdis of their subjects' destitution. In navigating this sea of difficult choice, the governors' minds and hearts were on conflicting courses, and the difficulty of reconciling their actions with the law was reflected in vacillating official governmental policy toward Russian trade with the Spanish Californians.

Fort Ross

In 1812 the Russian-American Company established a colony on the coast of Alta California on land claimed by Spain. The new colony, which came to be called Fort Ross, was the dream of Russian-American Company governor Alexander Baranov, and came under the direct supervision of his able deputy, Ivan Kuskov. The company had two excellent reasons for their action: starvation and profit. The company's Alaskan colonies, unable to grow enough food to supply themselves, still endured frequent shortages. Profit, too, played an important role in this venture, for furs—particularly sea otter—were the basis of the Russian-American Company's colonization efforts, and the California coastline abounded with these valuable animals.

With the establishment of their California colony, the Russians were now strategically placed to interact frequently with their Spanish neighbors. Over the years of the colony's existence, the majority of interactions dealt with three subjects: trade, sea otter hunting, and the constant irritation the presence of a Russian settlement on California soil caused the Hispanic authorities. But the most important topic, and the lifeblood of both colonies, was trade.

In discussing barter ventures between Russian and Hispanic, it is important to note that trade with Russian America was one thing, trade with Fort Ross quite another. In the larger arena, ships from Russian-American Company headquarters in Sitka sailed several times a year to San Francisco, Monterey, or other stops for vitally needed food supplies. However, Fort Ross rapidly became the focal point for smaller, more frequent interpersonal activities between Russian and Spaniard, particularly after the founding of Mission San Rafael in 1817 and Mission Sonoma in 1823. Indeed, the inhabited region between Fort Ross on the north, San Francisco on the south, and Sonoma on the east appears to have acted much like the permeable membrane of a living organism: Russian and Spanish subjects traveled back and forth openly and often with the knowledge and permission of Spanish authorities. Indeed, there is plentiful evidence to suggest that by 1818 an extraordinary trade relationship existed between the Russians at Fort Ross and the citizens of Alta California.

In summer 1812, Governor Arrillaga learned of the Russian establishments at Bodega Bay and Fort Ross and sent Lieutenant Gabriel Moraga to investigate. Moraga was courteously received at Fort Ross, learned what he could of the Russians' plans, then reported to the governor that the Russians needed supplies badly. He also relayed Kuskov's offer to trade for food. Arrillaga, a longtime Californian who understood the poverty Spain's economic policy forced upon his soldiers, forwarded his report on Fort Ross to the viceroy in Mexico City and asked official permission to trade. However, pending arrival of the viceroy's answer, Arrillaga made the decision between law and necessity on his own initiative. On January 27, 1813, he ordered Lt. Moraga back to Fort Ross—but not empty-handed. Russian sources state that Moraga brought twenty cattle and three horses. Even more welcome was the verbal message he carried: announcement of Arrillaga's consent to limited trade. Kuskov immediately sent a ship to San Francisco with a cargo of goods valued at fourteen thousand dollars, which was exchanged for wheat and other supplies.

The result of the above interaction can surely be laid at the door of frontier pragmatism. Life in California was arduous for both Russian and Spaniard, and it was the duty of their respective authorities to acquire what was needed. Interestingly, one of the few differences between the two cultures on the California frontier lay in the way they achieved that goal. The Russians openly advocated formal, legal trade to better their circumstances, and maneuvered unceasingly for a permanent trade policy with their California neighbors. Spanish officials, prohibited from freely ameliorating their lives with the goods and services of the Russians, finessed conditions to attain their objectives. They took particularly good advantage of the distance separating them (and their actions) from their superiors in Mexico, and of the generally laissez-faire attitude toward Alta California. While trade relations between the two cultures might be affected by the attitude of new players in the game as well as relations between Russia and Spain in the geopolitical context, eventually each Spanish governor found a way to rationalize the existence of regular Russian trade. Because most trade arrangements were oral, such as the one Moraga relayed to

Kuskov, they were hardly likely to find their way into the Spanish records. After all, why spoil the beauty of a thing with legality? Indeed, with regard to their Russian neighbors, the Spanish of Alta California went well beyond mere nonenforcement of their law: not only did the

MARIANO *Guadalupe Vallejo, Spanish commandant at Sonoma in the 1830s, enjoyed a warm relationship with several directors of the Fort Ross colony. The Russians supplied Vallejo with muskets, gunpowder and cloth in return for foodstuffs.*

Bancroft Library, University of California, Berkeley.

Russians trade frequently with Alta California, but in addition they actually achieved an unofficial "most favored nation" status, particularly during the Spanish period.

Between 1812 and 1817 few actual recorded contacts between Russian and Spaniard have been found. Despite this fact, we know that California supplied the Russians with food for their people and stores for their colony. For instance, the first peach tree was brought from San Francisco to Russian territory aboard the *Chirikov* in 1814. In 1815 the *Ilmen* and the *Chirikov*, with Ivan Kuskov aboard, obtained large quantities of grain. The Russian ship *Suvarov* visited San Francisco around that time and sold most of its cargo to citizens there. All these ships carried the same types of goods the Russians traded to the Spanish throughout

FORT ROSS painting by an unknown artist, 1817. The Russians established an outpost near Rumiantsev Bay in northern California in 1812. Governor Baranov hoped to solve the colony's supply problems by developing agriculture at Ross, but the climate proved an enemy. More effective than the agriculture was the access to Spanish missions, which offered the prospect of trade for supplies. Although relations with the Spanish were generally good, the Russians turned in the 1840s to their nearer neighbor, the Hudson's Bay Company, as major provisioner, and sold the California fort to John Sutter in 1841.

Oregon Historical Society, Portland.

their relationship; i.e., tools, iron, and cloth.

Occasionally, Aleut hunters were by some mischance apprehended by Spanish authorities and held until they could be repatriated by Russian officials. One Aleut, at least, left a lasting impression on Spanish life. Camille de Roquefeuil, visiting San Francisco in 1817, noted "well-made tables and benches" in the San Francisco home of Luis Arguello; he was told by Arguello they were made by a Russian captured while illegally hunting otter. De Roquefeuil commented dryly upon the austere life at the presidio: "So, in an establishment founded forty years ago by Spain, a savage from the Russian possessions was found to be the most skillful workman."[3]

Kuskov's rapid reaction to Moraga's offer to trade, the proximity of Fort Ross to San Francisco, the desperate needs of each frontier, and the scarcity of written record, all combine to suggest that a great deal of unrecorded, undoubtedly furtive contact took place during this time. Much of this clandestine activity was probably conducted by Russian ships and launches from Fort Ross. However, one document has been located in the Spanish archives that details the cargo of such a vessel. While the document itself dates from the early Mexican period, the launch's merchandise was typical of Russian-Hispanic trade items, and included heavy cloth, iron, and nails.[4]

A New Governor

The death of Governor Arrillaga, in July 1814, dealt a blow to the status quo of Russian-Spanish trade. Arrillaga's replacement, Don Pablo Vicente de Sola, found Alta California in a state of destitution; unsurprisingly, his first letter to the viceroy discussed poverty among the soldiers and deplorable port conditions. Recently arrived from Mexico, Sola did not at first understand the extent of

California's economic malaise and sought to strictly enforce all Spanish laws. Yet, to his credit, he soon realized the importance of the Russian presence and the necessity of foreign trade. In 1816, Lt. Otto von Kotzebue, visiting San Francisco aboard the *Rurik,* summoned Ivan Kuskov from Fort Ross to confer with Governor Sola regarding the legal existence of Fort Ross in Spanish territory, a subject that was a thorn in the side of the Spanish during the entire existence of Fort Ross. Although other subjects were surely discussed, it is interesting that the records of this un-precedented meeting dealt solely with the problem of territorial encroachment. The question of commerce is not mentioned in the documents—an example, perhaps, of the way Spanish officials finessed such matters.

The missions were the primary source of food for the Russians, who in turn provided a major market for mission agricultural surplus. The fathers were friendly to Kuskov and probably negoti-ated as many illicit commercial activities with the Russians as they did with the Americans. Although Governor Sola undoubtedly deplored the situation, he apparently tolerated mission activities and occasionally even acted as intermediary in accepting goods from the Russians or the fathers. Indeed, activity between the missionaries and the Russians was so extensive that one Spanish source sug-gested that the site for Mission San Rafael was chosen with market proximity in mind. Numerous sorts of interactions in the Fort Ross/San Rafael/Sonoma triangle suggest that could be correct. For in-stance, tools and materials came from Fort Ross for construction of both Mission San Rafael and Mission Sonoma; in return the fathers sent cattle and other foodstuffs.

There is also the example of the San Rafael missionary who made a weekly trip on muleback to Fort Ross for brandy, and various relationships between local Spanish neophytes and the Native peoples at Fort Ross to ponder. By 1818 trade between Fort Ross and San Rafael was so habitual that Padre Luis Taboado had the early California equivalent of a charge account, according to correspondence from L. A. Hagemeister, governor of the Russian-American Company. Following a meeting with Fr. Taboado in Monterey, Hagemeister wrote to Ivan Kuskov in 1818:

> He [Taboado] complained about prices charged to him, so to preserve his friendship I took off 1-1/2 piasters from the price of the cherry-colored kitaika, setting it at 3-1/2 piasters, as it was sold before, and from an arroba of coffee 10, lowering it from 25 to 15 piasters, 1 real about which I made a note on your record. Thus I ask you to enter the indebtedness of the padre at 96 piasters, 1 real.[5]

A turning point in the relationship between Russian and Spaniard was reached in 1818, when Hagemeister made a return voyage to San Francisco. The soldiers of Alta California had received no supplies for seven years; military necessi-ties were so lacking that Hagemeister had to lend powder to the Spanish for the traditional salute to his ship. Sola had reached his point of compromise: To help his soldiers, he allowed them to trade with the Russian ship, and apparently negoti-ated some sort of trading agreement with Hagemeister as well. Thereafter, with Sola's semisecret, unofficial permission, two or three Russian-American Company ships traded annually at Alta California's ports, unhampered by Spanish officials. Sola also insisted on collection of import and export duties, but otherwise placed no further obstacles before the Russians.

On their part, the Russians traded for enormous amounts of food whenever possible, and large profits were made with each voyage. In 1817, for instance, the *Kutusov* traded at San Francisco for 537 bushels of wheat, 384 bushels of barley, 163 bushels of peas and beans, 2 tons of flour, and 2-1/4 tons of tallow and lard. The profit realized on this trip was 254 percent. In 1818 the *Kutusov* traded goods worth 36,719 rubles in Monterey for nearly 5,000 bushels of wheat, 7,509 bushels of beans, a ton of flour, 9 tons of tallow and lard, and a little over 6 tons of dried meat, for a profit of 150 percent on the voyage for the enterprising Russians. Similar amounts of supplies were obtained and profits made on all the Russian ships mentioned in either Russian or Spanish records until 1822.[6]

Spanish governmental and ecclesiastical authorities apparently put aside the economic quarrels that frequently divided them and worked together to assist the Russians in their trade efforts. By 1818 a system existed to notify local missions of the arrival of a Russian ship, its cargo, and what supplies the Russians needed. An example of how this system worked can be seen in the 1821 trip of the *Kutusov*, which reached Monterey in late July. On July 30, Governor Sola sent a circular to the missions from Soledad to San Luis Obispo that stated: "I am sending you all a list of the articles brought by the Russian war frigate *Kutusoff* [sic] and also of the wheat, pease and lard that it is asking for, so that each of you can assess and come to an agreement as to what each mission can give said ship." The letter was answered quickly: On July 31 replies were received from Fr. Esteban Tapis at San Juan Bautista and Fr. Jose Viader at Santa Clara; on August l from Fr. Ramon Olbes at Santa Cruz and Fr. Narciso Duran at San Jose; on August 2 from Fr. Antonio Jayme at Soledad; on August 3 from Fr. Pedro Cabot at San Antonio; on August 6 from Fr. Jose Altamira at San Francisco. In

these letters, the fathers generally noted what they had available for trade, and how soon such could be transported to Monterey. Within days of arrival, much of the *Kutusov's* cargo was spoken for and the foodstuffs that were the medium of exchange were en route to Monterey.[7]

By 1821, trade between the two cultures was so extensive that the Russians apparently took special orders from Spanish customers. For instance, on its 1821 trip to San Francisco the *Buldakov* carried several items for Governor Sola, such as one "delicate writing desk," "forty-four packages high quality white thread," and "one box containing two dozens small cups." On that same ship, Mariano Estrada received the two *arrobas* of ammunition he needed, while the padres at Mission San Francisco obtained the one thousand one-inch nails they ordered, along with two new sets of candlesticks. That same year, the *Golovin* brought treated canvas for *Comandante* Luis Arguello's barge, needles and thread for the presidio troops, and even "one pair small scissors for Mrs. Chepita."[8]

Russian America: Most Favored Nation

In light of the intricate trading and commercial relationships established during the Spanish period in Alta California, there is ample evidence to show that Russia was the favored trading partner. By comparison, the ships of other nations did not always fare well at the hands of Spanish officialdom. A good example of this can be seen in the experience of Camille de Roquefeuil, captain of the French ship *Bordelais*. During 1817, the *Bordelais* traded in California with no official difficulty. Following a trip to Sitka, where a joint venture with the Russians turned sour and left him owing them money, he returned to California in 1818 to recoup his losses, only to receive a cold shoulder in San Francisco. Roquefeuil applied to Governor Sola for help, but the

VALTAZAR, an Inhabitant of Northern California, *by Mikhail T. Tikhanov, 1818. Paper, watercolor, lead pencil, and India ink. The two images are of the youth in profile and full-face.*

Collection of the Scientific Research Museum of the Academy of Arts, USSR; photograph courtesy of Shur Collection, Elmer E. Rasmuson Library, University of Alaska, Fairbanks.

governor remained aloof. Then Roquefeuil discovered that the Russian frigate *Kamchatka* and the trading ship *Kutusov* were anchored in Monterey.

Roquefeuil immediately wrote two further letters, one to the governor informing Sola he owed money to the Russians, and the second to the captain of the *Kamchatka*, asking him to intercede with

Sola on Roquefeuil's behalf. Captain P. N. Golovin did so, and in his reply to Roquefeuil noted that the captain of the *Columbia* had experienced similar difficulties and also requested his assistance. Golovin's intercession helped: Sola's subsequent reply to the Frenchman was ambiguous enough to allow him to complete his trading and repay the Russians. Although some of Roquefeuil's difficulties may be laid to Spanish paranoia following recent attacks by Argentinean pirates, the fact that both Frenchman and American requested Russian aid suggests that Spanish partiality toward Russian traders on the California coast was common contemporary knowledge.

Mexican Independence

Mexican independence from Spain caused the repeal of many laws in Alta California, including the prohibition on trade, and in 1822 California's ports were thrown open to ships of all nations. With increasing competition from other countries, particularly the United States, the Russians lost control of the California market. Yet the "most favored nation" status enjoyed by the Russian-American Company continued even under Mexican rule. An 1831 letter from Manuel Victoria, recently appointed governor of Alta California, to Baron Ferdinand von Wrangell, governor of Russian America, expressed friendly feelings toward the Russians and indicated he would favor them as best he could, particularly in preference to American traders. Victoria backed his words with action by imposing new tonnage fees on American whalers anchored in Mexican waters that Russian ships were not required to pay. In addition, launches and small boats from Fort Ross or the Russian port at Bodega Bay were allowed to trade openly in San Francisco without submitting to inspection, appraisal of cargo, or payment of duties. Victoria's successor, Jose Figueroa, sent Mariano Guadalupe Vallejo, northern *comandante* at Sonoma, to Fort Ross to trade for guns, cloth for his troops' uniforms, leather, wax, and tobacco. In his report, Vallejo noted that Governor Figueroa already had an account with the Russians at Fort Ross, to which he charged the cost of his military supplies.[9]

The foundation of cooperation with the Spanish laid by Ivan Kuskov in the nine

years he served as commandant of Fort Ross served his successors well. Future Russian administrators inherited not only a physically well-built colony, secure and peaceful, but a nurturing matrix of numerous and varied Russian ties to Spanish California as well. These ties were complex, inextricably entwining numerous Russian and Hispanic business and personal interests. They included, for instance, marriage between Russian subjects and Hispanic neophytes, particularly in the Fort Ross-Sonoma-San Francisco area; dependence of the Spanish on Russian medical and defense assistance in time of Indian trouble; dependence of the Russians upon the Spanish for most food staples; and finally, simple friendship. In the end, the interdependencies of the two cultures were so strong that even a change of government could not truly affect them. In the face of changing times, these ties simply evolved.

Life in California

Some of the new dimensions in Russian/ California relationships following Mexican independence were visible by 1823, the year the Russian ship *Kreiser* wintered in San Francisco. In charge of procuring supplies for the *Kreiser*'s continued journey around the world was a young naval officer, Dmitrii Zavalashin, to whom we are indebted for his memories of that sojourn. Zavalashin's duties afforded him the opportunity to travel in Alta California, where he learned Spanish in order to conduct his business with missionaries and secular authorities. Because of this, his memoirs reflect a more accurate picture of conditions in California and the character of its people than is common.

While one could hope that frequent trade with the Russians would be reflected by better living conditions for San Francisco residents, Zavalashin indicates that presidio life had improved little since Rezanov's visit:

[The presidio was] a rather formless pile of half-ruined dwellings, sheds, storehouses and other structures. The floors, of course, were everywhere of stone or dirt, and not only stoves but also fireplaces were lacking in the living quarters.... They warmed themselves against the cold air over hot coals in pots or braziers. There was no glass in the windows; some people had only grating in their windows.

To facilitate his business, Zavalashin was given a room in the presidio, but extensive renovation was needed before the space was comfortable enough to use. One of the *Kreiser*'s carpenters remodeled it by laying a wooden floor, introducing glass panes to casements heretofore innocent of such extravagance, and furnishing it with European furniture. Zavalashin also had a spare copper hearth from the ship installed to supply heat. Such luxury was noticed immediately: the young man noted that "during my off-duty hours, this room became a gathering place for female company, who came there to work."[10]

While Zavalashin's memories of his months in California provide tantalizing hints of more intimate aspects of Russian-Hispanic relationships, he clearly held the young women of Alta California in high regard. The young officer wrote that most Spanish women were beautiful, and made dashing note of some nicknames Russian officers had for certain ladies, i.e., "Madonna" and "Butterfly." It is hardly surprising, then, that "...talk of love was the most common topic of conversation" between the Russian visitors and Spanish ladies. Zavalashin recorded the meaning and popularity of the California fandango, and from his remarks we can form some impression of how young Russians and Californians interacted at close quarters, so to speak. The fandango required that partners face each other and sing memorized or improvised verses appropriate to the feelings and situations of the dancers. Unsurprisingly, many Russian officers began to write *sequidillas*, fandango verses. Zavalashin wrote that the following Russian-authored *sequidilla*, written in Spanish rather than Russian, was very popular and known widely in California:

> *My breast is full of new feelings;*
> *I grieve and pine;*
> *I long for someone's soul*
> *With a mysterious, sweet yearning!*
> *My blood surges faster!*
> *Is it love?*
> *The idol of all tender hearts,*
> *The crown of earthly bliss![11]*

FORT ROSS, Alta California. Il'ia G. Voznesenskii, Russian America's great scientist and naturalist, made this watercolor in 1841 for Alexander Rotchev, the last commandant at Ross, who had loved the fort and was shocked by its sale in 1841.

Original in Museum of Anthropology and Ethnology, Leningrad; photograph courtesy of California State Department of Parks, Sacramento.

While not all poetry translates well, the impulses of young love are universal—and surely sympathetic. Yet the mere existence of this verse, quite apart from its popularity, suggests that Russian-Hispanic interactions had made great strides, progressing from a relationship based on privation to one of cultural cross-fertilization.

Permanent Russian Agent in California

Despite Russian assertions that the California trade was increasingly less profitable after Mexican independence, there is evidence to suggest that the Russians maintained a special relationship with Alta California. For instance, in 1826 Governor Jose Maria Echeandia granted permission to the Russian-American Company to establish a permanent commercial agent in Monterey. Apparently they also warehoused a substantial amount of trade goods there as well, for in 1827 Hudson's Bay employee Aemelius Simpson spoke of the company's depot as "well furnished with goods for the market with which they purchase grain and other provisions for their establishments."[12]

The first individual to serve as Russia's agent in Monterey was Kyrill T. Khlebnikov, who entered the service of the Russian-American Company in 1800 and filled progressively more important positions through the years. By 1817 Khlebnikov was second only to Governor Hagemeister. He served frequently as supercargo on company trading ships from Sitka to California, and often conveyed correspondence between officials of both nations. Khlebnikov learned to speak and write both Spanish and English along the way, and knew all the Spanish officials. Clearly knowledgeable regarding conditions on the Pacific coast, he was the right man for the job. As company agent, Khlebnikov dealt with everyone who was anyone in Alta California, and his acquaintances covered the length and breadth of the province. Khlebnikov made deep personal relationships and cemented numerous business enterprises for the company until 1832, when he was recalled to Russia for further promotion.

Most company officials were aware that there was little future in California for their colony within a few years of Khlebnikov's departure. Secularization of many missions in 1832 played a large role in reducing sources for food supplies to the Russians in later years, as did the inability of Fort Ross to supply the northern colonies with enough grain, and the talent of the Americans for undercutting the Russians in trade. Profit was the name of the game for the company, and Fort Ross was awash in a sea of red ink; yet the Russians hung on by their teeth in California until 1841, when Fort Ross was sold lock, stock, and samovar to John Sutter of the Sacramento Valley. The heady days of unfettered trading, high profits, and preferential treatment were at an end—but friendship was not. As late as 1852, when Peter Kostromitinoff, former commandant of Fort Ross and the Russian-American Company's commercial agent in San Francisco following the sale of Fort Ross, left his post, Mariano Vallejo, the sage of Sonoma, gave grace to his departure. Vallejo loaned one of his Sonoma houses to the Kostromitinoff family, and even dispatched his own carriage to convey them from Benicia to their new home.

Indeed, despite many years at close quarters, Vallejo himself maintained apparently friendly relationships with the Russians, who, ironically, supplied all his military needs, including muskets, gunpowder, and cloth for uniforms. Occasional friction arose, usually over prerogatives of one nation or the other, but still Vallejo spoke well of his neighbors, recalling them to be "good traders who paid a just price for goods; they treated the Indians fairly and put down rebellious Indian renegades; and in general were clean and industrious people." Vallejo appears to have had a particular friendship with Alexander Rotchev, the last commandant of Fort Ross, and his wife, the former Princess Elena Pavlovna Gagarina. In the collection of the California Pioneer Society, San Francisco, is a magnificent silver tea service and traveling set that Rotchev gave to Vallejo; Vallejo was equally munificent in his gifts, in one instance sending the Rotchevs a new carriage. Several letters between Rotchev and Vallejo detail how routine and necessary trade between Sonoma and Fort Ross continued, even in those last days.[13]

We look to the talented Kyrill Khlebnikov for a fitting obituary to the Russians' days in California—and to better understand the deep ties of interdependence and friendship that developed between Russian and Hispanic during the Fort Ross years and beyond—with these lines from a letter to W. E. P. Hartnell:

I beg to testify my respects to Mrs. Hartnell and her children, to Don Mariano [Vallejo], Don David Spence, Don Malorin with their families and in general to such of my acquaintances who did not yet totally forget their amigo viejo, who is continually remembering of them all, who loves them all, who implores God to conserve their fate if good, to better it if bad, and to fill their days with all prosperity....

Wishing you all the happiness which the human nature is capable of, I remain forever, your faithful friend and servant, K. Khlebnikov.[14]

Diane Spencer Pritchard is a Sacramento-based historian specializing in the history of Fort Ross and the California Hispanic period.

For Further Reading

Bancroft, H. H. *History of California.* 1885; 2 vols., Santa Barbara: Wallace Hebberd, 1966.

Colonial Russian America: Kyrill T. Khlebnikov's Reports, 1817-1832. Trans. Basil Dmytryshyn and E. A. P. Crownhart-Vaughan. Portland: Oregon Historical Society, 1976.

Gibson, James R. *Imperial Russia in Frontier America.* New York: Oxford University Press, 1976.

Ogden, Adele. *The California Sea Otter Trade, 1784-1848.* Berkeley: University of California Press, 1941.

Rudkin, Charles. *Camille de Roquefeuil in San Francisco, 1817-1818.* Los Angeles: Glen Dawson, 1954.

Zavalashin, Dmitrii. "California in 1824." Trans. James R. Gibson. *Southern California Quarterly* 55, no. 4, p. 379.

Notes

1. Georg von Langsdorf, *Voyages and Travels in Various Parts of the World during the Years 1803, 1804, 1805, 1806 and 1807,* 2 vols. (London, 1813-14), 2, p. 173.
2. Ibid., pp. 175-176.
3. Charles Rudkin, *Camille de Roquefeuil in San Francisco, 1817-1818* (Los Angeles: Glen Dawson, 1954), p. 14.
4. Mariano Guadalupe Vallejo, *Documentos para la Historia de California, 1769-1850.* (36 vols.), 18, p. 178.
5. *The Russian-American Company, Correspondence of the Governors, Communications Sent: 1818* (Kingston, Ontario: Limestone Press, 1984), letter #212, pp. 124-125.
6. Kyrill T. Khlebnikov, *Colonial Russian America,* trans. Basil Dmytryshyn and E. A. P. Crownhart-Vaughan (Portland: Oregon Historical Society, 1976), p. 64; H. H. Bancroft, *History of California* (1885; Santa Barbara: Wallace Hebberd, 1966), 2, p. 301.
7. Santa Barbara Mission Archives, #2200, #2205, #2206.
8. Vallejo, *Documentos,* 17, pp. 36, 52.
9. Vallejo, *Documentos,* 30, p. 189, Victoria to Wrangell; Arch. Calif., Dept. State Records, 9, p. 123. Fort Ross visits, Dept. State Papers, Benicia Dustoms, 2, p. 103. Vallejo's trip, see Vallejo, *Documentos,* 2, p. 120; Arch. Calif., Missions and Colonization, 2, pp. 98-112.
10. Dmitrii Zavalashin, "California in 1824," trans. James R. Gibson, *Southern California Quarterly* 55, no. 4, p. 379.
11. Ibid., p. 379.
12. Quoted in James R. Gibson, *Imperial Russia in Frontier America* (New York: Oxford University Press, 1976), p. 183.
13. "Establicimientos de California." Information taken by Enrique Cerruti from M. G. Vallejo, Bancroft Library (University of California, Berkeley), MS C-D 75, p. 6; Vallejo, *Documentos,* 7, pp. 257, 390; 8, pp. 74, 181, 213.
14. Vallejo, *Documentos,* 32, p. 80.

Russian Exploration *and* Trade *in* Alaska's Interior

by Katherine L. Arndt

Less well known than the history of Russian activities on the coasts and islands of Alaska are past Russian efforts to explore and tap the fur resources of Alaska's mainland interior. Broadly defined, this vast area stretches from Mount St. Elias west to the Bering Sea and from Bristol Bay and the Gulf of Alaska north to the Brooks Range. Russian activities there were concentrated within four major regions: the Copper River drainage, the region north and west of the Kenai Peninsula, the Nushagak and Kuskokwim river drainages, and the Yukon drainage.

The furs of the mainland interior, beaver, land otter, marten, and fox, promised the Russian-American Company profits long after the coastal sea otter catch had dwindled to a fraction of its former size. Recognizing its potential at a fairly early date, the company made a considerable investment in developing that aspect of its trade. Its emphasis on and involvement in the mainland trade did fluctuate in intensity over time, influenced by such factors as international politics, world fur prices, company finances, and the state of relations with local Native inhabitants. From 1818 on, however, development of the trade of the Alaskan interior was never far from the minds of the Russian-American Company's directorate.

Economic rationality in St. Petersburg was not easily implemented in the field.

The Early Years

The first Russian hunters and traders to focus their efforts on the Alaskan mainland were associated not with the forerunners of the Russian-American Company, but with the rival Lebedev-Lastochkin Company. Between 1787 and 1798 this firm was very active on Cook Inlet and Prince William Sound and had begun to penetrate adjacent regions of the interior. Records of this early period of Alaska's history are sketchy, but we do know that the Lebedev-Lastochkin men had at least three posts on the mainland, one at Nikolaevsk on the Kenai Peninsula, and two on Lake Iliamna. From Nikolaevsk they sent at least one small party to the lower Copper River for exploration and trade. From the Iliamna posts at least one party is reported to have reached the Kuskokwim drainage and perhaps as far north as the Yukon River.

Despite a promising start, the Lebedev-Lastochkin Company did not survive long enough to consolidate its hold on the mainland. Crippled by squabbles among its own traders that on occasion bordered on open warfare, the company withdrew in 1798. Its posts were quickly occupied by employees of the United American Company, immediate forerunner of the Russian-American Company.[1]

In its early years the Russian-American Company, preoccupied with its territorial claims on the Northwest coast and problems of colonial supply, could devote little energy to extending the mainland trade. While the company continued to occupy the old Lebedev-Lastochkin posts at Nikolaevsk and at Konstantinovsk on Hinchinbrook Island, Prince William Sound, the Iliamna posts were apparently abandoned and replaced by a seasonal trader. Post personnel made little effort to travel inland to expand their trade contacts

PRINCE DMITRII Maksutov, the last governor of Russian America, 1865-67. A champion of Russian America, Maksutov worked tirelessly to make the colony pay its way, including streamlining the network of interior posts.

Dimitrii P. Maksutov Collection, Alaska State Library, Juneau.

among the Natives. Rather, any Natives interested in participating in the trade were expected to bring their furs to the existing posts.

Such a policy did not handicap the spread of the mainland fur trade as much as one might expect. Even before the arrival of the Russians, there existed among Alaska's Native peoples a network of traditional trade relations. A strategically placed Russian post needed only to attract and cultivate a few of the better-connected local Natives to tap into that network and extend its trade into distant regions no Russian had ever seen. Moreover, direct access to the goods sold at a post frequently allowed a Native to expand his trade ties—and by extension the Russians'—far beyond traditional bounds and to enhance his own wealth and prestige. Though a Native trader who became too powerful in his middleman role could also hinder Russian trade if he chose, such associations were more often mutually beneficial and were common in the interior trade in these and later years.

The half-dozen exploratory expeditions

known to have been dispatched inland during the Russian-American Company's early years all focused on the Copper River. Most went in search of minerals, not furs, seeking the sources of copper and mica known to come from that region. Only after nearly twenty years of existence did the company find the resources to embark on a major program of exploration of the interior with an eye toward expanding its trade.

Branching Out

Of first priority was the region north of Bristol Bay, rumored since the days of the Lebedev-Lastochkin Company to abound with beaver. In 1818 an expedition under Petr Korsakovskii examined the lower reaches of the major rivers flowing into Bristol Bay from the north and ascended the Kvichak River to Lakes Iliamna and Clark. One detachment of the expedition continued north from there, possibly reaching the Kuskokwim River. The explorers returned with promising reports of rich fur resources and of a Native population that seemed willing to trade. Encouraged by this information, the company established a new post at the mouth of the Nushagak River the following summer. Korsakovskii returned to the region in 1819 expressly to explore the Kuskokwim, but turned back without reaching his goal.[2]

Two years later colonial chief manager Matfei I. Murav'ev attempted to expand upon Korsakovskii's explorations from a different tack. In 1821 and 1822 he dispatched expeditions by sea to explore the coast north from Bristol Bay to Norton Sound and beyond. Geographical discovery was but a minor goal of the undertaking, for a Russian naval expedition had explored the same waters in 1820 and was returning in 1821. Much more important from the company's perspective were any trade contacts the expeditions could make with local inhabitants and any information they could gather concerning the mainland interior.

In this, expedition commander Vasilii S. Khromchenko and his assistant Adolf Etholen were quite successful. At Golovnin Bay and Stuart Island they met a number of local Natives and traded with them on a modest scale. They also recorded valuable information on a thriving trade in interior furs between the Natives of Alaska and Natives of the Siberian shore carried on by way of Bering Strait.[3]

Also receiving attention in this period of exploration were regions of the mainland interior with which the company had a somewhat longer acquaintance. In 1819 the Creole Afanasii Klimovskii was dispatched up the Copper River. The information he recorded on the country, its inhabitants, trade routes, and fur resources encouraged the company to establish a small trading station there sometime between 1821 and 1822.[4] From Nikolaevsk, the company began to send an Aleut trader "beyond Sukhotna"

[Susitna?] each winter at the request of Natives who found it difficult to transport their furs to the post. The trader was instructed to collect all possible information about trade routes and the Kuskokwim and Yukon drainages while on his rounds, but his results were not recorded.

By 1822 the Russian-American Company's first push to explore the mainland interior had lost momentum. Over the next five years company officials both in Russia and in the colonies were preoccupied with more urgent matters: implementation of the company's new charter, settlement of North American territorial boundaries with the United States and Great Britain, administrative reorganization of the Atka district, and plans to return the colonial capital from Sitka to Kodiak.

Nonetheless, the mainland trade was not forgotten in this period. In fact, the proposed capital move was partly motivated by a desire to be more centrally

DOG-TEAM DRIVING in the Alaskan interior.

From an engraving in William H. Dall's Alaska and Its Resources (Boston, 1870). Washington State Historical Society, Tacoma.

located in relation to the increasingly important mainland fur resources. But while every effort was made to keep the mainland posts well stocked, they sometimes had to share in shortages of trade goods or in economizing measures that affected the frequency of supply trips.

Mainland fur returns were particularly vulnerable to such shortages. Stations located elsewhere in the colonies equipped their own crews of Native conscripts, primarily Aleuts, and Creole and Russian employees to hunt marine mammals and island furbearers, whereas the mainland posts acquired furs almost exclusively through barter with the surrounding Native peoples. Moreover, only a few types of goods were acceptable to both parties. The mainland Natives as yet found little to recommend European

clothing, and the Russians were loath to accustom them to European foods, of which they themselves were often short, or to firearms and liquor, which they considered dangerous. The most desired and frequently traded items were instead tobacco, beads, and various small metal goods such as knives and axes. Lacking these, a post found it difficult to persuade even its regular Native customers to part with their furs, and to pursue new avenues of trade was nearly impossible. In the face of irregular supply of these goods, the mainland posts merely held their own through the mid 1820s and their trade remained static.

In 1828, citing the great decline in the annual catch of sea otter, the main office issued a call to resume the expansion of the fur trade far into the interior. Though the decline in sea otter was of long standing, the company had suffered no immediate hardship because prices for both sea otter and most other types of furs had remained high. Recently, however, prices had been down, especially for foxes, which now accounted for a large part of the annual returns.

The company's directors responded quickly and innovatively to these altered conditions. They believed that river beaver and land otter skins were their surest hope for profits after fur seals. Fur seal populations were already known to be on the decline, whereas there was still great potential to expand the beaver and land otter hunt. In addition, prices for these species promised to remain stable, both due to the seemingly insatiable demand for them in China and because of restrictions on importing foreign beaver and land otter skins into Russia.

Drawing upon the 1821 and 1822 reports of Etholen and Khromchenko and upon Murav'ev's comments on the trade

MARGARETHA Etholen, wife of the governor of Russian America, accompanied her husband to Sitka and introduced the Lutheran church to the cultural life of the capital city.

Photograph from the original oil, National Museum of Finland, Helsinki.

potential of southwestern Alaska, the directors instructed Chief Manager Chistiakov to focus attention upon two areas. The first was the heart of beaver and land otter country at the headwaters of the Nushagak, Kuskokwim, and Kvikhpak [Yukon] rivers, then thought to lie close together. The other was the coast of Norton Sound, where coastal Aziiagmiut middlemen purchased interior furs for resale to the Chukchi of the Siberian shore. In effect, this directive set the agenda for company explorations for the next decade.

In 1829 and again in 1830, Chistiakov dispatched expeditions under Ensign Ivan I. Vasil'ev up the Nushagak River toward the Kuskokwim and Yukon drainages to investigate the courses of the major rivers, gather information on the Native populations, trade, and fur resources, and find an advantageous location for a new trading station. In the first season he got no farther than the Nushagak, Wood, and Togiak rivers and the adjacent lake systems. In the second season he explored the middle Kuskokwim and descended the river to the coast. Though he did not manage to reach the Yukon drainage, everything he was able to learn about it indicated that it, too, would be rich in beaver and land otter. Based on what he could learn of local trade patterns, Vasil'ev recommended Stuart Island, near the mouth of Norton Sound, as a promising site for a new post.[5]

Chistiakov's successor as chief manager, Ferdinand P. von Wrangell, considered it unwise to continue to send special exploring parties into the interior of southwestern Alaska. Led by people who were relative strangers to the region, such expeditions had the potential of inadvertently offending the Natives with whom they came into contact and ruining any chance for future trade. Wrangell therefore assigned Vasil'ev to other tasks and entrusted the continued exploration of the

region to its long-resident traders, Fedor Kolmakov, his Creole son Petr, and the Creole Semen Lukin.

In 1832 and 1833 Kolmakov and his men took the trade directly to the Holitna and middle Kuskokwim rivers. Leaving their own post on the Nushagak River understaffed, they traveled extensively among the Native villages and camps to establish trade ties with local leaders and to encourage everyone to hunt furbearers more intensively. At several places they built small huts to serve as seasonal way stations, collection points, and storage depots. The groundwork laid, Kolmakov returned to his administrative duties at the Nushagak River post and delegated the Kuskokwim trade to Semen Lukin, under whom it flourished.[6]

Chief Manager von Wrangell more closely followed Chistiakov's lead when it came to investigating the trade potential of Norton Sound. In 1830 Chistiakov had sent a vessel under Lieutenant Adolf Etholen to trade there on an experimental basis. Etholen's relative success, combined with Vasil'ev's recommendation of Stuart Island as a permanent trading site, prompted Wrangell to dispatch Lieutenant Mikhail Teben'kov to the Bering Sea and Norton Sound three seasons in a row. His missions were to trade, to select a site for a post, and, in 1833, to oversee the establishment of Redoubt St. Michael on St. Michael Island, just south of Stuart Island and not far north of the mouth of the Yukon River.

As was typical of company posts designated "redoubts," St. Michael was roughly square in plan and surrounded by a stout, high fence, or palisade. Forming the sides of the square, and sometimes incorporated into the palisade itself, were the post's main buildings: barracks for the workers,

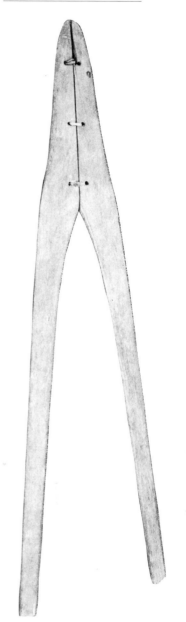

FOX STRETCHER, wood, nineteenth century. The stretcher was used to clean and shape the pelt. Fox was a popular fur in China and the animals abounded in the Alaskan interior. They also were plentiful on some of the Aleutian Islands.

Kodiak Historical Society.

OTTER STRETCHER, wood, nineteenth century. Otter hides were stretched on such forms for cleaning and shaping.

Kodiak Historical Society.

the manager's house and office, a kitchen and bathhouse, the trading shop and warehouses, and, at two opposite corners, tall blockhouses or watchtowers, all of log construction. Outside the palisade were gardens, work areas, a forge, a chapel, and a communal house or two for visiting Natives. Similar in size to other company redoubts, St. Michael had a permanent staff of twenty-five to thirty men.

The St. Michael post was not expected to capture the whole trade of the Yukon drainage by itself. Not only was it located some distance from the river, but local Native middlemen resented its presence as an intrusion on their lucrative trade with the Chukchi of far northeastern Siberia. Being situated on the coast, however, the post could be fairly easily supplied by seagoing vessel and was thus a convenient base from which explorers and trading parties could be dispatched into the interior.

Between 1833 and 1838, half a dozen small expeditions explored the lower Yukon drainage and various portages between the Yukon and the coast and between the Yukon and Kuskokwim drainages. All were led by Creoles trained in navigation who were quite capable of taking the observations needed to compile the first rough maps of the region. The explorers also collected information on local trade routes. Based on their recommendations, two small trading stations had been established on the Yukon by 1839, one at Ikogmiut and the other at Nulato.[7]

Epidemic

While the Russian-American Company focused considerable attention on developing the trade of the Kuskokwim and Yukon drainages in the 1830s, it did not intend to do so at the expense of the older branches of its interior trade. The same period saw the resolution of transporta-

tion problems that had been inhibiting the Copper River trade, the reestablishment on Lake Iliamna of a permanent post administered out of Nikolaevsk Redoubt (Kenai), and plans to launch an expedition north and west out of Nikolaevsk in order to explore unknown regions and establish new trade contacts with the resident Natives. To the disappointment of company officials, however, the proposed explorations had to be postponed repeatedly due to the smallpox epidemic then spreading unchecked into the region. The Natives' unsettled state in the wake of the terrible mortality, and the likelihood that they would blame the epidemic's appearance on any strangers then entering their country, finally convinced colonial authorities that it would be best to cancel the expedition altogether.

The region north of Nikolaevsk was not the only portion of the Alaskan interior affected by the smallpox epidemic. Despite the company's best efforts to contain the disease, it reached the mainland in 1838, and spread an unknown distance up the Copper River, through southwestern Alaska north to the shores of Norton Sound, and up the Yukon River for an unknown distance beyond Nulato. Wherever it appeared, it disrupted all normal pursuits, including the hunting of furbearers and the fur trade. From Tanaina territory north of Nikolaevsk and from the Copper River drainage came reports of major dislocations of people from their usual hunting areas and rumors of warfare between peoples. In the Nushagak and Kuskokwim drainages the disease killed many of the Native leaders with whom the company had cultivated its strongest trade relations. On Norton Sound and in the Yukon drainage it killed many of the people whom the company was trying to attract to the trade, but large numbers of the company's Native competitors there also succumbed.

The epidemic had everywhere run its

course by 1839 or 1840, but its effects on the interior trade lingered. Most of the Natives were too busy rebuilding their lives to give much thought to the fur trade. Others had become extremely wary of any unnecessary contact with strangers, Native or Russian, lest they be re-exposed to the disease. Still others blamed the epidemic on the Russians and sought retaliation. An attack on Ikogmiut, an attempt against the Kuskokwim River post, and rumors of other intended attacks at this time were all thought to be so motivated. In an effort to revive the trade, the company sent out emissaries to convince the Native inhabitants of the Russians' innocence in the epidemic and of their continued goodwill toward Native peoples. To keep up fur production in the meantime, company personnel temporarily increased their own hunting efforts.

Back to Business

By late 1840 and early 1841 the interior posts' relations with surrounding Natives had recovered sufficiently for the company to resume its program of exploration and expansion on the mainland. The new colonial chief manager, Adolf Etholen, turned his attention first to the Copper River drainage. Between late 1840 and mid 1844 three small expeditions were dispatched toward Tazlina Lake to locate a site for a forward base from which to launch explorations still deeper into that country. No suitable site was found and the proposal was abandoned.

Etholen also hoped to intensify the beaver trade out of Nikolaevsk. His plan was to equip parties of Tanaina Athabaskans with everything they would need for an extended hunting trip (guns, ammunition, food) and send them out after furs. On their return, they would be paid the company's set rate for each fur brought in plus a gratuity in tobacco, and sizable rewards in goods were promised to the party leaders. The Tanaina leaders readily agreed to the proposal, but rather than hunting, some of them used the supplies provided as capital in their own trading

AN INDIAN fishing village on the lower Yukon River, ca. 1865, an engraving.

From William H. Dall's Alaska and Its Resources (Boston, 1870), courtesy of Washington State Historical Society, Tacoma.

ventures into the interior. At first colonial officials were chagrined, but they quickly realized that it did not matter how furs were obtained as long as the pelts came to the company. Having failed in their own attempt to find a route into the interior by way of the Susitna River in 1844, they were soon happy to encourage the Tanaina in their middleman role.

The most elaborate expedition of Etholen's administration was reserved for the Yukon and Kuskokwim drainages. Though considerable geographical information on the region had been gathered piecemeal over the previous decade, much of the region remained unexplored. Etholen hoped that a single major expedition could verify and tie together all the earlier locational data and then push on into areas not yet known. The chief manager also wanted information on the state of the region's trade. Though posts had proliferated there, their yields were not as high as expected. This was due in part to competition with Natives involved in the Siberian trade, in part to unwitting competition among the company's own posts. Without detailed data, Etholen could not hope to sort out these relations.

The Yukon-Kuskokwim expedition was entrusted to Lieutenant Lavrentii Zagoskin, who, like some other young officers of his day, had taken advantage of a government policy that allowed him to transfer from the Russian navy to Russian-American Company service without loss of rank or seniority. Since 1839 he had been gaining valuable practical experience as a commander of company vessels on routine voyages between Okhotsk, Sitka, and California, but he longed to distinguish himself in exploration. In appointing him to command the proposed expedition, Etholen now gave him that opportunity.

Resident in the Yukon-Kuskokwim region from the fall of 1842 through the

early summer of 1844, Zagoskin did not accomplish all that had been assigned to him, but he did manage to integrate most of the information garnered from the earlier expeditions, ascend the Yukon another hundred miles beyond Nulato, and gather the requisite trade information. His travel notes, published in Russia in 1847 and 1848, introduced a little-known corner of Russian America to European scientific circles and won scholarly acclaim. The expedition's chief value for the Russian-American colonies, however, lay in Zagoskin's private recommendations for restructuring the region's trade.[8]

Etholen ordered a number of changes based on the information Zagoskin had gathered. To counter Native involvement in the Siberian trade, St. Michael and the Yukon River posts were to stock the Siberian reindeer clothing and coastal subsistence items for which the inland peoples most readily bartered their furs. For greater efficiency in operation and supply, the Nushagak River post was reduced to a small trading station. Kolmakov Redoubt, established on the Kuskokwim River in 1841, would now be supplied through St. Michael rather than through Nushagak. The post at Ikogmiut, long in competition with the Kuskokwim River stations, was to be moved down the Yukon to Andreevskaia, though a small seasonal station and a newly opened church mission would remain at the site. Finally, the Nulato post was to receive greater support as a forward base from which to advance the trade up the Yukon.

To coordinate the company's operations in the region as a whole, Etholen asked Zagoskin to compile detailed instructions for the Kolmakov, Andreevskaia, and Nulato posts. The explorer recommended specific staffing and salary levels, defined the trade territory to be covered by each, and proposed efficient schedules for the annual round of trading trips and supply runs. These recommendations guided regional operations for the remaining twenty years of the company's presence there. Though the company did not always have the resources to implement them in full, they remained the ideal toward which it always strove.

Through the end of the 1840s, company personnel carried the fur trade farther into the interior. Semen Lukin of Kolmakov Redoubt pushed to the very headwaters of the Kuskokwim and Nulato's Vasilii Deriabin instituted an annual spring trading trip far up the Yukon toward the western edge of the Yukon Flats. At Nikolaevsk the post manager was content to rely on the Tanaina middlemen, for the company had not the resources to attempt another exploration of the Susitna.

The last exploratory expedition of the decade was instead dispatched toward the headwaters of the Copper River in the hope that it could cross to the Yukon drainage and thus overlap the explorations completed by Zagoskin. Led by the young Creole Ruf Serebrennikov, recently returned from navigational training in St. Petersburg, the unfortunate party was killed en route along the Copper River in 1848. It was reported that Serebrennikov

ARVID ADOLF Etholen, governor of Russian America, 1840-45, was an explorer and able administrator. He took particular interest in expanding Russian influence into the interior, organizing explorations of the Copper River drainage and the Yukon-Kuskokwim basin.

Photograph from the original oil, National Museum of Finland, Helsinki.

ST. MICHAEL REDOUBT, ca. 1865, an engraving from a drawing by William H. Dall. Dall was a member of the Smithsonian scientific team that accompanied the Overland Telegraph Expedition of 1865-67.

From William H. Dall's Alaska and Its Resources *(Washington, D.C., 1870). Washington State Historical Society, Tacoma.*

had offended his Native hosts, but some suspected that the true motivation had been the desire of the upper Copper River's Native middlemen to protect their share of the trade.

Due to the company's worsening financial position, the Serebrennikov expedition proved to be its last major attempt at geographical exploration in Alaska's interior. In fact, in the late 1840s the company found the very foundation of its interior trade to be threatened. Beginning in the mid 1840s, the price of beaver declined drastically on world fur markets, and many pelts remained unsold in company warehouses. Since beaver had always been the most abundant of the mainland furs, a sharp reorientation of the interior trade was required. The mainland posts were directed to shift their emphasis to land otter and especially to marten furs, which were increasing in price, and henceforth to accept only the higher grades of beaver pelts.

Market Changes

Economic rationality in St. Petersburg was not easily implemented in the field. First, both the post personnel and the

Native fur hunters and traders had to be reeducated. The former were loath to turn away any fur, no matter how poor the quality, lest they lose business, and the latter viewed any attempt to change the rules of the trade as capricious and even insulting. Fur prices were, of course, always open to a certain amount of negotiation. The official price schedule for the interior posts, set at Sitka and approved at St. Petersburg, defined only the average price to be paid for each type and grade of fur. Within those limits, it was up to each company trader to find a price that was neither so low that the Natives refused to sell nor so high that the Natives could buy all the European goods they wished and give up fur hunting for the season. A company trader could also influence what types of fur were brought in by paying out the most desirable goods only for the types he wanted most. Those involved in the interior trade were just becoming accustomed to the price schedule instituted in 1842, under which the amount paid for beaver had increased. It was difficult to reopen the topic so soon.

More importantly, neither land otters nor martens were as readily obtained as beaver. They were harder to catch, harder to clean, and present in much smaller numbers in those areas most closely integrated into the company's trade network. The region most abundant in marten, the Tanana River drainage and the upper middle Yukon, was accessible to the company's traders only indirectly through Native middlemen and as yet figured only peripherally in their fur returns. Despite the post managers' best efforts, their aggregate annual fur returns never fully regained their former value.

The Difficult 1850s

Declining revenues continued to plague the Russian-American Company through the 1850s. A pair of weak colonial chief managers in the first half of the decade and the disruptions in shipping and supply brought on by the Crimean War in mid decade only exacerbated its problems. When a series of setbacks hit its trade in the Alaskan interior, the company lacked the resources to address them promptly, and the trade suffered accordingly.

During a famine in the Copper River country in the spring of 1850, starving Natives stripped the company post there of its stock of provisions, thus forcing the post manager and his family to leave. With the loss of the Serebrennikov party still fresh in their minds, colonial officials interpreted the raid as further evidence of local Native enmity. Lacking personnel to reinforce the post, they reduced it to a seasonal station visited only in summer.

On the Yukon River the Nulato post fell victim to a dispute between the Nulato Natives and their rivals in the fur trade, Natives of the lower Koyukuk River. In the spring of 1851, a party from the Koyukuk destroyed the Nulato Native village and killed several at the company station, including the post manager. Though the post was quickly reinforced in personnel and defenses, it became much more cautious in its dealings with Natives,

and trading trips up the Yukon were sharply curtailed.

At the same time, the company was beginning to feel the effects of competition from the Hudson's Bay Company post at Fort Yukon, surreptitiously established within Russian territory in 1847. Before the interlopers could be expelled, the fact of their trespass had to be documented with precise cartographic information. The chief manager laid detailed plans for an expedition to do just that, but could not muster the wherewithal to dispatch it, and the trespass remained unchallenged.

The Kuskokwim drainage trade fared well until the death in 1855 of Semen Lukin, longtime manager of Kolmakov Redoubt. Unable to find a replacement of the senior Lukin's experience and caliber, the colonial authorities left the post in the charge of his son, Ivan. In addition to the problems of supply that affected all the more distant colonial posts in the Crimean War years, the administration of Ivan Lukin was marked by mismanagement, disorder, and insubordination in the ranks. Accused of private trading on the side and issuing large, irrecoverable credit advances to the Natives, he was

HAND-WROUGHT *iron shears, nineteenth century. Although the purpose of these large shears is not known, they were made in Russian America, one of the products of the support industries that sprang up as part of the colony's effort to become self-sufficient.*

Kodiak Historical Society.

replaced in 1860.

The net result of the Russian-American Company's difficulties in the 1850s was an overall contraction of its activities in Alaska's interior. That its fur returns did not drop as sharply as might be expected must be credited to the activities of various Native middlemen. Throughout the decade, the company grew much more dependent upon their services to carry its trade to the far reaches of the colonies.

Regrouping

The arrival of a new colonial chief manager in 1860 marked a change in policy toward the interior trade. Perhaps because the company's charter would soon be up for renewal and was even then a topic of heated debate in Russia, Chief Manager Johan H. Furuhjelm was bent on regaining ground lost in the previous decade. In 1860 the manager at Nikolaevsk once again began sending a winter trader to the head of Cook Inlet. At Kolmakov Redoubt an entire turnover in personnel was ordered in an effort to end petty corruption there. Though the Hudson's Bay Company post at Fort Yukon was too well established to be readily expelled, Ivan Lukin was dispatched there from St. Michael in 1862 to gather intelligence on its prices and trade. In 1863 the annual spring trading trips upriver from Nulato were reinstituted

with great success, and Furuhjelm's orders to reopen the Copper River post as a year-round station were implemented. Through these efforts and continued strong participation by the Native middlemen, the interior trade began to look more promising, but the business acumen displayed in redirecting the company's efforts could not overcome the external pressures it faced.

Until the end, the company's colonial officials kept struggling to raise profits. The company's last colonial chief manager, Prince Dmitrii P. Maksutov, was determined to make the colonies a paying enterprise. Between the summers of 1865 and 1866 he formulated an ambitious program to streamline operations and develop new industries. Establishments that did not earn enough to repay the expense of maintaining them were to be closed or turned to other uses. The mainland interior posts affected by Maksutov's sweeping orders were the Copper River station, Kolmakov Redoubt on the Kuskokwim, and Andreevskaia on the Yukon, all closed in 1866.

The efficacy of Maksutov's reforms went untested. In 1867 Russia sold its colonies to the United States and the Russian-American Company was forced to liquidate its holdings. Because of the remoteness of the region, the company's Yukon

ST. MICHAEL REDOUBT,
Norton Sound, 1843. A
drawing by Il'ia G.
Voznesenskii, scientist and
naturalist who studied and
explored in Russian America
in 1839-49. The fort was the
base from which explorations
of the Yukon set out,
beginning in 1833.

Museum of Anthropology and Ethnology, Leningrad; photograph courtesy of Oregon Historical Society, Portland.

drainage stations operated for an additional year, but in the summer of 1868 they, too, ceased to be Russian posts.

The sale of Alaska brought a number of changes to the interior fur trade, most notably the end of an era of monopoly and the arrival of a multitude of competing traders. And yet, the trade also retained a certain continuity. Many of the Russian-American Company's former Russian, Creole, and Native employees stayed on to work for the new trading firms or tried their hand at operating independently. Moreover, the Alaska Commercial Company, which had acquired most of the Russian-American Company's colonial assets and soon came to dominate the trade, chose to organize its Alaskan operations along much the same lines as its Russian predecessor. In this manner, the Russian legacy continued to shape the fur trade of Alaska's interior until nearly the twentieth century.

Katherine L. Arndt is a research consultant in Fairbanks who has published articles on Russian-American policy and translations of primary documents.

For Further Reading

Ketz, James A. and Katherine L. Arndt. "The Russian-American Company and Development of the Alaskan Copper River Fur Trade." *Le Castor Fait Tout: Selected Papers of the 5th North American Fur Trade Conference, 1985.* Ed. Bruce G. Trigger et al. Montreal: Lake St. Louis Historical Society, 1987, pp. 438-455.

Lieutenant Zagoskin's Travels in Russian America, 1842-1844. Trans. Penelope Rainey, ed. Henry N. Michael. Toronto: University of Toronto Press, 1967.

Russian Exploration in Southwest Alaska: The Travel Journals of Petr Korsakovskiy (1818) and Ivan Ya. Vasilev (1829). Ed. James W. VanStone, trans. David H. Kraus. Fairbanks: University of Alaska Press, 1988.

V. S. Khromchenko's Coastal Explorations in Southwestern Alaska, 1822. Ed. James W. VanStone, trans. David H. Kraus. *Fieldiana Anthropology,* vol. 64. Chicago: Field Museum of Natural History, 1973.

Notes

1. Svetlana G. Fedorova, *The Russian Population in Alaska and California, Late 18th Century - 1867,* trans. and ed. Richard A. Pierce and Alton S. Donnelly (Kingston, Ontario: Limestone Press, 1973), pp. 121-130.

2. *Russian Exploration in Southwest Alaska: The Travel Journals of Petr Korsakovskiy (1818) and Ivan Ya. Vasilev (1829),* ed. James W. VanStone, trans. David H. Kraus (Fairbanks: University of Alaska Press, 1988), pp. 7-8, 11-75.

3. *V. S. Khromchenko's Coastal Explorations in Southwestern Alaska, 1822,* ed. James W. VanStone, trans. David H. Kraus, *Fieldiana Anthropology* 64 (Chicago: Field Museum of Natural History, 1973).

4. James A. Ketz, *Paxson Lake: Two Nineteenth Century Ahtna Sites in the Copper River Basin, Alaska,* Anthropology and Historic Preservation, Cooperative Park Studies Unit, Occasional Paper 33 (Fairbanks: University of Alaska, 1983), pp. 4-45; and James A. Ketz and Katherine L. Arndt, "The Russian-American Company and Development of the Alaskan Copper River Fur Trade," *Le Castor Fait Tout: Selected Papers of the 5th North American Fur Trade Conference, 1985,* ed. Bruce G. Trigger et al. (Montreal: Lake St. Louis Historical Society, 1987), pp. 438-455.

5. VanStone, *Russian Exploration,* pp. 9-10, 77-109.

6. Wendell H. Oswalt, *Kolmakovskiy Redoubt: The Ethnoarchaeology of a Russian Fort in Alaska* (Los Angeles: Institute of Archaeology, University of California, 1980), pp. 9-13, 79-84.

7. James W. VanStone, *Ingalik Contact Ecology: An Ethnohistory of the Lower-Middle Yukon, 1790-1935, Fieldiana Anthropology* 71 (Chicago: Field Museum of Natural History, 1979), pp. 43-103; and James W. VanStone, "Russian Exploration in Interior Alaska: An Extract from the Journal of Andrei Glazunov," *Pacific Northwest Quarterly* 50, no. 2 (1959), pp. 37-47.

8. *Lieutenant Zagoskin's Travels in Russian America, 1842-1844,* trans. Penelope Rainey, ed. Henry N. Michael (Toronto: University of Toronto Press, 1967).
among the Natives. Rather, any Natives interested in participating in the trade were expected to bring their furs to the existing posts.

Charles Sumner
and the Alaska Purchase

by Margaret Shannon

The deal was cut in the midnight hours of March 29-30, 1867. Rumors of the treaty ceding Russian America to the United States quickly spread to the nation's newspapers, whose editors were at first puzzled, then outraged. Where and what was this Russian America, said to be a snow-shrouded dreariness of "glaciers, icebergs, white bears and walruses?" Why did the Russians want to sell it? Why the haste and secrecy? And why would the United States want to buy it? "Russia Has Sold Us a Sucked Orange!" fumed the *New York World*. But Secretary of State William Seward was elated. An ardent supporter of Manifest Destiny and eager to cap his lifelong career of government service with a bold diplomatic coup, Seward staked everything on his Alaskan venture. Besides, the price was right: $7.2 million for some half-million square miles of presumably valuable real estate.

The gamble, however, had little chance of success unless Seward could get the backing of Charles Sumner, the powerful chairman of the Senate Committee on Foreign Relations. At first, Senator Sumner was skeptical. Like most Americans, he knew virtually nothing about Russian America. However, the habits of a lifetime compelled him to search for sufficient knowledge upon which to make an informed decision.

Sumner turned to the Congressional Library. There, working with his clerk, C. C. Beaman, and friends such as ethnologist George Gibbs and journalist Ben. Perley Poore, he culled a treasure trove of information on Russian America from the library's books, manuscripts, journals, maps, atlases, broadsides, newspapers, prints, pamphlets, and periodicals, in English as well as in German, French, and Russian.

What Sumner discovered about the value of Russian America transformed him from a skeptic into a powerful persuader. Armed with the knowledge gained in only ten days of research, Sumner spoke to his Senate colleagues on April 8, 1867, for nearly three hours in defense of the treaty. Influenced both by Sumner's dazzling command of information about Russian America, as well as his acknowledged preeminence in the field of foreign policy, the Senate, in a remarkable demonstration of the relationship between knowledge and power, overwhelmingly approved the treaty the next day.

Sumner subsequently acknowledged publicly the role of information discovered within the Library of Congress and expressed his satisfaction that "the chief sources of original information on Alaska may be found in the Congressional Library." What were these "sources of original information" in the Congressional Library of 1867 upon which Sumner relied? In what ways had the library evolved to that time? What is known about Sumner's research odyssey into the history of Russian America?

The Congressional Library[1]

The Library of Congress was founded in 1800, when the government moved from New York City to the new District of Columbia. Its sole purpose was to gather the information members needed for their day-to-day work on the floor of Congress. The Founding

What Sumner discovered about the value of Russian America transformed him from a sceptic into a powerful persuader.

Fathers—primarily lawyers and merchants and plantation owners with large personal libraries that they used in their daily work—used books as working tools in the temporary capitals of Philadelphia and New York. In those established cities, the working bookmen of Congress' existing libraries were housed just down the hall in the same buildings where the senators and representatives met.

When the national government was finally moved to its permanent home in Washington, D.C., in 1800, there were no literary facilities of any kind in the city, so the law transferring the seat of government created a library for Congress, to be housed in the new Capitol building. Between 1800 and 1812, the first Librarian of Congress accumulated three thousand volumes across a very broad, general span of interest. Besides current English plays, poetry, and novels, as well as the law, history, and political science that would be expected, the library soon contained books on medicine and agriculture, and an amazing number of maps and atlases of the North American continent. The latter were instruments of national defense, their purchase justified as a way of proving borders and presence in defense of expected conflicts with England, Spain, and France, which still owned and occupied the land surrounding the United States. Senator Charles Sumner referred to these maps and atlases for the same purpose in 1867, namely, to defend American title to Russian America.

After a British force burned the Capitol in 1814, destroying the original Library of Congress, retired president Thomas Jefferson offered his personal library as a replacement. Jefferson had accumulated his collection during a public career of many years in this country and abroad, and the result was a library that was not only one of the largest in America, but

also probably the broadest in scope on the continent. The Congress acquired the entire collection, paying $23,950 for its 6,487 volumes.

Recognizing from the outset that the Jefferson collection was a national treasure, Congress added new materials across the entire subject range to keep it as comprehensive and catholic as it had been when Jefferson first created it.

After fires in 1825 and 1851 destroyed two-thirds of the cumulated holdings, some thirty-five thousand volumes, Congress constructed a large multigalleried series of rooms across the mall side of the Capitol building exclusively for the library. By the close of the Civil War, the Library of Congress had grown to eighty-two thousand volumes.

The library, with its fireproof iron shelving, was intended for members of the legislature (comments like "left the floor and went to the Iron Room to get proof of my assertion" appear frequently in contemporary records), although occasionally a researcher from a federal agency was permitted to sit at a table and use a book. The "Congress-only" years lasted until the arrival of Librarian of Congress Ainsworth Rand Spofford, appointed by President Lincoln in 1864. Spofford was convinced that in order to give the legislators the finest possible library service, he needed a much larger collection of books. He thus dedicated himself to bringing in "oceans of books and rivers of information," and set out to gather the printed word in quantity for his employers. He soon acquired the library of Peter Force, the greatest private collection of Americana of its day, and nonscientific volumes from the library of the Smithsonian Institution. In fact, the transfer of the Smithsonian materials to the congressional library took place during the same ten-day period as Sumner's research on Russian America. There were still no congressional office buildings except the Capitol itself, so the library remained "just down the hall" from the legislators.

The Making of the Alaska Treaty

[March 29, 1867]
Friday evening

My dear Sir,
Can you come to my house this evening? I have a matter of public business in regard to which it is desirable that I should confer with you at once.

Yours very truly,
William H. Seward

The Honorable
Charles Sumner[2]

This cryptic message—which would plunge the unsuspecting chairman of the Senate Committee on Foreign Relations into days of intensive work ultimately stretching over two months—was delivered on heavy black-bordered and crested stationery to Senator Sumner's rooms by Frederick Seward, son of the secretary of state. After hastening the short distance across Lafayette Square to Seward's home on a clear, cool evening, Sumner received from Frederick Seward and Russian minister Edouard de Stoeckl his first information on the negotiations by Secretary Seward to buy Russian America from Russia. Meanwhile, the secretary of state had summoned his aides back to the State Department late that night and the treaty was hastily engrossed, translated, and signed.

Saying nothing about the treaty itself, Sumner responded to Secretary Seward's search for a sense of the Senate's willingness to consider the treaty ("executive business") on the eve of adjournment.

322 I Street
Friday evening

My dear Secy,
You wished me to let you [know] how the Senate would feel about a called session. Congress has voted to adjourn at 12 o'clock noon tomorrow. I think the Senate would be glad to proceed at once with Executive business so as to dispose of it promptly.

Very truly yours,
Charles Sumner

P.S. By at once I mean as soon as the legislative session is closed.

At 12 o'clock noon on Saturday, March 30, the appointed hour for adjournment having arrived, no doubt more than a few of the senators present were startled to hear the clerk announce, "Mr. President, a message from the President of the United States."

I transmit to the Senate, for its consideration with a view to ratification, a treaty between the United States and His Majesty, the Emperor of all the Russias, upon the subject of a cession of territory by the latter

SENATOR CHARLES Sumner (R., Mass.) took up the defense of the Alaska Purchase at the urging of his friend Secretary Seward and spoke eloquently for three hours on the floor of the Senate, April 8, 1867. His words carried the day, as the Senate approved the treaty on the next day by a vote of 37-2.

Library of Congress.

ARTIST'S CONCEPTION of the treaty signing. The original oil by Emmanuel Leutze hangs in the Seward home in Auburn, New York. In 1934 two copies of this painting were made by Lynn Faucett and Helen Wassells. One hangs in the U.S. Department of Interior and the other in the Alaska State Museum. The significant players are Seward (seated to the left of the globe), Baron Edouard de Stoeckl, the Russian minister to Washington (standing with his hand on the globe), and Senator Charles Sumner (seated next to Stoeckl).

Alaska State Museum, Juneau.

to the former; which treaty was this day signed in this city by the plenipotentiaries of the parties.

According to more than one diarist, conversation around Washington's dinner tables was given exclusively "to talk over the purchase of Russian America." Critics like the *New York Tribune's* Horace Greeley derided "the acquisition of this territory of ice, snow and rock" or proposed that the money would be better spent reducing the income tax. Sumner himself wondered whether the needs of states undergoing Reconstruction were greater: "Which is better? To spend money for South to help Union or for this?"[3]

While the politicians worked the dinner tables, the assistant secretary of the Smithsonian, well-known naturalist Spencer Fullerton Baird, sent this note to Sumner on Sunday afternoon, March 31:

I hope the purchase of Russian America as proposed, will be authorized by the Senate. The shores of the North Pacific are swarming with animals of enormous importance…. We have received much informa-

tion respecting the resources of the region in consequence of the operation in Natural History connected with the exploration of the Russian Telegraph Co. The published maps are very defective as regards the interior. We have with us now two persons, one of whom spent a year in Norton Sound below Behring Straits, the other fifteen months at Sitka. Would you care to see them?[4]

That evening, Sumner's longtime friend and Harvard classmate George Gibbs took Baird to Sumner's rooms to talk about cession of Russian America. Baird was about to become a very busy man. Beginning Monday, April 1, the Senate convened at noon each day of the Senate's special session, meeting in closed "executive session," to consider business proceeding from the executive such as treaties and nominations. The treaty remained in the Committee on Foreign Relations, where it had been referred at Senator Sumner's insistence, for ten days, during which the committee met four times: Monday, April 1; Wednesday, April 3; Friday, April 5; and Monday, April 8.

On Monday, April 1, the committee met

to consider the treaty with six of its seven members present: five Republicans—Chairman Charles Sumner (Massachusetts), William Pitt Fessenden (Maine), Simon Cameron (Pennsylvania), James Harlan (Iowa), James W. Patterson (New Hampshire)—and one Democrat, Reverdy Johnson (Maryland). Only Oliver P. Morton (Republican, Indiana) was absent. Deliberations around the committee table were rambling and inconclusive. Sumner listened, speaking only to give information on the territory using a map, a globe, and Keith Johnson's *Atlas of Physical Geography.*

On Wednesday, April 3, Sumner summoned Baird to the Senate Chamber to discuss his appearing before the committee; Baird, in turn, aware that public sentiment was based on uninformed opinions instead of reliable information, proposed that Sumner prepare "a report of the extensive resources and character of the country to be furnished perhaps in advance of the meeting of Congress." Baird asked George Gibbs whether he had a copy of the work on the Russian-American Fur Company: "If so, please let me know at once. I could put [Henry Martyn] Bannister [who read Russian] to look it over and see what there is in it bearing on the *qualities.*" Then he "spent rest of day getting up memoranda for [Friday's testimony]." Mr. Sumner's case for the character and value of Russian America was taking shape.

While Baird set about gathering raw data from experts such as Bannister and Frederick Bischoff, Sumner enlisted Poore, Beaman, and Gibbs in a search-and-seizure expedition into the congressional library's collections.

At noon on Wednesday, Sumner chaired a second inconclusive session of the Committee on Foreign Relations. On Friday, April 5, Smithsonian Assistant Secretary Spencer F. Baird, accompanied by Bannister and Bischoff, testified before the Committee on Foreign Relations from ten in the morning to noon.

After the witnesses were dismissed, Sumner finally spoke. "I wish there were not so many New England men on the committee. If we should go against it, it would be put down against New England and I don't want to deal her such a heavy blow." Sumner had privately come to the conclusion, however, that he could not oppose the treaty. "I regret very much," he told his colleagues, "to go for this treaty. I've a heavy load to carry it."[5] When the reluctant chairman announced he wanted to report the treaty favorably without amendments, only Fessenden and Patterson did not accede to Sumner's wishes. With the committee vote of 5-2, the die was cast.

WILLIAM H. SEWARD, secretary of state during the administrations of Presidents Abraham Lincoln and Andrew Johnson, was convinced that the purchase of Alaska from Russia was in the best interests of the republic. Portrait commissioned by Seward is by F. B. Carpenter.

Anchorage Museum of History and Art.

Throughout the week, Sumner continued to pore over both the printed materials that he and his scouts had assembled both from the Congressional Library and the unpublished firsthand accounts provided through Prof. Baird and his Smithsonian colleagues. By Saturday, the floor of his room at 322 I Street was strewn with over one hundred books, pamphlets, maps, and atlases. Among the books were the Russian work of Müller, *Voyages from Asia to America*, William Coxe's *Russian Discoveries*, Sir John Barrow's *Voyages into the Arctic Regions*, Burney's *Northeastern Voyages*, and one on the third voyage of Captain Cook.

Two large and showy volumes were entitled *An Historical Survey of the Formation of the Russian-American Company, and Its Progress to the Present Time*, by P. A. Tikhmenev, St. Petersburg. Another Russian work was entitled *Materials for the History of the Russian Colonies on the Coasts of the Pacific*, appearing in *Morskoi Sbornik* [*Naval Review*], published in St. Petersburg. Accounts of the voyages of Billings, Lisianskii, Kotzebue, Litke, and Vancouver were side by side with Campbell's *Pleasures of Hope*, portraying in poetry "Earth's loneliest bounds and Ocean's wildest shore," and "the wolf's long howl from oonalaska's shore."[6]

Geographers were represented by works of Wrangell, Erman, Petermann, Wappaus, and Kittlitz. Sumner also had at hand a new work by Murray, *Geographical Distribution of Mammals*; the work of Sir John Richardson, *Fauna Boreali-Americana*; Latham's *Nationalities*; Blodgett's *Climatology of the United States*; and the *Encyclopedia Britannica*. He also drew data from articles in *The Nautical Magazine* (1849) and the *Journal of the London Geographical Society* (1841).

For maps, he had before him a "General Map of the Russian Empire" published by the Academy of Science at St. Petersburg in 1776 and one of the Aleutian Islands appearing in *Transactions of the Imperial Mineralogical Society of St. Petersburg*, a map of North America published by the Geographical Institute of Weimar in 1859, and an outline map newly prepared by the United States Coastal Survey.[7]

The one book *not* in Sumner's possession was an extraordinarily handsome work with color plates entitled *Les Peuples de la Russie*. Undoubtedly, it was George Gibbs who brought the work to his attention. Gibbs had acted as librarian of the Astor Library (now The New York Public Library), where resided the only known copy of this book.

On April 17, Spencer Baird set out to remedy that deficiency. In a letter to Waldemar Bodisco at the Russian Legation, Baird presented "a list of wanting volumes of 'Morskoi Sbornik' " and then casually slipped in his request:

Some years ago the Russian Government published a very fine work on the different races composing the empire entitled "Les Peuples de la Russie." This we have long desired to procure and if you could secure a copy from your government, you would put us under many obligations.

The fourth and final two-hour session of the Committee on Foreign Relations met at ten in the morning on Monday, April 8, during which Reverdy Johnson scribbled a note to Secretary Seward: "The treaty case reported finally. Expect today." The Senate convened at noon; consideration of the Alaska treaty commenced at one o'clock.

Though outside the day was hazy, inside the Senate Chamber the Chairman of the Committee on Foreign Relations was not. Charles Sumner rose from his third-row seat, holding in his hand a single sheet of notes from which he spoke

TREASURY DEPARTMENT.

To the Treasurer of the United States, GREETING:

PAY to *Edward de Stoeckl, Envoy Extraordinary & Minister Plenipotentiary of his Majesty the Emperor of Russia*

or order, out of the appropriation named in the margin,

Seven millions, two hundred thousand dollars, being in consideration of certain territory ceded by the Emperor of Russia to the United States, as described in the treaty of 30th March 1867

WARRANT.

No. *927*

APPROPRIATION.

To carry into effect the treaty with Russia, of March 30th 1867, per Act appd. 27 July 1868

Alaska Purchase

Agreeably to a Certificate of the Comptroller of the Treasury No. *45615* dated *29 July 1868,* recorded by the Register. For so doing, this shall be your WARRANT.

Given under my hand and the seal of the Treasury, this *first* day of *August*, in the year one thousand eight hundred and sixty-*eight* and of Independence the *93*

Secretary of the Treasury.

COUNTERSIGNED.

$7.200.000

RECORDED.

Register.

Comptroller.

August 1

RECEIVED for the above Warrant, Draft No. *9750*, on *New York*

WARRANT FROM the U.S. Treasury authorizing issuance of a check for $7.2 million to be paid to Russia for the territory of Alaska. The date is July 29, 1868, more than a year after the Senate had approved the Treaty of Purchase and nine months after the actual transfer had taken place at Sitka.

National Archives, Washington, D.C.

in support of the treaty's adoption. By the time Sumner concluded some two and three-quarter hours later, he had presented an encyclopedia of all the facts then known about Russian America.

The Massachusetts orator relied on his prodigious memory of all that he had read in original sources found in the congressional library. The former

Harvard lecturer upon the Law of Nations formulated his arguments in the style of a legal brief. Dispassionately, he spelled out the transaction at hand, traced the right of title to Russian America, presented four advantages to the future interests of the United States, and concluded with a brilliant summary of scientific data on the topics of population, climate, productions of soil, mineral products, and fisheries. At five o'clock the Senate, no doubt exhausted, adjourned for the day without voting.

Debate on the treaty resumed at eleven the next morning. A motion by Senator Fessenden to postpone consideration was defeated 29-12. After six hours of further debate, the resolution of advice and consent was agreed to by thirty-seven yeas to two nays. Seward's dinner parties and Sumner's scholarship had carried the day.

The Publication of Charles Sumner's Speech

Senator Sumner spoke in a closed executive session, so his actual remarks were not recorded. On April 13, Sumner asked that the injunction of secrecy be removed from the text "so that the same may be published in authentic form," giving new meaning to the right of a Member to "revise and extend" his remarks. Despite Fessenden's efforts to block Sumner, there were widespread calls for his monumental assemblage of knowledge to be made available to the public.

Sumner immediately launched into writing out his speech, a task that would consume his energies completely over the next six weeks. On April 15, one week after his speech, Sumner wrote to his close friend Henry Wadsworth Longfellow:

I have been tried a good deal by the Russian Treaty which has given us a new world with white foxes & walruses not to be numbered. At last I made up my mind that I could not take ground against it. My course had a decisive influence & I feel the responsibility, and am now trying to write out the speech which I made. I spoke 2 hours & 3/4ths. How I envy you quiet days of beautiful labor.

The first half of his "speech" was a review of the geography of the territory, its history and right to title, the negotiations preceding the treaty, and the sources of original information about the territory.

TREASURY DRAFT no. 9759, the check that paid for the purchase of Alaska. The sum amounted to less than two cents per acre. The check is dated more than a year after the treaty signing, due to the press of more urgent business in the House of Representatives: the impeachment proceedings against President Andrew Johnson. (The purchase was not part of the indictment!)

National Archives, Washington, D.C.

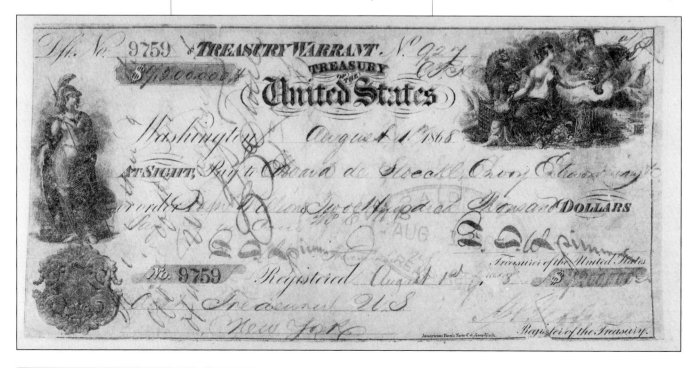

The second half was an assessment of "the character and value of these possessions as seen under these different heads: (1) government, (2) population, (3) climate, (4) vegetable products, (5) mineral products, (6) furs, and (7) fisheries."

Written on a ruled legal pad, Sumner's original draft is 225 pages long. Extant galley-proof fragments document his exacting attention to detail. In his summation of the sources of original information on Russian America, a marginal note in Baird's handwriting suggests a reference to "an elaborate article by Holmberg in the transactions of the Finland Society of Sciences at Helsingfors [which] *is replete with information.*" Not having direct knowledge of the work, Sumner, ever the lawyer, carefully edited Baird's note to read "*said* to be replete with...." That Baird reviewed Sumner's manuscript for accuracy is confirmed by his handwritten notation on galley sheet twelve: "Better let me see the whole slip. S.F.B."[8]

As April gave way to May, Baird's

SENATOR SUMNER'S speech amplified his brief notes. The printed paragraphs below left are the first two of seven paragraphs expanding four lines of notes (below right): "Important to consider character of country. But — treaty will be ratified with reference to other considerations. Advantages to Pacific coast."

Sumner Papers, Massachusetts Historical Society, photo courtesy Library of Congress.

GENERAL CONSIDERATIONS ON THE TREATY.

From this survey of the Treaty, as seen in its origin and the questions under it, I might pass at once to a survey of the possessions which have been conveyed; but there are other matters of a more general character which present themselves at this stage and challenge the judgment. These concern nothing less than the unity, power, and grandeur of the Republic, with the extension of its dominion and its institutions. Such considerations, where not entirely applicable, are apt to be controlling. I do not doubt that they will in a great measure determine the fate of this treaty with the American people. They are patent, and do not depend on research or statistics. To state them is enough.

Advantages to the Pacific Coast.

(1.) Foremost in order, if not in importance, I put the desires of our fellow-citizens on the Pacific coast, and the special advantages which they will derive from this enlargement of boundary. They were the first to ask for it, and will be the first to profit by it. While others knew the Russian possessions only on the map they knew them practically in their resources. While others were still indifferent they were planning how to appropriate Russian peltries and fisheries. This is attested by the resolutions of the Legislature of Washington Territory; also by the exertions at different times by two Senators from California, who, differing in political sentiments and in party relations, took the initial steps which ended in this Treaty.

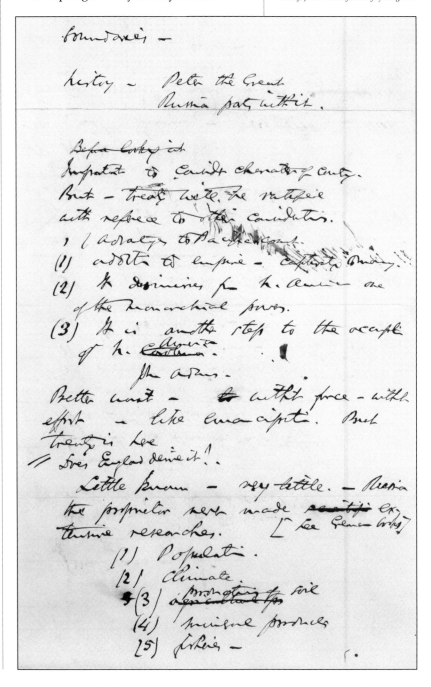

diary records almost daily communication with Sumner: "...at Mr. Sumner's in afternoon," "Sumner at house in afternoon," "...in even Mr. Sumner called with proof of Russian American speech." Sumner complained to Longfellow on May 19:

I have been busy enough lately on Russian America, and have a pamphlet—called a speech—in press, more elaborate than any former product of mine. I am weary. The grind of proofs is nearly over. There has been no end of work. It has been like notes to Dante. Pardon. Thus do I advertise my small wares...!

THE *"ADVICE and Consent" of the United States Senate approving the signing of the Alaska Treaty of Purchase, dated April 9, 1867.*

National Archives, Washington, D.C.

The Washington bicycle messengers of today would have had a very good day on Tuesday, May 21, so frequent was the exchange of materials between Sumner and Baird. In the morning Sumner sent another batch of proofs over to the Smithsonian with the hope "that you can glance at these during the morning.... I confess that I should be glad to return them to the printer soon.... I long to have this work off my hands."

Sumner's carefully crafted defense of the character and value of Russian America was published on May 24, 1867. Printed at the Congressional Globe Office, the "Speech of Hon. Charles Sumner, of Massachusetts, on the Cession of Russian America to The United States" filled forty-eight double-columned pages, and was accompanied by the new Coast Survey map entitled "Northwestern America showing the territory ceded by Russia to the United States compiled for the Department of State at the U.S. Coast Survey Office. May 1867." The first edition, dated April 1867, is in the Geography and Map Division of the Library of Congress.

Public acknowledgement of the quality and magnitude of Sumner's efforts was swift. The *Boston Journal* published this assessment of Sumner's speech:

This speech...coming from the Chairman of the Committee on Foreign Affairs, and abounding in a mass of pertinent information not otherwise accessible to Senators, exerted a most marked if not decisive effect in favor of the ratification of the treaty. As might be expected, the speech is a monument of comprehensive research, and of skill in collection and arrangement of facts. It probably comprises about all the information that is extant concerning our new Pacific possessions, and will prove equally interesting to the student of history, the politician, and the man of business.

At the very last minute, Sumner, the onetime Harvard law librarian, had picked up a five-by-seven-inch sheet of blue "U.S. Senate Chamber" notepaper and scribbled out one final insert:

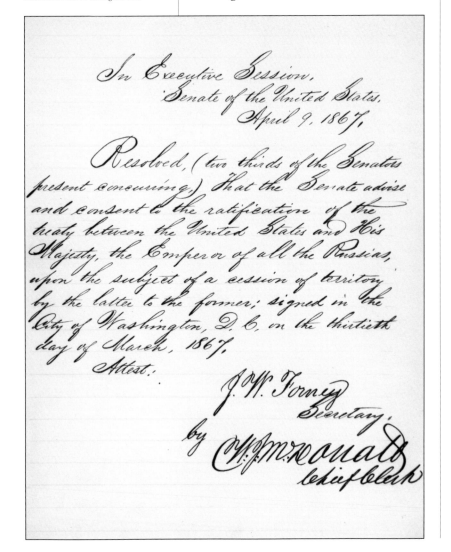

In closing this abstract of authorities, being the chief sources of original information on this subject, I cannot forbear expressing my satisfaction, that, with the exception of a single work [here, he crossed out the phrase "in the Astor Library"] all these may be found in the Congressional Library now so happily enriched by the rare collection of the Smithsonian Institution.

What about that "exception of a single work" *not* found in the Library of Congress? By June 4, having received a book shipment from Mr. Gustavus V. Fox, Baird dashed off a note to Sumner that,

Among a great variety of delightful Russian books [is] the "Peuples de la Russie," the only work wanting among the sources of information actually in your hands.

Les Peuples de la Russie is today in the Rare Book and Special Collections Division of the Library of Congress, 123 years later the world's largest repository of knowledge and information.

The decisive influence of Charles Sumner's "monument of comprehensive research" on the acquisition of Alaska and the role of the Library of Congress in that research vindicate Thomas Jefferson's belief that, within the Library of Congress collections, "there is, in fact, no subject to which a Member of Congress may not have occasion to refer."

Margaret Shannon is with the Division of Interpretive Programs, Library of Congress.

For Further Reading

Donald, David Herbert. *Charles Sumner and the Rights of Man.* New York: Knopf, 1970.

Libby: The Sketches, Letters and Journal of Libby Beaman, Recorded in the Pribilof Islands, 1879-1880, as Presented by Her Granddaughter Betty John. Tulsa, Oklahoma: Council Oak Books, 1987.

Miller, David Hunter. *The Alaska Treaty.* Kingston, Ontario: Limestone Press, 1981.

The Papers of Charles Sumner. Microfilm edition, ed. Beverly Wilson Palmer, 85 reels. Alexandria, Virginia: Chadwyck-Healey, Inc., 1988.

Sumner, Charles. *Speech of Hon. Charles Sumner, of Massachusetts, on the Cession of Russian America to the United States.* Washington: Congressional Globe, 1867.

Notes

1. A portion of this section on the history of the Library of Congress is adapted from the "Guide to the Library of Congress," Washington, D.C., 1988.

2. All communications to and from Sumner are indexed by date and available on the microfilm edition of *The Papers of Charles Sumner*, ed. Beverly Wilson Palmer, 85 reels (Alexandria, Virginia: Chadwyck-Healey, Inc., 1988).

3. Sumner's comments were recorded by his clerk, Charles Cotesworth Beaman, whose notes of the four meetings constitute the only written record of committee deliberations. Beaman's unpublished notes are in the "Sumner Mss." at the Massachusetts Historical Society, Boston. The income tax suggestion came from Lemuel Shaw, April 2, 1867, in the Sumner microfilms, 038/609.

4. All quotations, here and later, from Spencer Fullerton Baird's letterpress books, journals, and diaries are from the Smithsonian Institution Archives, Record Unit 7002, Spencer F. Baird Collection, 1793-1923.

5. Sumner's comments are in Beaman's notes cited in Note 3.

6. Thomas Campbell, *The Pleasures of Hope; with Other Poems*, 4th ed. (Glasgow, 1800), p. 8.

7. The lettering on the Coast Survey maps of Alaska was done by a woman. Libby Beaman, the first female entrant in the Corcoran School of Art in Washington, D.C., became the first nonnative woman to travel to the Pribilof Islands. As a draftsman in her father's office, Libby was assigned "to work on the details of the map.... Perhaps there was no one more familiar with the details of this part of the world than I was at the time, for the maps of the Alaskan Purchase Territory were my project." *Libby: The Sketches, Letters and Journal of Libby Beaman, Recorded in the Pribilof Islands, 1879-1880, as Presented by Her Granddaughter Betty John* (Tulsa, Oklahoma: Council Oak Books, 1987).

8. Sumner's handwritten draft, fragments of galley-proofs, and the single sheet of notes from which he spoke are in "Sumner Mss." at the Massachusetts Historical Society, Boston.

LIFE IN RUSSIAN AMERICA

Health *and* Medical Care *in* Russian America

by Robert Fortuine, M.D.

The work was...hard and dangerous, with serious accidents a constant threat to health and future livelihood.

Russian mariners—followed later by a few from Spain, England, and France—had been exploring the islands, bays, sounds, and inlets of Alaska for more than a half-century when the Russian-American Company was established in 1799. Many sojourned only briefly while trading for sea mammal pelts, but toward the end of the century some Russian traders were wintering over in the Aleutians and Prince William Sound, and others had established permanent settlements in the Aleutians, on Kodiak Island and the Kenai Peninsula, and in Prince William Sound. In 1799, Alexander Baranov founded his first outpost on Sitka Sound.

These Europeans—mostly Russians—were not a healthy lot. The sailors were drawn from the lowest strata of society, where alcoholism, tuberculosis, syphilis, gonorrhea, and nutritional diseases were rife. By the time they reached Alaska, they had been at sea anywhere from a few months to several years, during which the cramped and poorly ventilated quarters, wretched shipboard diet, dangerous working conditions, and frequent physical abuse only aggravated their already marginal health. The diet aboard the ships consisted largely of ship biscuit (or "hardtack") and salt beef, both of which through spoilage often became quite unfit to eat. This diet frequently led to the bane of all seafarers—scurvy—which decimated the crews of several eighteenth-century voyages and greatly endangered the survival of some of the early settlements, notably those at Three Saints Bay and New Archangel (Sitka). During the early years of the Russian-American Company, in fact, health conditions ashore were nearly as bad as those on board ship. The workers were drawn from the same general labor pool as the sailors. They ate much the same poor diet and lived in wretched housing that bred disease. The work was also hard and dangerous, with serious accidents a constant threat to health and future livelihood.

The health of the Alaska Natives at the time of first contact was also far from ideal, although it represented an equilibrium with an unforgiving environment. Probably the greatest cause of death and disability was trauma, either from the hazards of subsistence or from warfare. Infectious diseases were widespread and affected every body system. Skin infections, including sores, impetigo, and boils, were particularly common, many of them traceable to constant scratching from the ubiquitous head and body lice and the seasonal plague of biting insects. Other common sites for infections were the respiratory tract, ears, and gastrointestinal tract. Nor were the Natives spared chronic and degenerative diseases. Early human remains and narrative accounts show that arthritis, blindness, deafness, and many other crippling disorders were prevalent. Even cancer and arteriosclerosis, usually thought of as "diseases of civilization," have been found in precontact human remains. Scurvy, however, spared the Natives completely since their traditional diet contained adequate amounts of ascorbic acid throughout the year.[1]

Natives living in close contact with the Russians, such as their Aleut and Koniag hunters and the Tlingits who lived near New Archangel, soon acquired new health problems. The most devastating were the periodic epidemics of smallpox and respiratory disease, which caused heavy mortality among those with no previous exposure and hence no immunity to the microorganisms. Tuberculosis was probably also introduced among the Natives in the eighteenth century and, although its spread was less dramatic, it caused no less disability and death over the long run. Finally, new forms of trauma resulted from the introduction of firearms and other Western technology.

A health problem that affected both Russians and Natives was the abuse of alcohol, introduced to the Aleuts as early as 1741. Even in the eighteenth century many of the traders manufactured *kvass,* a kind of fermented drink, and at an early stage taught the process to the Aleuts and other Natives. Most Russians were fond of distilled beverages, especially vodka, and the poor living and working conditions in the colonies in the earlier years fostered excessive drinking among both the workers and the officers. On holidays and other special occasions the workers and Creoles were given a ration of vodka or rum, which they were sometimes able to supplement with *kvass* or contraband liquor from American trading vessels or the Hudson's Bay Company. The Russian-American Company made attempts to control the consumption of alcohol, especially in the Native villages, but it was only after an 1842 agreement with the Hudson's Bay Company that it achieved a measure of success.

Early Medical Care

The first "Western" medical care available in Alaska was provided by the physicians and surgeons sailing on the larger ships visiting Alaska for the purposes of exploration, trade, supply, or

administration. Some of these ships in the last quarter of the eighteenth century were Spanish, English, or French, but after 1799 they were almost exclusively Russian naval vessels or ships belonging to the Russian-American Company itself. The first duty of these practitioners, of course, was to render care to the officers and men of their ships, but they also, on occasion, treated company employees ashore or Natives they encountered.

Beginning in 1804 with the voyage of the *Neva* under Captain Lisianskii, some of these vessels spent extended periods in the colonies, either at New Archangel or at St. Paul's Harbor (Kodiak). The *Neva* carried two medical men, one of whom, Assistant Surgeon Alexei Mutovkin, was injured by an arrow in the Battle of Sitka in October. The ship wintered at Kodiak, where the two surgeons almost certainly treated patients during their months ashore. Count Nikolai Rezanov's personal physician, Dr. Georg H. von Langsdorf, spent the following winter at Sitka, where he found himself in the midst of a major scurvy outbreak, which he attributed to the poor housing, diet, and clothing of the workers.

Other ship's surgeons spent long periods ashore during the next few decades. Dr. Karl Mordgorst of the *Neva* wintered at Kodiak in 1807-08, during which time he amputated both feet of the Scottish seaman Archibald Campbell, who had suffered severe frostbite following a shipwreck. Dr. Georg Anton Schaeffer arrived at Sitka in November 1814 on the *Suvorov* and remained in the capital for a year.

In July 1817, the *Suvorov* returned to Sitka, this time carrying as surgeon Vasilii Bervi, who remained at the capital until the departure of the *Kutuzov* in November 1818. During his sixteen-month stay, Bervi performed a variety of medical tasks, including a fitness-for-duty examination, the treatment of the victim of a domestic quarrel, the examination of the

FORTUINE

THE ONLY IMAGE of the hospital in Sitka, taken in the 1870s. This was the second hospital built at Sitka, the larger structure replacing the first, which had been built between 1821 and 1826. In 1861, it was reported to have forty beds.

Muybridge Collection, Anchorage Museum of History and Art.

body of a murder victim, and care of the survivors of a Tlingit attack. As a result of his faithful service, Chief Manager Leontii Hagemeister awarded him a sea otter pelt "of medium quality."[2]

The Establishment of a Medical Service in Alaska

Baranov had recognized the need for medical services in the colonies as early as 1795, when he suggested the establishment of a pharmacy to provide needed drugs for the sick. Rezanov noted in the report of his inspection trip in 1805-06 that sick company employees deserved medical care in appreciation of their services, and further, that good applicants to the company might be discouraged from accepting appointments by the lack of such care.

In 1810 Baranov remarked to Captain-Lieutenant Vasilii M. Golovnin of the *Diana* that it would have been wiser if the company had sent out doctors to the colonies rather than the paintings that adorned the walls of his residence. "I do not know whether the directors trouble themselves to think about it," he went on, "but we doctor ourselves a little, and if a man is wounded, so as to require an operation, he must die."[3] This exchange must have made some impression on Golovnin, for eight years later, when he returned with the *Kamchatka*, he observed in his report that for lack of medical assistance some employees were becoming gravely ill and losing their lives. That same year the new chief manager, Hagemeister, had to return to Russia because of ill health. The following year his successor, Semen Yanovskii, found himself in the midst of a fierce epidemic in Kodiak, where many were dying around him without the benefit of medical care.

By March 1817 the directors had decided to station a doctor in the colonies, but the appeals of Baranov, Golovnin, Hagemeister, and Yanovskii probably hastened the fulfillment of their promise. In March 1820 they selected Dr. Vasilii Volkov for the post and sent him via

Okhotsk to New Archangel, where he arrived probably late that year. The directors instructed the chief manager, M. I. Murav'ev, to establish a permanent hospital, for which drugs and supplies would be sent from Russia. He was also to see to it that the doctor taught Creole apprentices, who in the future could provide medical services to the people.

The New Archangel Hospital

The new hospital, built between 1821 and 1826, was a two-story wooden structure some sixty-three feet in length that contained an infirmary (ward), pharmacy, quarters for the doctor and priest, an office, and two rooms for officials. The ward initially had eight beds for the seriously ill, while ambulatory patients stayed in their own quarters and received their medications at the hospital each morning. By 1825 "three good rooms" had been set aside for the pharmacy and the medical personnel working there. The drugs were kept in jars in an orderly fashion and were of good quality. Surgical instruments (probably those shipped in 1818 from Kodiak, where no one knew their use) were said to be of excellent workmanship.

Initially, patients were charged seventy-five kopeks per day for their hospitalization, but by 1821 Murav'ev rescinded this rule. Instead, the medical service was supported by funds set aside from 0.5 percent of company profits, a policy dating back to 1802. Other support derived from the proceeds of auctions held when officials left the colonies, or from the sale of confiscated furs held illegally by company employees.

Sometime after a visit by Captain Litke in 1827, the hospital was enlarged to twenty beds. Governor Ferdinand P. von Wrangell noted in the early 1830s that the hospital was in a large, well-maintained building that was generously supplied with all the necessities. Later in the decade both a men's and a smaller women's hospital are mentioned. The men's hospital, probably at the site of the original building, had three eight-bed wards, but its capacity could be expanded, as in an epidemic, by setting up additional beds in the reception room. The second floor had a special room where medicinal plants could be dried and otherwise prepared for use. The hospital was situated on a small peninsula near the water, where the latrines could be washed by the incoming tide. Lt. Belcher of the H.M.S. *Sulphur* described the building in 1837 as "comparatively" clean and comfortable, and was particularly struck by the practice of placing over each patient's bed a sign giving his name, date of admission, and diagnosis so that visitors

DR. GEORG H. von Langsdorf was a physician who visited Russia's American colony with Nikolai Rezanov in 1805. He spent 1805-06 treating illness, wounds, and scurvy in Sitka.

From Georg H. von Langsdorf's A Voyage Around the World, 1803-1807 (Frankfurt, 1812). Alaska and Polar Regions Dept., Elmer E. Rasmuson Library, University of Alaska, Fairbanks.

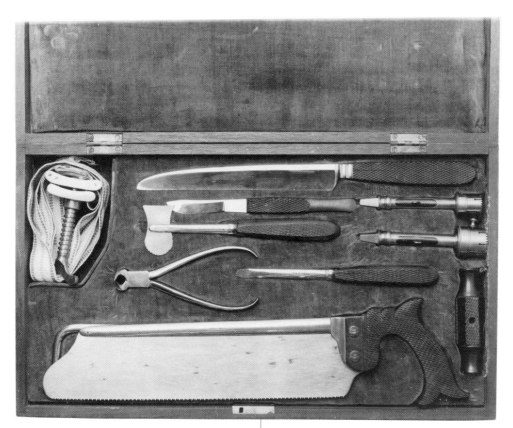

AMPUTATION KIT, typical of nineteenth-century medical science. Medical equipment as well as food and fabric came to Russian America through the United States trade network. This kit was made by J. F. (T.) Cassell of Baltimore, 1823-27.

National Museum of American History, the Smithsonian Institution.

could protect themselves from contagion. The women's hospital normally housed four beds and was contained within a damp, dilapidated private dwelling some distance away in the settlement.[4]

In the early 1840s, under Governor Adolf Etholen, the men's hospital was enlarged to forty beds. Following his visits to New Archangel in 1841 and 1842, Sir George Simpson, chief factor of the Hudson's Bay Company, remarked that "in its wards, and, in short, in all the requisite appointments, the institution in question would do no disgrace to England." This from a man who on the same visit called Sitka "pre-eminently the most wretched and dirty" place that he had ever seen.[5]

Probably in 1858, the hospital was relocated to a large building that stood next to the orphanage. In his 1862 report, Lt. Capt. Pavel N. Golovin described this building as a two-story wooden structure with forty beds. As previously, there was no special ward for women, who were usually treated in their own quarters. An exception was made for Tlingit women,

who were confined to a special room while undergoing forced treatment for syphilis. Other patients visited the hospital early in the morning or were treated in their quarters.

Golovin felt that the hospital was not being adequately cleaned, nor were the patients' linens changed often enough, considering the poor hygiene of most of the workers. He also complained that the hospital diet was unsatisfactory, since the patients were rarely given fresh meat, but rather maintained largely on rice and a kind of soup made from salt fish or salt meat, with occasional fresh fish in the summer. Golovin recommended that, whenever fresh meat was available from the Tlingit hunters, some of it be set aside for the sick in order to speed their recovery. He further suggested that the seriously ill receive chicken from time to time, despite its high cost, and preserved foods from the company warehouses. Recent excavations of the hospital trash pit by the National Park Service have revealed that the patients did indeed receive meat, but usually from the more undesirable cuts.[6]

The hospital was operated by the Russians until the sale of the territory in 1867, following which the United States Army maintained it until their departure in 1877. Subsequently, the building was taken over by the navy, which in turn gave it to Sheldon Jackson in 1881 for use as an industrial training school for the Tlingits. The structure was totally destroyed by fire in January 1882.

Other Hospitals

After Mordgorst's departure from St. Paul's Harbor in 1808, no further mention of a hospital at Kodiak occurs until the 1820s. Although one authority suggests that a ten-bed hospital was built there between 1818 and 1820, Litke specifically states that at the time of his 1827 visit the only hospital in the colonies was located at New Archangel. By the early 1830s,

however, a hospital was definitely in place on the island. By 1862 it had ten beds and a small annex for women.

In 1827 a small medical facility was built at Unalaska. Two years later a similar one was erected at Atka. Neither was a true hospital, but rather a clean, warm place where the sick could receive proper care. By 1862 both had closed.

Medical Practice

The quality and number of physicians improved after 1820. In the earlier years especially, staff turnover was high since few doctors saw a tour of duty in the colonies as a step up the career ladder. Nor was it likely that the best and brightest would volunteer for the post. Volkov found himself in debt at an early stage, and Wrangell was forced to send a Dr. Simon home, probably because of alcohol abuse.

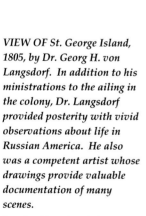

VIEW OF St. George Island, 1805, by Dr. Georg H. von Langsdorf. In addition to his ministrations to the ailing in the colony, Dr. Langsdorf provided posterity with vivid observations about life in Russian America. He also was a competent artist whose drawings provide valuable documentation of many scenes.

From Georg H. von Langsdorf's A Voyage Around the World, 1803-1807 (Frankfurt, 1812). Photograph courtesy of Bancroft Library, University of California, Berkeley.

The earlier years of the company were the so-called Age of Heroic Medicine, in which the chief methods of treatment were extensive bloodletting, clysters, and strong drugs, especially purgatives. Others prescribed drugs prepared from wild and cultivated plants. Poultices and other external treatments were popular, as was the use of mineral baths, such as the volcanic springs several miles south of Sitka. Surgery was crude and swift, at least until the discovery of anesthesia in 1848. Obstetrical techniques had advanced considerably, but many women still died of post-partum infection due to contamination.

Following Dr. Volkov's departure in 1822, the company tried to maintain at least one physician, and preferably two, in New Archangel. In 1827 only one physician was available at the hospital, assisted by four apprentices, but a few years later two naval physicians were assigned,

together with three apprentices. Two physicians, Dr. Eduard Blaschke and Dr. Volynskii, were in the colonies during the great smallpox epidemic of 1835-40. They were assisted by several Creole feldshers, a kind of "mid-level practitioner" trained either in Russia or in the colonies. Besides leading the smallpox efforts, Dr. Blaschke wrote a significant book on the geography, climate, population, geology, and zoology of New Archangel and its environs.

Russian medical care at this time was heavily influenced by German medicine, since many of the physicians and surgeons on Russian ships or in the colonies were ethnic Germans. The use of feldshers was also of German origin, being derived from the German "feldscher," or "field barber" (surgeon). German medicine at this time, incidentally, was not at the forefront, as it was later in the nineteenth century. Many practitioners embraced vague philosophical "dead ends" of medicine, including mesmerism and homeopathy, to the neglect of the scientific advances being made in this period by the French, Italians, Dutch, and others.

The medical service was, of course, established primarily for the benefit of the employees of the Russian-American Company, who, besides Russians, included Creoles and Aleut and Koniag hunters. Probably from the earliest days, however, the doctors and other practitioners treated other Natives living near the settlements or in the more distant villages. The Russians, knowing all too well what devastation smallpox could cause, were particularly interested in ensuring that the Natives were vaccinated. They also made a special effort to treat Tlingit women and other Natives suffering from syphilis, to prevent further spread of the disease.

The Natives themselves were initially very suspicious of Russian medicine,

ENGRAVING OF *Three Saints Bay, from a drawing by Luka Voronin. Voronin was expedition artist with the Billings-Sarychev expedition of 1790-92. This view of Grigorii Shelikhov's first permanent establishment in America was made six years after its founding in 1784.*

Alaska and Polar Regions Dept., Elmer E. Rasmuson Library, University of Alaska, Fairbanks.

especially the Tlingits, who vehemently rejected vaccination. During the smallpox epidemic the Koniag and the Yup'ik Eskimos also firmly resisted vaccination, with disastrous consequences for each group. Gradually a majority of Natives came to accept and even seek Russian care. By the 1850s most Tlingits preferred treatment by the Russian doctors to their own highly developed system of healing.

Dr. Alexander Romanovskii, who worked at New Archangel from 1840 to 1845, and his colleague Dr. Alexander Frankenhaeuser, there from 1841 to 1848 or 1849, are remembered especially for the detailed medical reports on the colonies published after their return to Russia. These papers are a mine of information on medical problems, especially syphilis and tuberculosis, which plagued the people during those years. In the 1850s Dr. Z. Govorlivyi spent some eight years at the capital and is also remembered for his medical reports, which dealt extensively with the health problems of the Tlingits.[7]

A Medical Care System

By the end of their sojourn in Alaska, the Russians had developed a well-thought-out system of health care that extended to all company employees and to many of the Native peoples as well. Beginning with a single physician at New Archangel in 1820, the company went on to establish a forty-bed hospital there, which by 1861 was staffed by two physicians, three feldshers, four apprentices, a midwife and her assistant, and normally a pharmacist. At the same time, a ten-bed hospital at Kodiak was headed by a senior feldsher, who himself supervised two feldshers, five apprentices, and a midwife and her assistant. Other feldshers were stationed at Unalaska, Atka, St. Michael, and the coal mine on the Kenai Peninsula.

In settlements too small for a feldsher, the local priest or trader was entrusted with a medical kit containing basic drugs and instruments, with instructions for their use. Besides attending to injuries and illnesses, the local official was expected to provide care, including vaccinations, on his periodic trips to the outlying settlements of his district. Likewise, on the smaller company ships, the captain was responsible for medical care of those under his command.

One of the physicians at New Archangel was assigned to take care of the hospital patients, while the other treated patients in their quarters. During the summer months when sea travel was safer and the medical workload was down, one of the physicians regularly visited the outlying company posts to supervise the work of the feldshers and provide consultation on difficult cases. The senior feldsher at Kodiak also visited the field stations for consultation and supervision. During the great smallpox epidemic, both doctors, at least a half-dozen feldshers and apprentices, and priests and traders assisted in the vaccination effort throughout the far reaches of the colonies.

Training was also an important responsibility of the medical service. Both the main hospital at New Archangel and the smaller one at Kodiak trained Creole apprentices to become feldshers who were later sent out to the more remote stations. Pharmacists and midwives presumably also trained their own assistants.

Although the Russian-American Company's health care system was far from perfect, it was a well-organized effort that was effectively adapted to the living conditions and geography of Alaska. Except for the recruitment of physicians and the annual drug and supply shipments from Russia, the system was largely self-sufficient and self-perpetuating. Unfortunately, soon after the American flag was unfurled over Baranov's Castle in October 1867, this valuable legacy of experience was allowed to go undeveloped.

Robert Fortuine, M.D., now with the Biomedical Program of the University of Alaska Anchorage, directed hospitals in Dillingham, Bethel, and Anchorage during seventeen years with the U.S. Public Health Service in Alaska.

For Further Reading

Colonial Russian America: Kyrill T. Khlebnikov's Reports 1817-1832. Trans. Basil Dmytryshyn and E. A. P. Crownhart-Vaughan. Portland: Oregon Historical Society, 1976.

Fortuine, Robert. *Chills and Fever: Health and Disease in the Early History of Alaska.* Fairbanks: University of Alaska Press, 1989.

_____. "Scurvy in the Early History of Alaska: The Haves and Have-Nots." *Alaska History* 3 (Fall 1988), pp. 21-44.

Ivashintsov, N. A. *Russian Round-the-World Voyages, 1803-1849, with a Summary of Later Voyages to 1867.* Trans. Glynn R. Barratt, ed. R. A. Pierce. Kingston, Ontario: Limestone Press, 1980.

Langsdorf, Georg H. von. *Voyages and Travels in Various Parts of the World during the Years 1803, 1804, 1805, 1806, 1807.* London, 1814; New York: Da Capo Press, 1968.

Lisiansky, Iurii. *A Voyage Round the World in the Years 1803, 4, 5, and 6.* London, 1814; New York: Da Capo Press, 1968.

Litke, F. P. *A Voyage Around the World 1826-1829.* Trans. Renee Marshall, ed. R. A. Pierce. Kingston, Ontario: Limestone Press, 1987.

Sarafian, Winston Lee. "Russian-American Company Employee Policies and Practices, 1799-1867." Ph.D. dissertation. Los Angeles: University of California, 1971.

Notes

1. Robert Fortuine, "Early Evidence of Infections among Alaska Natives," *Alaska History* 2 (Winter 1986/87), pp. 39-56.
2. R. A. Pierce, *The Russian American Company. Correspondence of the Governors. Communications Sent: 1818* (Kingston, Ontario: Limestone Press, 1984), p. 150.
3. *Documents on the History of the Russian-American Company,* ed. R. A. Pierce, trans. Marina Ramsey (Kingston, Ontario: Limestone Press, 1984), p. 105.
4. Edward Belcher and Francis Guillemard Simpkinson, *H.M.S. Sulphur on the Northwest and California Coasts, 1837 and 1839,* ed. R. A. Pierce and John H. Winslow (Kingston, Ontario: Limestone Press, 1979), p. 22.
5. George Simpson, *Narrative of a Journey Round the World during the Years 1841-1842* (Philadelphia: Lea and Blanchard, 1847), two vol. in one; 2, p. 79.
6. Catherine Blee, *Wine, Yaman and Stone: The Archeology of a Russian Hospital Pit. Sitka National Historical Park, Sitka, Alaska* (Denver: National Park Service, 1986).
7. I am indebted to Tanya DeMarsh for a translation of Govorlivyi's medical reports.

Industries
in Russian America

by Timothy (Ty) L. Dilliplane

EXHIBITION
■ ВЫСТАВКА ■
ИНФОРМАЦИЯ ИНФОРМАЦИЯ
■ RUSSIAN AMERICA ■
INFORMATION

...We see a colonial establishment capable of exercising a good deal of ingenuity in its day-to-day business affairs.

Shrouded in mystery as if enveloped by the mists of Yakutat and Sitka, the Russian settlements of Alaska, California, and Hawaii have traditionally been overshadowed and forgotten. Today only a few anthropologists, historians, and geographers dedicate themselves to the study of this period. This is so despite a rich heritage and important research areas that await both appreciation and inquiry.

Investigating daily, weekly, or monthly activities relating to work and recreation is perhaps the only way to understand Russian America. Such study may reveal important data about attitudes, living conditions, occupational and free-time priorities, and the degree of adaptation to foreign and sometimes hostile environments. This approach requires detailed examination of specific industries. Since other contributors to this volume describe the most important industry, the fur trade, I will concentrate on four other industries that in varying degrees complemented it: shipbuilding, mining, brickmaking, and the ice trade.

Shipbuilding

Because most of the colonies were situated on the coast, one of the most important industries in Russian America was shipbuilding. Ships were needed to support sea otter and fur seal hunting, for trading with the Natives, and for the transportation of personnel, supplies, and colonial products. This industry was initiated early, and continued on an intermittent basis throughout most of Russian America's history. Four, and possibly six, shipyards were established, turning out a minimum of twenty-three vessels.

Grigorii Shelikhov, a major figure in the initial colonization of Russian America, encouraged shipbuilding at an early date. Construction of Voskresenskoe, a shipyard and settlement in Resurrection Bay, had definitely begun by 1793. Although a shortage of manpower and materials posed a major challenge, the first vessel constructed in the colonies, the *Phoenix*, was built here. Christened in 1794, she had two decks and three masts, and "was 73 feet long, 23 feet wide, and 13-1/2 feet deep, and of 180 tons capacity. In place of pitch and tar Baranov caulked her with a durable compound of his own invention consisting of fir pitch, sulfur, ocher, and whale oil." Usable timber was hard to find, and other basic materials needed for a European-style ship were in short supply. Baranov reported having "only half a flask of pitch, not a pound of caulking, not a single nail, and not enough iron for such a big vessel." The settlement needed iron for axes, and the canvas had been used up on tents and sails for smaller craft. Old canvas had become "so worn out that it was difficult to make...10 pairs of pants for the Native workers, and even these pants fell to pieces after they had been used for two days."[1] Two forty-foot vessels were subsequently built, although there is disagreement as to where.

No vessels of major proportions were built in Russian America following this activity until a decade or so later. In part that was because the *Phoenix* project had taken the combined efforts of more than seventy-six men, over half the total number of Baranov's workers. Baranov noted that the workers threatened to mutiny, being worried about "danger in the places not subjugated."[2] Two ships, the *Rostislav* (forty-one feet; approximately eighty-five tons) and the *Ermak* (fifty-one feet; one hundred-plus tons), were built at the settlement of New Russia (near modern-day Yakutat). A primary reason for their construction was to help counterattack the Tlingit Indians, who had destroyed major Russian settlements in 1802 and 1805.

Ships were also built at the Russian settlement of Fort Ross in California. This work was initiated in 1816, resulting in a total of six ships. Two of these were made to order for use by Spanish missionaries. Because of the use of improper lumber and/or the lack of needed treatment, the four Russian-American Company vessels constructed there suffered badly from wood rot; none of them saw a period of active service longer than six years. Perhaps the carpenter in charge was unfamiliar with shipbuilding. Kyrill Khlebnikov wrote that "One must give credit to the common carpenter who built two ships on Sitka and later four ships at Fort Ross. But one must also acknowledge ...that any person boarding these ships for a stormy passage cannot have full confidence in an individual who has no understanding of the art of shipbuilding."[3]

Without a doubt, the colonial capital of New Archangel (Sitka) was the location of Russian America's most important shipyards. Shipbuilding there began not long after the founding of the settlement in 1804, despite the danger of Tlingit attack. A visitor in 1806 reported that even though the shipyards were only "three hundred *sazhens* [twenty-one hundred feet] from the fort, we always had loaded guns with us. Sentries are on the lookout on the hill and now we have a cannon ready in the shipyards, so that they do not set the ship on fire at nighttime."[4] It would continue on an on-and-off basis until the sale of Russian America to the United States in 1867. Suitable timber was nearby, including the popular shipbuilding woods larch and cypress. Skilled personnel based in the capital were available to support shipbuilding or ship-repairing activities. Included here were shipwrights, coopers, woodworkers, boatwrights, ropemakers, and painters. Blacksmiths would have also played an important role. As of January 1, 1825, there were twenty-one shipwrights and carpenters in the population of New Archangel. At the same time, there were also ten boatwrights, joiners, and turners. Perhaps the most remarkable vessel produced by such colonial specialists, either in New Archangel or anywhere else in Russian America, was the *Mur*. A small steamship, this vessel was built *entirely* at New Archangel in 1840-41, including the manufacture of all engine components.

Mining

While the gathering of furs was the primary intent of the Russian *promyshlenniki* (fur trappers/traders) in Alaska, the Russian government was interested in mining from the start. For example, in 1758 the government agent assigned to the ship *Iulian* was tasked with the collecting of *iasak* (tribute) as well as locating materials such as gold, silver, iron, and mica. Years later, Grigorii Shelikhov anticipated the need for at least one "mining expert" in the settlements. In his 1787 proposal, he included a force of one hundred military men, one officer in this group to have expertise in mining techniques. A year earlier, Shelikhov had ordered his Three Saints manager to obtain information about the minerals known to exist in the various regions of Alaska. The concern about mineral wealth in the new land was also expressed in the first charter of the Russian-American Company. As granted in 1799, the monopoly rights of the firm extended to mining as well as to fur-gathering.

Despite the sensitivity, however, very little was done in the colonies in the way of mineral extraction. A primary reason was that most of the labor force was needed for fur-gathering. Hence, most of the mining in Russian America was intended solely to support colonial and related needs. Examples include salt and even sandstone. Certain types of the latter were extracted for use with grindstones and whetstones. Salt was in demand throughout the colonies and in Siberia.

necessitated the processing of seawater.

With the depletion of fur resources, the Russian-American Company became increasingly interested in alternative ways to make a profit. But, with the exception of coal, commercial mining continued to be shunned, despite long-standing reports of deposits of gold and copper. According to S. B. Okun, the Russian-American Company's reluctance stemmed from a fear that it might lose its monopoly rights as a result of governmental intrusion into prospective mining operations.[5]

The one major attempt by the Russian-American Company to commercially

In 1827, fifty-four to ninety tons were required on an annual basis for the people living in the Okhotsk Seaboard/Kamchatka area. By an 1828 order of the tsar, the Russian-American Company was obliged to provide salt for Kamchatka. Some of this was purchased in Hawaii and California. One large shipment, with the permission of California officials, was "mined" (so to speak) by Russian-American Company employees from salt-water lakes in California. Salteries existed in Russian America; they may have been needed since, at times, salt shortages

exploit a mineral resource in its colonies involved coal and took place on the Kenai Peninsula, at a site known as Coal Village, on the northern shore of Port Graham at Coal Cove. Coal had initially been discovered here by the English naval officer Nathaniel Portlock in 1786. Baranov visited Coal Cove in 1795 and conducted tests on coal samples taken from the deposit. Coal was noted in other regions of Russian America as well, including Kodiak Island, Atka, and Unga. The Russians opened mining operations in the latter two places. While the Atka coal was intended only for local use, the effort

ENOCH HJALMAR
Furuhjelm, Finnish mining engineer hired by the Russian-American Company to establish a coal-mining facility on the Kenai Peninsula near present-day Port Graham. Arriving in 1855, he oversaw the construction of a large town (behind only Sitka and Kodiak) and the production of five thousand tons of coal before his departure in 1862. The coal mainly served company ships, but was of insufficient quantity or quality to attract the California market.

From a portrait in the National Museum of Finland, Helsinki.

on Unga was larger in scale. Unga coal was shipped to Sitka in the 1840s. The historian H. H. Bancroft does not speak favorably of the Unga coal: "When used by steamers, it was found to burn so rapidly as to eat into the iron and endanger the boilers...."[6] Kodiak coal was judged to be of a poorer quality than some deposits found on the Kenai Peninsula.

It was not until 1852 that the company began any systematic investigation of the various coal deposits in Alaska. Peter Doroshin, a Russian mining engineer, was tasked with this responsibility. The coal sample taken from Coal Cove was found to have 4,294 "heat units" (calories?). Although this was the deposit that was later the subject of mining operations, Doroshin did not consider it to be the highest-quality coal in Russian America. A sample taken from the Mt. Katmai

region proved to have a total of 5,774 heat units. Nevertheless, probably due to logistical considerations, Doroshin recommended that Coal Cove deposits be mined by the Russian-American Company: the adjacent harbor was ice-free during the winter months. The commercial reason behind the company's desire to mine coal is explained by P. N. Golovin:

> *The need to supply Company steamers with coal at a lower price than California offered, and the hope to profit from the sale of coal, the consumption of which in California in 1855 had already reached 20,000 tons a month and was constantly increasing, forced the Company to give special consideration to this subject, and they began to increase mining operations wherever it seemed profitable to do so.[7]*

Consequently, the Russian-American Company reached an agreement with a California firm known as the American-Russian Trading Company: The latter wished to buy, on a yearly basis, ten to twelve thousand tons of coal. A major step in the development of this business was the initiation, in 1855, of the Kenai Mining Expedition. This would be the organization actually conducting the mining. Enoch Furuhjelm, a Finnish mining engineer, was designated the director of the operation. Having purchased needed equipment in San Francisco, Furuhjelm and his expedition landed at Coal Cove. The engineer was definitely not impressed with the quality of his crew:

> *Our expedition was made up of myself, as the leader, the two German coal miners, a stock keeper and a clerk, a surgeon's aide, a petty-officer, 15 army regulars and 25 laborers, among them Russians, more Finns, Creoles, Yakuts and Kodiak Indians. With this motley crowd I was to place the*

WOODEN PLANE, *typical of hand-wrought tools. This and many of the other tools displayed in the exhibit are from the Russian "retirement" community of Afognak, which retained its Russian identity in customs and language well into the twentieth century.*

Kodiak Historical Society.

steam engines in the primeval forest and start rational mining operations. Fortunately I had with me three young Finns from Orijarvi, Finland—they had been hired through the shipowner Julin for Sakhalin Island—and an old drunkard, a journeyman bricklayer from Helsingfors. The soldiers hardly knew how to use an axe, and most of the other company workmen were hard-drinking good-for-nothings that the company had enticed to come from St. Petersburg and Siberia to the colony.[8]

Although men were sent specially to Russian America to work in the coal mines (seventy-seven in 1857, twenty-four in 1858, forty-nine in 1861, fifty-two in 1862), the emphasis was not on skilled workers. Nor was the machinery the best available.

A settlement to support the operation was built at the site between 1857 and 1858, and was known as Coal Village. Fourteen houses made up the heart of the settlement when Sergei A. Kostlivtsev visited in 1861. Other buildings there at the time were a chapel, a store, a barracks building, a kitchen, a cattle shed, and a structure evidently enclosing the entrance to the main shaft. The total value of these buildings is given as 32,850 rubles, or $6,570. Those living in the settlement received some of their food supplies from the area of Nikolaevsk Redoubt (present-day city of Kenai). Provisions were sold to the expedition by colonists living there raising cattle and tending gardens, and fish from this area were provided by the Russian-American Company.

Kostlivtsev noted that fifty-two people were employed at Coal Village (including twenty-nine Russians). There is reason to believe that thirty-three of these worked in the mining activity, per se. At one time, the total number of workers was 131. At least ninety-three employees directly associated with the actual mining were needed at the site: forty-five miners, eighteen hod carriers, six carpenters, six loaders, three steam engine maintenance personnel, two stokers, a blacksmith, six coal sorters, and six coal carriers. In addition, twenty-eight administrative/support personnel were required.

The coal vein on the Kenai Peninsula was estimated to be nine to twelve feet thick, with a probable extension inland of at least three to four miles. It was possible that a naturally occurring pit of coal had more depth than the strata. The latter yielded as much as 70 percent coal. Picks appear to have been the primary tool used. At least several vertical shafts were dug, and a horizontal shaft as well. The latter was meant to be a temporary expedient for coal needed locally.

The initial mining effort produced low-grade coal. This was used as fuel on Russian-American Company steamers; up to five hundred tons were also shipped to the California market. Selling price: 12.50 rubles (approx. $2.50)/ton. Kostlivtsev withheld judgment on the coal, noting that, "As yet the coal vein is not far enough developed to judge the quality of the mineral, but there is a prospect of reaching good coal." Golovin also held out hope, reporting that, "There is no reason not to expect that they will find coal of excellent quality, although it may be at a considerable depth."[9]

A total of 2,760 tons was mined by the expedition from 1857 to 1860, valued at 45,800 rubles ($9,760). This was not good, given an average yearly loss of 23,214 rubles ($4,156). Adding to the company's headache was a fire at the steam engine building in 1860, halting work for a time. An early student of the mines, F. A. Golder, tells us that this calamity "wiped out the whole plant and ruined the machinery."[10] Operations did resume, however, and 850 tons were extracted in 1862.

The final blow to the mine evidently was the discovery of coal deposits in the San Francisco area. In 1864 coal from Vancouver Island was being shipped to Russian America, and the Kenai effort was scuttled with considerable loss in 1865.

Although his operation was not a

success, Furuhjelm was optimistic about the potential of future coal-mining activities in Russian America. The engineer worked out a seven-year agreement with the Russian-American Company following his return to Europe; however, questions concerning the company's charter renewal prevented this from being implemented.

Brickmaking

Brickmaking in the Russian colonies was an important support industry. This certainly is not readily apparent, given the lack of emphasis on the construction of brick buildings. Almost all structures were built of wood. One reason for this may have been the traditional reliance on

ENGRAVING OF Sitka Bay by Freidrich H. von Kittlitz, expedition artist with the Seniavin on its round-the-world voyage, 1826-28, under command of F. P. Litke. The building in the foreground—a warehouse and workshop— and the ships at anchor in the bay give a lively impression of the capital city's industry.

From the F. P. Litke Atlas, Alaska and Polar Regions Dept., Elmer E. Rasmuson Library, University of Alaska, Fairbanks.

wooden buildings, another a possible shortage of personnel who knew how to build with brick. Both in turn stemmed from the company's emphasis on fur acquisition. Nevertheless, bricks were needed in the colonies for chimneys and ovens. Indeed, Shelikhov had proposed that bricks made there could be used to help fill needs in Russian Asia as well.

Bricks came to be a highly prized commodity in the settlements. In a letter dated September 3, 1824, Governor Matfei I. Murav'ev speaks of New Archangel as having a "critical" need for bricks. In fact, this was not a new situation. Early in 1823, the governor instructed the Kodiak manager that, "As many bricks as are on hand, that is all bricks without exception,

are to be loaded onto the brig *Golovnin,* even those that have not been fired, but well dried." In December of that year, Murav'ev wrote to the main office in St. Petersburg that:

Our need for bricks here in Sitka is very great. Presently, we received from Kodiak 3500 bricks, but in view of extensive construction going on here, this quantity is far from sufficient. I hope to receive the same or even greater quantity with the next transport out of Kodiak.

Nor was the requirement for bricks limited to this time frame: in 1851, Governor N. I. Rosenberg chided the

Kodiak office for the small quantity of bricks received at Sitka, and requested that the brick kiln at Nikolaevsk Redoubt (under the jurisdiction of the Kodiak office) produce at least twelve to fifteen thousand bricks yearly.[11] As a step to help increase production, the Russian-American Company authorized one of its brickmakers to go to the Hudson's Bay Company post of Fort Vancouver (present-day Vancouver, Washington) to learn how bricks were made there.

Within Russian America, bricks were produced at Kodiak Island, Long Island, Unalaska, the Kenai Peninsula, Fort Ross, Atka, Nushagak, and St. Michael. A brickmaking site has also been reported at Nuchek. With reference to the Kodiak Island enterprise, Tikhmenev writes:

ICE TONGS used in the ice trade on Woody Island, near Kodiak. Beginning in 1852, the Russian-American Company sold blocks of ice to the San Francisco market in such quantities that in some years the profits outstripped all fur sales. Ice was "harvested" at Sitka as well. In all, a total of 27,500 tons of ice packed in sawdust from sawmills at Woody Island and Ozerskoi Redoubt, near Sitka, cooled Californians.

Kodiak Historical Society

Every year from three to six thousand bricks were made on Kodiak Island, and their production might have been increased to fifteen thousand, if there had been more lime, which had to be burned from shells, and clay suitable for brickmaking.[12]

Ten thousand bricks were made on Kodiak Island in 1831. The brick kiln at Nikolaevsk Redoubt on the Kenai Peninsula, constructed in 1841, was also important, and the bricks produced here were "of good quality"; they were primarily sent to New Archangel, although some went to Kodiak. The brickyards on Atka and at St. Michael existed to fill local demands. Bricks manufactured at Nushagak (New Alexandrovsk Redoubt) were reported as being substandard. Yet even Nikolaevsk bricks were more expensive than and inferior in quality to those from Victoria, on Vancouver Island.[13]

Documentary and archaeological research have uncovered interesting details relating to those who made the bricks and the process used. The work ranged from grueling to tedious, and Natives appear to have borne most of it. In a letter dated May 18, 1795, the head of the Russian Orthodox clergy in Alaska counsels Shelikhov that:

I would not advise you to ship bricks from here because it is unprofitable. The discontent comes mostly from Russians and not from Aleuts. The Russians, especially the ones who do not like you, say that this work is a cruelty towards the native workers. And it is true that even for local needs the bricks are made with great difficulties. The clay has to be brought from an island, dried, and sifted before bricks can be made. The native workers have lots of work to do besides this. They, together with Russians, are very busy with construction work.[14]

Russians were evidently scarce at the brickyards. S. G. Fedorova notes that, "A very small number of settlers was engaged in working...clay for the brickworks on Kodiak and Unalashka." Tikhmenev notes that part-time employees drawn from the Native population assisted in the production of bricks made at Nikolaevsk Redoubt.

Archaeological investigations at a Russian brick-kiln complex on Kodiak Island occurred on an intermittent basis from 1979 to 1983. The project, directed by the author and accompanied by historical research, revealed data not previously known about the brickmaking industry in the colonies.[15] The complex had been built by 1823 and may have been permanently shut down by 1861. It is possible that all of the bricks made in the Kodiak area from 1823 on were manufactured here. When initially built, the site consisted of at least the kiln (furnished with a "roof on posts to house the firing oven"), a barn, and laborer housing. It is located on the shoreline, which no doubt facilitated pick-up and transport of the bricks.

The kiln itself was completely excavated, and covered an area of over sixteen square meters. Interestingly enough, it closely resembles a style of kiln used by the ancient Romans, and which is still being used today in the Near East. One of the trademarks of the style is the use of arches to support the floor and contain the kiln's fires. The structure had been dug into the adjacent hillside. This matches a Roman kiln excavated in England, and would have allowed for more efficient heat conservation. Indications are that wood was used as fuel, although it is possible that coal was burned as well. Bricks found at the site characteristically had a high gravel content, which appears to at least partially account for their brittle nature. The brick bond used in the kiln's construction seems to have been the stockbond style: bricks stacked one on top of another in a nonalternating way.

Investigations in an area immediately adjoining the kiln discovered a number of other features. One of these was a large, unnatural-looking accumulation of gravel: this may have resulted from sifting activities of the type mentioned earlier. Several of the features revealed aspects of the production process not yet seen in colonial records or accounts. Evidence of a pit having an accumulation of out-of-context clay was uncovered; nothing else of note was found in it. General technical references relate that the raw clay had to be of the correct consistency prior to being molded into brick forms, and that this was commonly done via focused mixing. Hence, the pit may have been used for such a purpose. The remains of a lightly built structure were also found; molding the clay into the "green," or unfired, brick forms might have taken place here. Yet another facet of the manufacturing process not seen elsewhere, but recovered during the field work, was that of "signing" the bricks. Parts of two bricks were found with undecipherable script and, although this could have been done in Russia, signing could also have been an additional step pursued in the colonies immediately prior to firing the clay forms.

Ice Industry

The ice industry in Russian America began in 1852. Ice had previously been shipped to California from Boston, but California's growing population caused a demand for a more speedily delivered, less expensive alternative. Three thousand tons were needed yearly. Lake ice was obtained from Lesnoi Island (Woody Island, near Kodiak) and New Archangel (present-day Sitka), although the climate in both locales was not always conducive to stockpiling large amounts. This was especially the case for New Archangel.

Nevertheless, all of the ice retrieved during the first two years of the operation came from the colonial capital. In 1852, 325 tons were taken, with most of this (250 tons) being shipped to California on board

OFFICIAL SEAL of the San Francisco-based American-Russian Commercial Company. Established in 1851 by a number of prominent Bay-area businessmen to capitalize on trade possibilities with the Russians in Sitka, the firm's first interest was importing ice, but coal and fish were soon added. Timber followed. During the Crimean War, this company was also the largest single supplier of goods to Russian America.

David Walker Collection, Alaska State Library, Juneau.

the *Bacchus*. This was to be resold by a firm known simply as the Ice Company. The purchase price was $18,750, or $75 per ton. Following this, the first of four agreements on the ice trade was reached between the Russian-American Company and the American-Russian Trading Company. Under this pact, good until September of 1855, the Russian-American Company would export as much as one thousand tons on a yearly basis at a selling price of thirty-five dollars per ton.[16] Storage facilities and dockworkers needed to support the operation at New Archangel would be sponsored by the United States firm. United States ships would transport the ice. The terms were renegotiated in

1854 for a twenty-year period. One of the highlights of the new contract was that the two companies would share the profits on a fifty-fifty basis; another was that the Russian-American Company was given by the tsar a monopoly on the shipment of ice from the northeastern coast of Siberia.[17] The next agreement may have been brought about by a warmer-than-usual winter in 1856. The price per ton was now set at three dollars, a considerable drop from the initial rate of 1852! The fifty-fifty profit sharing would continue. Other terms included a five-percent commission and a per ton export tax of seventy-five cents. On January 9, 1860, a fourth agreement took effect. Covering a three-year period, this latest convention bound the Russian-American Company to sell, on an annual basis, three thousand tons of ice to its California partner for seven dollars per ton, although a deduction of 20 percent could be taken for ice lost due to melting.[18]

According to Golovin, during the eight-year period from 1852 to 1859 (inclusive), a total of 17,860 tons of ice was cut at New Archangel (with 13,960.5 tons actually exported), while Lesnoi Island contributed 19,200 tons (7,403 tons exported). The figures given would indicate that these shipments earned the Russian-American Company a combined total of at least $121,956.04. Looking at the ice trade from its inception until July 1, 1862, Tikhmenev writes that altogether 27,500 tons had been shipped, bringing in a total of $250,000.

Company employees and specially hired Creoles and Natives made up the work force. The pay varied greatly. Evidently, Russian-American Company personnel were awarded a cup of vodka per day, regardless of their work areas. Salaries for the company men on the Lesnoi operation were not found; however, their counterparts at New Archangel annually earned anywhere from three hundred to five hundred paper rubles, plus food. The Creoles and Natives working on Lesnoi Island received a daily salary of one paper ruble, with food and vodka thrown in. Tlingit Indians hired at New Archangel were also paid a daily wage of one paper ruble, with their *toiens* (chiefs) receiving gifts as well.

The most difficult facet of the industry was retrieving ice lying under a three- to four-inch cover of frozen slush. A "special scraper" pulled by three horses was called on in such instances. Once this surface had been removed, the ice was ready to be cut. Golovin tells us how this was done at a New Archangel lake:

> The weather held, and the ice was superb, with no slush; it was as sparkling and clear as crystal. Yesterday I went to the lake to watch them cutting ice. The operation is performed with marvelous ease and speed. A horse is harnessed to an iron cutter with one smooth runner and one with a sawtooth edge. The horse moves along at an even gait and the saw gouges the ice about two inches deep. Then they turn it back again and set the sledge so the smooth runner goes along the cut line and the saw cuts a new one. In this manner they mark the ice with absolutely straight lines and then cut lateral marks in the same way. Thus they cut a large surface and mark it in perfectly uniform squares just like a checkerboard. Then along these marked lines they drag a saw-like plow, which cuts the ice eight inches thick. After that a single blow is enough to separate one block from the next. They heave these pieces up on the ice, and several Kolosh, who are barefoot as usual, pile up pieces one on top of another, and use a rope to drag them along wooden rails to the harbor.[19]

The wood rail system would have played a critical role in the acquisition process. More specifically, this was used to transport the blocks to temporary storage in icehouses, as well as from the latter to awaiting transports. The Lesnoi Island operation had two icehouses, each with a three-thousand-ton capacity. The three such structures at New Archangel could individually hold at least two thousand and possibly three thousand tons. It appears that ice could be stored year-round in the Lesnoi sheds, although whether this could be done at New Archangel remains to be determined. Colonial ice-cutting facilities and equipment were reported by Golovin as having a total worth of fifty thousand paper rubles.

The cutting of eight-inch ice slabs,

POLITKOFSKY, *a steamer built entirely of Alaskan products in the Russian shipyard at Sitka in 1863. The fittings included hand-hammered copper spikes holding the cedar planks prepared in the sawmill at Sitka, and a boiler entirely made of Alaskan copper. The ship was sold to the Alaska Commercial Company after the Alaska Purchase and served primarily as a tug, then a barge, plying the northwest coast.*

Photograph courtesy of Washington State Historical Society, Tacoma.

described above, is peculiar because Golovin officially reported that anything under ten inches was "useless," and New Archangel ice thicknesses usually did not exceed that figure. Perhaps slabs thinner than ten inches were permitted when warmer-than-usual winters (as was the case for New Archangel in 1859-60) prevented that dimension from being reached. Because of the undependable climate, Golovin had his doubts as to whether the then-existing industry in Russian America could be counted on to support any future expansion of the ice trade. He notes that the Amur River in eastern Siberia was a dependable source of large quantities of ice without significant problems.

Conclusion

The industries summarized above deepen our insight into the realities of Russian America. Beyond the very clear, and expected, emphasis on profit-making and saving money, we see a colonial establishment capable of exercising a good deal of ingenuity and aggressiveness in its day-to-day business affairs. As extensive hunting depleted fur resources by the middle of the nineteenth century, the Russian-American Company experimented with mining and the ice trade. One measure of the fur trade's extraordinary and irreplaceable contribution to the Russian-American economy is that the Russian-American Company could create no other industry remotely as lucrative.

Yet these alternatives to fur suffered from personnel problems stemming from low-level Russian recruits. Poor quality of personnel injured three of the four industries reviewed here: the rotten ships at Fort Ross, the incompetent miners at Coal Cove, the crumbling bricks at New Archangel. More research might even show lack of expertise in the ice trade; if that industry turned out to be free of personnel problems, the reasons may lie in its late start, when dwindling fur resources may have caused more employees of better quality to be available, and its relative lack of need for specialized expertise. Only close study of documentary, oral, and archaeological records will answer questions like these, and permit valid comparisons of the colonial Russian experience with those of other eighteenth- and nineteenth-century European nations.

Timothy (Ty) L. Dilliplane is a Ph.D. candidate in Anthropology, Brown University.

For Further Reading

Davydov, G. I. *Two Voyages to Russian America, 1802-1807.* Trans. Colin Bearne, ed. Richard A. Pierce. *Materials for the Study of Alaska History, No. 10.* Kingston, Ontario: Limestone Press, 1977.

Dilliplane, Timothy (Ty) L. "Mining in Russian America: A Research Objective." *Mining in Alaska's Past.* Ed. Michael S. Kennedy. Office of History and Archaeology Publication, No. 27. Anchorage: Alaska Historical Society, for the Office of History and Archaeology, Alaska Division of Parks, 1980.

_____. "Shipbuilding in Russian America: A Sampling of the Literature." *Transportation in Alaska's Past.* Ed. Michael S. Kennedy. Office of History and Archeology Publication, No. 30. Anchorage: Alaska Historical Society, for the Office of History and Archaeology, Alaska Division of Parks, 1982.

Fedorova, Svetlana G. *The Russian Population in Alaska and California, Late 18th Century - 1867.* Trans. Richard A. Pierce and Alton S. Donnelly. *Materials for the Study of Alaska History, No. 4.* Kingston, Ontario: Limestone Press, 1973.

Gibson, James R. *Feeding the Russian Fur Trade.* Madison, Wisconsin: University of Wisconsin Press, 1969.

_____. *Imperial Russia in Frontier America.* New York: Oxford University Press, 1976.

Golovin, Pavel N. *The End of Russian America: Captain P. N. Golovin's Last Report, 1862.* Trans. Basil Dmytryshyn and E. A. P. Crownhart-Vaughan. Portland: Oregon Historical Society, 1979.

_____. *Civil and Savage Encounters: The Worldly Travel Letters of an Imperial Russian Naval Officer, 1860-1861.* Trans. Basil Dmytryshyn and E. A. P. Crownhart-Vaughan. *North Pacific Studies Series, No. 5.* Portland: Oregon Historical Society, 1983.

Colonial Russian America: Kyrill T. Khlebnikov's Reports, 1817-1832. Trans. Basil Dmytryshyn and E. A. P. Crownhart-Vaughan. Portland: Oregon Historical Society, 1976.

Makarova, Raisa V. *Russians on the Pacific, 1743-1799.* Trans. and ed. Richard A. Pierce and Alton S. Donnelly. *Materials for the Study of Alaska History, No. 6.* Kingston, Ontario: Limestone Press, 1975.

Pierce, Richard A. "The Russian Coal Mine on the Kenai." *Alaska Journal* 5, no. 2, 1975.

Tikhmenev, P. A. *A History of the Russian-American Company.* Trans. and ed. Richard A. Pierce and Alton S. Donnelly. Seattle and London: University of Washington Press, 1978; *Vol. II. Documents.* Trans. Dmitri Krenov, ed. Richard A. Pierce and Alton S. Donnelly. *Materials for the Study of Alaska History, No. 13.* Kingston, Ontario: Limestone Press, 1979.

Wrangell, Ferdinand P., von. *Russian America: Statistical and Ethnographic Information.* Trans. Mary Sadouski, ed. Richard A. Pierce. *Materials for the Study of Alaska History, No. 15.* Kingston, Ontario: Limestone Press, 1980.

Notes

Special thanks are due the Office of History and Archaeology (OHA), Alaska Division of Parks and Recreation, for permission to reprint extracts from several articles concerning shipbuilding and mining in Russian America, written by T. L. Dilliplane and previously published by OHA.

1. P. A. Tikhmenev, *A History of the Russian-American Company, Volume II, Documents,* trans. Dmitri Krenov, ed. Richard A. Pierce and Alton S. Donnelly (Kingston, Ontario: Limestone Press, 1979), p. 31.

2. Ibid., p. 60.

3. *Colonial Russian America: Kyrill T. Khlebnikov's Reports, 1817-1832,* trans. Basil Dmytryshyn and E. A. P. Crownhart-Vaughan (Portland: Oregon Historical Society, 1976), p. 79.

4. Nikolai Rezanov, quoted in Tikhmenev, *History: Documents,* p. 226.

5. S. B. Okun, *The Russian-American Company,* ed. B. D. Grekov, trans. Carl Ginsburg (New York: Octagon Books, 1979), p. 245.

6. Hubert H. Bancroft, *History of Alaska, 1730-1885* (Darien, Conn.: Hafner Publishing, 1970), p. 695.

7. *The End of Russian America: Captain P. N. Golovin's Last Report, 1862,* trans. Basil Dmytryshyn and E. A. P. Crownhart-Vaughan (Portland: Oregon Historical Society, 1979), p. 86.

8. Richard A. Pierce, "The Russian Coal Mine on the Kenai," *Alaska Journal* 5, no. 2 (1975), p. 106.

9. Sergei Kostlivtsev, Tabular Statement of the Present Condition of the Russian American Colonies, in T. L. Dilliplane's files; Golovin, *End of Russian America,* p. 87.

10. F. A. Golder, "Mining in Alaska before 1867," *Washington Historical Quarterly* 7, no. 3 (1916), p. 236.

11. Matfei I. Murav'ev, Letter to the Main Office of the Russian-American Company, December 18, 1823, trans. Lydia T. Black, National Archives, *Records of the Russian-American Company, Correspondence of Governors General, Communications Sent* 4, folios 427 and 428, no. 393. Kostlivtsev in 1860 recorded that the brick yard at Nikolaevsk Redoubt was producing twenty thousand bricks per year for use within the colonies; no mention is made of these bricks being exported to places outside Russian America.

12. P. A. Tikhmenev, *A History of the Russian-American Company,* trans. and ed. Richard A. Pierce and Alton S. Donnelly (Seattle and London: University of Washington Press, 1978), p. 87.

13. James R. Gibson, *Imperial Russia in Frontier America* (New York: Oxford University Press, 1976), p. 41.

14. Quoted in Tikhmenev, *History,* p. 84. In a letter dated two days later, Baranov writes that seven thousand bricks made the previous year, completely with Native labor, suffered because the workers "did not separate the stones from the clay." Letter to Shelikhov and Polevoi, May 20, 1795, in Tikhmenev, *History,* p. 71.

15. Timothy (Ty) L. Dilliplane, "Excavations at a Possible Colonial Russian Brikkiln Site," paper presented at the seventh annual Alaska Anthropological Association conference, Anchorage, 1980.

16. Tikhmenev's account again differs. He writes that a *minimum of twelve hundred tons of ice, with a price range of twenty to twenty-five dollars per ton,* were contracted for on a yearly basis (emphasis added). Tikhmenev, *History,* p. 335.

17. Actually, this compact included more than just ice: Alaskan lumber, fish, and coal were also included in a deal that authorized the sale of these items in western ports of North America as well as Australia. Tikhmenev, the official historian of the Russian-American Company, writes that this agreement did not work out well, and he unhesitatingly points the finger of blame at the American-Russian Trading Company. He reports that the decline of the ice business in California might have been forestalled had better fiscal management been provided by this firm. In an attempt to put things back on track, the 1860 agreement was worked out. Tikhmenev, *History,* pp. 335-337.

18. However, data taken from Golovin indicates that significantly higher prices may have been offered. One of the ships (*Tsarita*) could carry as much as twelve hundred tons of ice. In the spring of 1861, the chief manager of the colonies, Johan H. Furuhjelm, projected that three cargoes of ice shipped via the *Tsarita* would bring fifty thousand dollars. If this was based on a full twelve-hundred-ton load per trip, the going rate for ice at the time was $13.98 per ton. Pavel N. Golovin, *Civil and Savage Encounters: The Worldly Travel Letters of an Imperial Russian Naval Officer, 1860-1861,* trans. Basil Dmytryshyn and E. A. P. Crownhart-Vaughan (Portland: Oregon Historical Society, 1983), pp. 109, 126.

19. Ibid., p. 99.

The Russian-American Company Currency

by Richard A. Pierce

The Russian-American Company's worn, frequently illegible parchment tokens were a perpetual reminder of the crudity and precarious quality of life at the far reaches of the Russian Empire.

Visitors to the Russian colonies in North America usually remarked on the small pieces of parchment or heavy paper that served as currency. Known officially as *marki* (singular, *marka*), or tokens, or *assignatsii*, but more often referred to familiarly as "skin money" or "leather money" (*kozhannye*), they were in denominations of twenty-five, ten, five, and one ruble and fifty, twenty-five, and ten kopeks. To help the illiterate distinguish between denominations, some issues were in color—the same pastel tints as had been used for the first Russian paper money issued in the second half of the eighteenth century. Some had holes punched in them or had two or four corners clipped. Most pieces were rectangular, a few were oval in shape. The face of most bore the printed words *"Marka v Amerike"* (marka in America), the denomination, a hand-written serial number, and the signature of Andrei Severin, a member of the board of directors. The reverse side bore the Russian-American Company seal printed or stamped and the denomination.

According to H. W. Elliot, who lived in Alaska in the early 1880s, the notes were originally of walrus hide used by the Russians to cover packages of furs sent from Sitka, the colonial capital, to Okhotsk and from there overland and by barge for more than two thousand miles to Kiakhta, the trading center on the Chinese border. There the skin was stripped and again used to cover the chests of tea that were received in exchange for the furs, to protect them for the nearly three-thousand-mile trip to Moscow or St. Petersburg. The soundest portions of the hide remaining on the boxes were then cut up and stamped with the denominations, and sent back to the seas where they had originated, for use as a circulating medium throughout Alaska.[1]

Today this company scrip is exceptionally rare, although up to three hundred thousand pieces were probably issued during the half century it was in use. The largest collection, of fifteen specimens, is in the Numismatic Section of the State Historical Museum in Moscow. In Finland the National Museum has nine, and a private collector has five specimens of an even rarer subvariety, made up in Russian America for use at the Russian-American Company coal mine that operated for several years at English Bay, on the Kenai Peninsula, in the 1850s. The Ulster Museum in Belfast, Northern Ireland, has seven specimens, the Hermitage Museum in Leningrad has four, the Smithsonian Institution in Washington, D.C., has three, and a few others exist in various private collections and museums. Small, soiled, and worn, others have probably been overlooked, lost, or discarded. Seldom on the market, units of this currency are so rare that it is difficult to arrive at any idea of their value. Specimens of the lower and therefore more numerous pieces, in good condition, have sold for over a thousand dollars. The rarest would seem to be those of the twenty-five-ruble denomination, of which only two specimens are known, one in Canada and one in Alaska, in private hands. Occasional attempts at counterfeiting, in the Russian time and more recently, have complicated the picture.

TEN-RUBLE parchment scrip in a rare red color. At the urging of Governor Baranov, the Russian-American Company began in 1816 to issue a special money for use only in the American colony. These pieces of scrip were produced in denominations of twenty-five, ten, five, and one ruble(s), and fifty, twenty-five, and ten kopeks, and in various sizes and colors. More than three hundred thousand pieces of this scrip were produced, but today only a few survive in museums and private collections around the world.

National Museum of Finland.

Little has been written of this currency. K. T. Khlebnikov, the longtime (1818-1832) manager of the company's Sitka office and diligent collector of information concerning the colonies, barely mentions it. Neither the company historian P. A. Tikhmenev nor the Soviet historian S. B. Okun gives the currency more than passing mention in his comprehensive history of the Russian-American Company. Many references to this currency have been erroneous—one writer thought the notes might have been used to pay for the dispatch of letters. Specialized studies since 1980, mostly by Soviet scholars, have cleared up some of the mysteries. Others remain only because scholars have not used two important sources, a report to the emperor in 1804 and correspondence from the chief managers (governors) to the Russian-American Company's authorities in St. Petersburg. Using this additional material, I will present here another history of the currency, and suggest solutions to some of the problems.

The Currency

From the first years of the Russian-American Company after its founding in 1799, there was a shortage in the colonies of means of exchange. Coins, like all other goods, had to come across Siberia to Okhotsk and then by sea to the colonies, and they were in perpetually short supply. Constantly low on trade goods, Alexander Baranov never had enough to barter with the indigenes or pay them. Instead, he had to make articles for payment from local products. He set the Aleuts to catching birds and ground squirrels, and making parkas from the skins, then used these to pay the Aleuts for their work. Moreover, the company paid the *promyshlenniki,* or hunters, in shares, giving them part of the fur catch. In the market these furs sold at lower prices, giving serious competition to those sold by the company.

In a secret report to the company board of directors on June 20, 1803, Baranov, the longtime (1790-1818) chief manager, or governor, of the colonies, described the difficulty he was experiencing with receipts, expenditures, purchases, and other transactions because of lack of coins.

This was causing errors in calculation and losses for the company, the *promyshlenniki,* and the indigenes. He therefore proposed that he be supplied a means of exchange, either gold, silver, or some other coin as the company preferred, "or some form of obligations on parchment, of various colors." Deliberations on this matter led to a document dated May 20, 1804, "A report of the board of directors of the Russian-American Company to the Emperor...." Although published in a Russian historical collection in 1876, and referred to by this writer and the late Alexander Dolgopolov (Doll) in a popular article on the tokens in 1969, this document seems so far to have been ignored by other researchers.[2]

In its report to the emperor, the board of directors opposed the idea of sending coins to the colonies. It was still too early, they said, "because the untutored local people, eager for all kinds of metal, can transform coins into finery, and from copper can make spears, arrows and other harmful weapons...." Transforming coins into finery would remove them from circulation, defeating the purpose of introducing coins in the first place. Bringing raw material for weapons into the colony at a time of endemic warfare between Natives and Russians seemed even more foolish. Instead, the board eagerly grasped the idea of parchment tokens. The company would send at the first opportunity the sum of fifty thousand rubles in notes, printed on parchment, in various colors, in denominations of one, two, five, ten, and twenty-five rubles. These tokens would be in the following form:

Token No. _____

....
The Russian-American Company under the protection of His Supreme Imperial Majesty will pay the bearer 20 rubles.
No. _____

The numbers on the top and on the reverse of each note would be entered, not in numerical order, in a special book, in order to distinguish real from counterfeit notes. The numbers below would be entered in the same book in numerical order. The row of dots, corresponding to the value of the notes, would help illiterate company personnel and "islanders" (the Aleuts) distinguish between the denominations. On the reverse side the company directors would sign their names. Personnel leaving the colonies could redeem the notes in Okhotsk, and those on their way to the colonies could exchange their ordinary rubles there for the colonial currency. Authorization for issue of the currency, the document stated, had to come from the emperor, but in practice the government willingly left issuance of the colonial currency in the hands of the company, as a privately owned organization.

The Governors and the Currency: A Detailed Record

For reasons not yet understood, the first issue of tokens seems not to have taken place until twelve years later, 1816. From that year, the record becomes clearer, thanks to another fundamental but neglected source, the correspondence of the chief managers, or governors, of the Russian-American Company at Sitka, turned over to the United States by the Treaty of Sale in 1867. These files are now in the United States National Archives and are readily available on microfilm. The files for most of the Baranov era, before 1817, were sent back to St. Petersburg, where they and other company files were destroyed in about 1870, after liquidation of the company. Remaining, however, are about sixty thousand documents comprising copies of communications sent from Sitka to districts and to the main office in St. Petersburg, and the originals of incoming correspondence from the main office.

These documents show the many vicissitudes accompanying issuance and use of the company scrip. Nothing displays the recurring problems so clearly as quotations from the actual letters, presented here chronologically with the date and number of the document. The same problems appeared again and again for half a century, never solved.

There was soon a shortage of tokens. The 1816 issue did not satisfy the need in the colonies. On November 3, 1820, #52, Governor Matfei I. Murav'ev wrote: "Because of a lack of Company marki I have found it necessary to issue 400 rubles worth of *bilety* [notes] of 50 rubles, 1000 rubles worth of 25 ruble notes, and 1000 rubles worth of 10 rubles. They are written in the hand of Nikolai Gribanov and signed by me and bookkeeper Petr Aleksandrovich Anikiev."

This local issue was evidently deemed insufficient, for on December 31, 1820, #108, Murav'ev wrote: "Because of the shortage of *marki* I am putting out 3000 r. worth of notes. Up to 1,250 rubles at 25

rubles each, on white paper; up to 1000 rubles worth at 10 rubles, up to 750 rubles worth of 5 ruble ones on blue paper. They will be good only here in the port of Novo-Arkhangel'sk." Khlebnikov, the office manager, was to enter them in a book with a list of numbers. On December 19, 1821, #199, Murav'ev stated that he had ordered the office to redeem the notes.

On May 9, 1822, #166, Governor Murav'ev again wrote: "Please send 5000 *marki*; we often need them in internal exchange."

On November 16, 1827, #88, Murav'ev's successor, Chistiakov, informed the office that new *marki* had been received via the Okhotsk office and would be put into circulation on December 1, "and the old ones withdrawn from use. At the proper time they will be sent to the Main Office."

On February 28, 1835, #9, Governor von Wrangell wrote that he would make four hundred tokens of five rubles each, to be called in upon arrival of real ones from the main office.

On November 12, 1835, #44, Governor von Wrangell wrote to the Sitka office informing them that the main office in its communication of July 31, 1834, #768, stated that it was sending to Sitka on the military transport *Amerika* "new colonial *marki* worth 30,056 to replace old ones, [now] so worn and dirty that it is impossible to tell them apart." All of the four hundred temporary notes of five rubles (worth two thousand paper rubles) were turned in and redeemed. These temporary notes were to be collected and presented to the governor for burning.

RUSSIAN LEAD weights for use in trade, nineteenth century. The lead pieces were ground through the center to achieve the correct weights of two, three, ten, and twenty funty (pounds).

Alaska State Museum, Juneau.

AN ABACUS was the
universal calculator in
Russian America.

Alaska State Museum, Juneau.

At this point an early case of counterfeiting occurred, for on March 18, 1838, #325, Governor Kupreianov wrote to the Kodiak office regarding the appearance the preceding fall of false *marki* that made one ruble piece worth five. "The office will try to find out who is doing this and report to me."

In 1839, #219, Governor Kupreianov asked the main office for forty thousand rubles' worth of new *marki* of various denominations to replace old, worn ones.

On December 12, 1840, #241, Governor Adolf Etholen, having heard a report from the New Archangel (Sitka) office about the number of old *marki* that had become completely useless, proposed that the office put into circulation eighteen hundred rubles' worth of new *marki*, transferring the old, useless *marki* to the main office from time to time, as they accumulated.

On May 13, 1841, #271, Etholen requested new *marki* from the main office.

On January 28, 1842, #15, Etholen informed the main office that he was putting into circulation 110 notes of one hundred, fifty, and twenty-five rubles to a total of eight thousand rubles to replace completely worn-out colonial *marki*. These were to circulate only at Sitka and the nearby Ozerskoi redoubt. Elsewhere they would have no value.

On May 9, 1842, #257, Etholen wrote that, as the new *marki* requested in #271 the previous year had not arrived, the office should follow the example of Governor Wrangell (in 1830-1835) and put into circulation *bilety* (notes) of whatever worth was needed, namely 210 of one hundred, fifty, and twenty-five rubles—eight thousand rubles in all—under his signature, with the seal of the Sitka office, on January 28, recalling and destroying the superseded ones. Any not turned in would have no value in the future.

On September 25, 1842, #539, Etholen reported that new *marki* sent by the main office were now in the Sitka office. On better white parchment with various stamps (*shtempel*, evidently referring to the company seal), in six colors, they included the ten-kopek note in brown, the twenty-five-kopek in black, the fifty-kopek in lilac, the one-ruble in green, the five-ruble in blue, and the ten-ruble in rose, in all, 51,039 pieces of *marki* worth over forty thousand rubles. The new *marki*, sent to all places in the colonies, would replace the old ones, which were to be returned to the Sitka office from the nearest places by January 1, 1844, and from those more distant by January 1, 1845, after which the office would accept none of the old *marki*.

Moreover, since several denominations of the new *marki* were the same size, namely ten rubles and fifty kopeks, five rubles and twenty-five kopeks, and one ruble and ten kopeks, in order to avoid any sort of mischief and to achieve greater convenience in their circulation, the Sitka office would distinguish between them as follows: In order to differentiate fifty-kopek *marki* from ten-ruble ones, they

TWENTY-FIVE-KOPEK parchment scrip (top), and ten-kopek parchment scrip (bottom).

National Museum of American History, Smithsonian Institution, Washington, D.C., and the National Museum of Finland.

would cut off the two upper corners; in order to differentiate twenty-five-kopek notes from those of five rubles, they were to cut all four corners; and to differentiate ten-kopek notes from those of one ruble, they would make a round hole on the two upper corners. Old notes were to be exchanged for new ones at Sitka only from October 1 to November 1, after which none would be accepted.

On May 15, 1845, #381, Etholen complained that in all, 20,360 rubles' worth of tokens were sent instead of the 40,000 rubles' worth originally supposed to be sent.

On May 5, 1846, #383, Governor Teben'kov wrote that *marki* then in circulation were worn out, and, moreover, the amount, 62,461 rubles, was insufficient for all transactions, particularly accounts with the clergy, which sometimes involved considerable sums. Therefore, he requested new *marki*, including fifty thousand rubles in twenty-five-ruble notes, ten thousand rubles in ten-ruble notes, six thousand rubles in five-ruble notes, twenty-five hundred rubles in one-ruble notes, and fifteen hundred rubles in twenty-five-kopek notes. Teben'kov asked the main office to use thicker material and press the stamp deeper, for as the *marki* became worn with use, the words on them disappeared. As for the twenty-five-ruble note, Teben'kov requested that it be made in the size of two one-ruble notes on white paper with a black stamp. This denomination of *marki* would be new in the colonies, but with constantly increasing turnover and needs, it would be much more convenient than the smaller denominations. Larger denominations were a greater share of this issue than in 1842: Notes over five rubles were 37 percent of the total value of the 1842 issue, but 75 percent of the 1846 issue.

On May 10, 1848, #264, Teben'kov wrote that new colonial *marki* worth eighty thousand rubles had been received and would be exchanged for ones then in circulation that were worn out.

On May 24, 1851, #492, Governor Rosenberg wrote to the main office that on January 16, 1851, by order of the main office (July 23, 1847, #1139), 12,900 rubles' worth of worn-out *assignatsii* had been destroyed. Just as in 1850, it was impossible to report the numbers of the destroyed *marki*. To avoid this, he had ordered that none with an illegible number or denomination be redeemed in the office.

After destruction of such a significant number of useless *marki*, wrote Rosenberg, there were no more in the Sitka office, and because of the impermanence of the parchment *marki* then circulating in the colonies, sent in 1848, they could not serve more than two years. Therefore, he asked the main office to send another eighty thousand rubles' worth of new *marki*. Also, to avoid frequent changes, the main office should ask that the new *marki* be printed by the very best means, and on durable, first-quality parchment. "The Novo-Arkhangel'sk office has reported to me," he wrote, "that *marki* sent to the colonies before 1842 were incomparably more permanent and better than those supplied here in 1842, 1844, and 1848, and moreover these *marki* were numbered in the main office and all were signed by one of its members. It is very desirable that this order be revived now, with sending new *marki* to the colonies. Those received in the colonies from 1842 to 1848 are to be given consecutive numbers."

On February 10, 1853, #30, Rosenberg reported that the main office had stated on April 5, 1852, #483, that the round-the-world vessel sent that year would take the colonies the requested thirty-five thousand new *marki* worth eighty thousand rubles, but these, like the previous ones, would lack the director's signature.

On September 3, 1853, #521, Rosenberg wrote that upon receipt of these he would replace the old ones, which as before would be destroyed. Rosenberg informed the main office that the new *marki* of ten, five, and one rubles and fifty kopeks had the same stamp (*shtempel*) as before, but were of different colors than former *marki* of the same value, namely ten rubles' worth, with a black *shtempel* on a red field; five rubles' worth, with a black *shtempel* on a blue field; one ruble's worth, with a black *shtempel* on a light yellow field; and fifty kopeks' worth, with a black *shtempel* on a white field.

On May 15, 1857, #188, Rosenberg reported the destruction of 6,689 old *marki* worth 25,398 rubles and 18 kopeks in *assignatsii*. Also, he urged the main office to send better ones. The last ones, which were red, blue, and yellow, with the *shtempel* on top, had not held their colors. The *shtempel* and number had disappeared entirely. "The *marki* of former shipments were much more durable."

On May 6, 1858, #150, Rosenberg reported that on December 17, 1857, 19,959 rubles' worth of colonial *marki*, found completely useless, had been destroyed.

On February 23, 1860, #73, Governor Johan H. Furuhjelm reported to the main office that 32,900 rubles' worth of colonial *marki* sent in 1858 had been received, but were in circulation only four months before they were defaced and torn. "The ones sent to the colonies in 1842, 1844 and 1848 were better." Notes of those issues were still good, he wrote, and it was desirable "that in the future we receive ones as satisfactory for their permanence."

(This issue of 1858 appears to have been the last. Thereafter, the story is one of steady deterioration of existing *marki* and vain requests for replacements.)

On May 13, 1860, #275, Furuhjelm wrote that, "on 3 March, upon ascertaining them entirely worthless for use, we destroyed colonial *marki* worth 23,531 r. 95 k. paper."

In 1863, #33, Furuhjelm asked that fifty thousand rubles' worth of *marki* be sent.

On June 2, 1864, #65, 2nd ser., Governor Maksutov asked for a fresh issue of one hundred thousand rubles' worth, mainly of one-ruble, fifty-kopek, and twenty-five-kopek notes, "as the existing ones are entirely useless."

On October 10, 1866, #242, Maksutov reminded the main office of his request of June 2, 1864. He had thought the re-quested notes would be on the ship *Kamchatka*, but they were not, so "at present only the 25 and 10 rubles ones are in circulation. The small ones are so worn that they cannot be distinguished from common *laftak* [walrus skin]. It is hard to keep accounts. Please send new ones via Siberia so we can have them in the fall."

On December 19, 1866, #321, com-plained Maksutov, "lack of tokens hinders accounting."

Summary

Thus, at the time of transfer, on October 18, 1867, only very worn notes were in cir-culation, and it would have been difficult to find whole and legible ones. However, legible or not, some continued to circulate for a while. Years afterward, Elmer M. Montague, a boy when the transfer occurred, wrote: "The Russians had skin money...when the two upper corners were cut off it was taken for 8 cents, so they soon demoralized the currency system till the natives were afraid to take any skin money." The unprepossessing appear-ance of the notes then still in use probably explains why the newcomers to Sitka did not take more as souvenirs. Captain E. G. Fast, stationed at Sitka in 1867, managed to find nine good specimens, which he included in a collection of curios he assembled and put up for sale when he re-turned home the next year. The collection, purchased by the Peabody Museum, is still intact except for the tokens, which dis-appeared long ago.

The above information permits certain conclusions about the date of various tokens:

1. There seem to have been more issues than previous research has indicated, namely of 1816, 1822, 1826, 1834, 1841, 1844, 1848, and 1858.
2. The modification of tokens of the 1841 issue reported by Governor Etholen in 1842 makes it possible that tokens so treated are of that date or later.
3. The twenty-five-ruble denomination was requested in 1846 and presumably supplied in the issue of 1848, so none of that denomination would be earlier than that.
4. Governor Rosenberg in 1852 indicated that the tokens of the 1848 issue were the last to be signed. Andrei Severin seems to have been the only director to sign the tokens, and he ceased to do so about 1847.
5. In 1853, Rosenberg wrote that the new 1852 issue was of different colors than the same denominations of earlier issues.
6. The five specimens in the Ulster Museum in Belfast, "collected in Canada by Gordon Augustus Thomson about 1835-1840 for the museum," can therefore be assumed to have been of that time or earlier.

There remain the anomalies. Notable among these are three specimens de-scribed in 1976 by a Czech numismatist, Eduard Polivka. Lacking the features of the later, more "conventional" notes, they are of a simple form that suggests that they may be of an earlier issue. One, of twenty-five kopeks, is a circle within a square, containing the words *"Marka v Amerike, 25 kopeek."* Another, of fifty kopeks, has the same inscription in an oval with that denomination; and a third, of one ruble, has the same inscription with the denomination *"odin rubl'."* On the back of each is the monogram "RAK" with a serial number. There is no signature.

There is also a one-ruble note of this type in the State Historical Museum collection in Moscow, on heavy paper, and of the same type of crude design, though not identical to that of the Polivka specimens. There are three possibilities: (1) that these simple, rather crude specimens were of some as-yet-unknown issue occurring before 1816, but there is no documentary evidence to support this; (2) that they are of the 1816 issue (there seems to be no description of the 1816 tokens, as to whether they had the company seal, etc.); or (3) that they were one of the temporary issues made in the colonies, as shown in the company correspondence. However, it would seem that the *bilety* (notes) mentioned in the correspondence were of larger denominations and done by hand. If the four anomalous specimens are printed, they would have to have come from St. Petersburg, as the Russian colonies never had printing facilities. Identification of these notes will require further research.

Broader Perspectives

The vicissitudes of the Russian-American parchment tokens suggest larger conclusions about Russian America. The colony was perpetually short of cash. For fifty years, Russian administrators in the colony and in St. Petersburg recognized the problem but were unable to solve it. In similar circumstances, British colonies in North America printed their own paper money to provide a circulating medium, but Russian-American Company officials lacked printing presses and, more significantly, waited for their superiors in St. Petersburg to act. By keeping currency under control of the home authorities, colonial officials precluded the kinds of local initiative that might have improved life in nineteenth-century Russian America in such areas as education, health, and industry. The Russian-American Company's worn, frequently illegible parchment tokens were a perpetual reminder of the crudity and precarious quality of life at the far reaches of the Russian Empire.

Richard A. Pierce is Professor of History, University of Alaska, Fairbanks.

For Further Reading

Berglund, Anders, et al. "Russian-American Company Scrip Notes: Some Observations." *Journal of the Russian Numismatic Society* 28, Autumn 1987.

Doll, A. and R. A. Pierce. "Alaska Treasure—the Russian Skin Money." *Alaska Journal* (November 1969), p. 22.

Elliott, H. W. *The Seal Islands of Alaska.* Washington, D.C., 1884.

Notes

1. H. W. Elliott, *The Seal Islands of Alaska* (Washington, D.C., 1884), pp. 96-97 n.

2. A. Doll and R. A. Pierce, "Alaska Treasure—the Russian Skin Money," *Alaska Journal* (November 1969), p. 22. The document is Sobstvennoi Ego Imperatorskago Velichestvo Kantseliarii. *Sbornik istoricheskikh materialov izvlechennykh iz arkhiva Pervago otdeleniia* [His Imperial Majesty's Office. Collection of historical materials from the archive of the First Section], Vyp. 1.

Education *in* Russian America

by Richard L. Dauenhauer

ormal education in the European sense is now entering its third century in Alaska. In the first hundred years, it was implemented by the Russian Orthodox church and the Russian-American Company. In the second hundred years, it was initiated by the Presbyterian church and the United States government, with increasing transfer of authority to local control at the territorial, state, and community levels. Unfortunately, basic historical facts of the first hundred years remain unfamiliar to the average American, even the average Alaskan, including professional educators and historians. Simply stated, the facts are these:

- Education existed in Russian America.
- It was bilingual.
- Literacy was taught both in Russian and the local Alaska Native language.
- Books were written and published in the four Alaska Native languages with which the Russians had the greatest contact: Aleut, Central Yup'ik, Alutiiq, and Tlingit.
- There was widespread popular literacy in Russian and the Native languages.
- The educational system had many illustrious graduates.
- The American Protestant philosophy regarding bilingual education and Alaska Native culture conflicted with the Russian Orthodox philosophy.
- Specifically, Alaska Native language and culture were forbidden in schools beginning with the American period.
- The momentum of the Russian era continued until about 1912.
- Although bilingual/bicultural education is now legally permitted, and in some cases encouraged or required, the antibilingual momentum of the second century is continuing into the third, and the value of bilingual education remains a topic of heated debate among American educators.

...In Russian-America, education was bilingual, and it produced many notable Native graduates who became middle managers in the Russian colony.

Beginning in 1794, the Russian Orthodox mission to Alaska established bilingual education as its norm, with literacy in Russian and the Native language of the particular area as the ideal. The result was the nineteenth-century flowering of Aleut literacy, whose momentum carried well into the American period.

Orthodoxy had particular influence on the self-identity of three distinct populations, each of which recognizes its difference from the other two, yet all of which call themselves "Aleut": the Unangan (Aleuts of the Pribilof and Aleutian Islands), the Central Yup'ik speakers of Bristol Bay, and the populations of the Alaska Peninsula, Kodiak Island, and Prince William Sound. These three groups all share a heritage of Orthodoxy, Russian intermarriage, and bilingualism.

Bilingual education grew out of similarities between the precontact Native and the Orthodox world views that contributed to the success of the Orthodox mission with minimal social disorientation. This is not to say that bilingual education was inevitable: in other places in the Russian Empire local languages were suppressed, primarily for political reasons. But in Russian America, education was bilingual, and it produced many notable Native graduates who became middle managers in the Russian colony. Michael Oleksa has compiled biographies of nineteenth- and twentieth-century "Aleuts" who were graduates of the Russian-American educational system. Most are Creole, with Native mothers and Russian fathers. They studied in local bilingual schools, went on to higher education in Russia, and returned to leadership positions. In general, their achievement has not been recognized by American historians, who consider them Russian and not Native because of their names. Ironically, some writers have minimized Creole achievement on the one hand and unknowingly cited Creoles on the other as examples of Russian achievement. Fr. Oleksa's article in this volume offers more detail on the Creole contribution in Russia and America.

The Russian and American views of religion and education are sharply con-trasted in the lives and philosophies of the Orthodox Bishop Innocent (Veniaminov, 1797-1879) and the Presbyterian Sheldon Jackson (1843-1909). Each was a missionary to Alaska, each founded schools, and at his death each man had been elected to the highest position in his church. Beyond these parallels, however, the two men differed drastically regarding the relationship of Native culture, Native language, and Christianity.

As an Orthodox theologian, Bishop Innocent considered the issue of cultural diversity resolved in Apostolic times, as recorded in *Acts*. A fundamental principle of Orthodox missionary spirituality held that as one did not have to become a Jew to become a Christian, neither did one have to become a Russian to be a Christian. Orthodoxy used Alaska Native languages liturgically and in the schools, encouraged translations of scripture, and at the Sitka seminary required several years' study of Alaska Native languages.

Jackson, on the other hand, argued that Alaska Natives could not become

AN ALPHABET BOOK in both Russian and Church Slavonic, the language of Orthodox church services.

Collection of the Alaska State Library, Juneau.

Russian School, Sitka Alaska

THE RUSSIAN SCHOOL at Sitka, ca. 1896. Students and staff gather in front of the old Russian Bishop's House and Seminary, which had become an orphanage. By the 1890s there was not a resident bishop in Alaska, the diocesan seat having moved to San Francisco in 1872 and the seminary to Irkutsk in 1858. But the school continued, with students from all over Alaska, girls as well as boys.

Photograph by Edward deGroff, Alaska State Library, Juneau.

Christians unless and until they had been acculturated or "civilized." Translation of scripture was abandoned on the grounds that the languages were too heathen and sin-ridden to express civilized Christian thought, and in Sheldon Jackson School the use of Native languages was expressly forbidden. All instruction was to be in English only. Jackson became superintendent of education for Alaska, and his policies and the laws based upon them continued in force in Alaska until well beyond the mid twentieth century.

Bilingual education was the norm in Russian America, with proven results. The bilingual schools of Russian America attempted to build on indigenous talent and potential, and channel them to new fulfillment in new directions, such as literacy. In the American period, the schools had the express purpose of destroying Native language and culture, with the following results: Most Native languages are on the verge of extinction, a very low level of self-esteem exists in most Native communities, and families and communities have suffered from extreme social upheavals.

The present paper establishes a simple historical record of early schooling in Alaska, mainly before Veniaminov;

explains its conceptual basis; and documents the lives of some interesting graduates. As researchers, Michael Oleksa and I do not want to become too deeply engaged in a debate over its success or failure. We make no claims to objectivity: we are advocates of bilingual education, and we are Orthodox. However, we do not intend to engage in a polemic or diatribe. Rather, we seek to establish a record, and let the record speak for itself. Our main point is to demonstrate the extent to which bilingual education, considered new and innovative—even radical—by many American educators who view it as a product of the 1970s forced on school districts by the federal government, is in fact old, with proven positive results. The monolingual policies considered "old" and "pioneer" by American educators are actually comparatively new.

Early History

Formal education in Alaska began with Grigorii and Natalia Shelikhov, who operated a small school in Three Saints Bay on Kodiak Island from 1784 to 1786. What meager records exist regarding this school show that it was bilingual, and that the Shelikhovs made an effort to write Alutiiq, the Native language of Kodiak Island, using the Russian alphabet. The school was short-lived, and was abandoned after their return to Russia.

In 1794 the first clergy arrived on Kodiak, including Fr. Herman. It is assumed, but not recorded in extant documents, that he initiated schooling in the 1790s. Alexander Baranov is recorded as subsidizing a school in Kodiak in 1801. The dearth of documentation does not preclude the probability that former students and company employees continued some educational work throughout this period.

The early nineteenth century witnessed a renewal of efforts in education. In 1804, Hieromonk Gideon reorganized the Shelikhov school. In 1805, Count Nikolai

Rezanov, who was deeply concerned with education, subsidized schools for boys and girls at St. Paul Harbor, site of the present city of Kodiak. By 1805, schoolbooks were produced in the Native language by Fr. Gideon, and Nikolai Rezanov officially appointed Fr. Herman as the head of the school in Kodiak. By 1807, the school had one hundred students, and Fr. Gideon and Paramon Chumovits had begun an Alutiiq dictionary and primer, but with Rezanov's death, the school was forced to close for lack of financial support.

When chief manager Matfei I. Murav'ev took over in 1820, he issued a directive reiterating the Rezanov goals of 1805 and directing the company to support education. Among the goals was that schools should produce seamen, military leaders, agriculturalists, artisans, shipbuilders, craftsmen, accountants, administrators, agents, navigators, and people skilled in medicine and surgery. Although there seem to have been some problems, the venture appears to have been successful on the whole.

The trail picks up again in 1823, when Fr. Herman, at the age of sixty-six, left Kodiak to establish his hermitage and school on nearby Spruce Island. This became the most successful mission school of the era and continued until Fr. Herman's death in 1836. Among the faculty were the Creole Sophia Vlasov and an Aleut named Gerassim Zirianov, who was an active writer in the Alutiiq language, and who became a church officer, but not a tonsured monk. Fr. Herman is remembered both for his school and his exemplary Christian life. His memory is greatly cherished by the Native people of Alaska, and in 1970 he was canonized as the first North American saint of the Russian Orthodox church.

Bishop Innocent (Veniaminov)

The greatest figure in Russian-American education in Alaska in the nineteenth

INNOCENT (Veniaminov) as Metropolitan of Moscow, ca. 1870. The great Orthodox bishop of Alaska, who began his American career as priest at Unalaska and Sitka, was elevated to the highest office in the Russian church in 1868, serving until his death in 1879.

St. Herman's Theological Seminary

century was Bishop Innocent (born Veniaminov, 1797-1879). He arrived in Unalaska in 1824, built the Church of the Holy Ascension of Our Lord, designed an alphabet for Aleut, and, with the help of Aleut leader Ivan Pan'kov, started translation into and original writing in Aleut. In 1834, he moved to Sitka, where he encouraged writing in Tlingit, and produced instructional materials in Tlingit and Russian. In 1840 he was ordained Bishop of Kamchatka, and the Kurile and Aleutian islands. He built the Cathedral of St. Michael the Archangel, 1844-48, and in 1845 moved the seminary from Petropavlovsk (Siberia) to Sitka. The seminary (high school) curriculum included navigation, medicine, Latin, trigonometry, and six years of Alaska Native language. Graduates of the Sitka All Colonial School established bilingual elementary schools, which developed into a full statewide system of forty-four parochial schools by 1900. In 1868, Bishop Innocent was elected Metropolitan of Moscow, head of the Russian Orthodox church.

Because so much has been written about him already, we will not discuss his life and achievements any further here, but simply make a few summary comments. Bishop Innocent was responsible for confirming bilingual education and Native language literacy in Alaska. He was aided in this by more support from both church and company than had been given to his predecessors, and he gained from the work of his predecessors. He also benefited greatly from the collaboration of numerous gifted colleagues, such as the Creole priest Iakov Netsvetov and the Aleut leader Ivan Pan'kov.

Our understanding and appreciation of the Russian era are limited by our lack of evidence. J. Lincoln Starr, writing twenty years ago, could not find bilingual materials attributed to Bishop Innocent, but there

BISHOP'S PANAGIA, or medallion, attributed to Bishop Innocent.

Collections of the Security Pacific Bank, Seattle.

are some materials in print, and we can assume that many more circulated in manuscript. The 1984 edition of *Notes on the Islands of the Unalaska District* includes a sample of his pedagogical work in Tlingit. New research is constantly locating fragments of manuscripts, lesson plans, notebooks, and related materials, if not used by Veniaminov, then certainly used by Orthodox teachers well into the American period.

Starr argues that Veniaminov's claims of widespread literacy are inflated, but I would disagree with Starr and agree with Veniaminov. Enough documentation exists, and enough Native language literacy has survived among the oldest generations despite sixty years of suppression, that we can imagine literacy was far more widespread in its heyday, and was spread as much tutorially and liturgically as in formal classrooms. Certainly some Eskimos and many Aleuts continued reading and writing their own languages in Cyrillic a century after the sale of

Alaska. Many of these literate Natives accomplished much.

Biographies

One of the most accomplished graduates of the Orthodox parochial schools, Ilarion Archimandritov received his basic education at Unalaska, 1827-33, and was sent at company expense to the Kronstadt Naval Academy near St. Petersburg for college-level studies in navigational science and cartography. A skilled seaman, he sailed the North Pacific from the Pribilofs and Atka to Sitka and San Francisco for two decades, and was decorated for heroism for rescuing passengers and crew when the *Naslednik Alexander* sank. Later he explored and mapped Kodiak Island by bidarka, producing the first accurate charts of the area, which were published in the 1852 Teben'kov atlas.

Major General Alexander Kashevarov, a Creole from Kodiak, also attended the Kronstadt Academy. Together with another Creole seaman, Nicolai Chernov,

he explored the Arctic coast of Alaska by kayak, mapping the coast to a point forty miles east of Barrow. Later Kashevarov conducted two round-the-world cruises and served as governor of the Siberian port of Ayan. He retired to St. Petersburg with a distinguished record of service to the company and his homeland spanning three decades and five continents.

Father Iakov Netsvetov studied at the Irkutsk Theological Seminary and returned to his hometown of Atka in 1829, where he immediately organized a bilingual school. After seventeen years serving his fellow Creoles and the Native and Russian residents of the western Aleutian Islands, he was transferred to the Yukon delta as the first missionary to the Yup'ik Eskimos. His detailed accounts of daily life in Atka and at Russian Mission constitute a fascinating record of village life in nineteenth-century Alaska. He was the first to devise a writing system and teach Yup'ik at his parish school on the Yukon. Old and nearly blind, he retired to Sitka, where he died and was buried. His two brothers also distinguished themselves, one as a navigator on a circumnavigation of the globe, the other as a shipbuilder.

Semen Lukin, whose trading post on the Kuskokwim is described in Lieutenant Zagoskin's journals, began his career on the Nushagak River after finishing elementary school at Kodiak. He earned the respect and admiration of Russian officials by his honest and energetic work among the Native people in the modern Aniak area during the 1830s and 1840s.

Modern-day Aleuts and Eskimos such as Matthew Berezkin (d. 1971), Nicolai Epchook (d. 1961), Vladimir Melovedoff (d. 1979), Sergei Sheratine, and others continued this tradition of bilingual (and even trilingual) literacy into the late twentieth century. As the paper trail becomes more defined through the work of a growing number of scholars, it becomes clearer that these talented Native

BISHOP INNOCENT of Alaska. In one of the few surviving oil paintings of Innocent, the missionary priest of Unalaska and Sitka is shown shortly after becoming Archbishop of Irkutsk, following eighteen years as bishop in Alaska. Bishop Innocent promoted education of Native and Creole children by encouraging the use of Native languages and development of alphabets and translations for them. He himself was a gifted linguist who translated many works into Aleut. He also established a seminary at Sitka to provide opportunities for Native Americans to rise in church or company service.

From a portrait in the collections of the Palace Museum and Parks of Petrodvorets, Leningrad.

RUSSIAN BISHOP'S House, Sitka, was built by the Russian-American Company in 1841-42 to serve as Bishop Innocent's residence and as a seminary for Alaskan Native and Creole students. The seminary operated until 1858, when its function was transferred to Irkutsk, Siberia, along with the bishop himself. Courses at the seminary included a general curriculum as well as church history, liturgics, and doctrine. In the 1870s the diocesan seat was transferred to San Francisco, and the building was used as an orphanage and a school.

Photograph by Winter and Pond, ca. 1900, courtesy of Historical Society of Seattle and King County.

and Creole people were not anomalies, but were part of a larger cultural context.

Conflicting Visions

This concluding section addresses the period in which education in Alaska's past became education in Alaska's present. As this era of "Conflicting Visions" is detailed elsewhere, I will only highlight that conflict here. It should be clear now that Fr. Oleksa and I do not consider Sheldon Jackson a "pioneer educator," but a relative latecomer who initiated the present educational era with a world view and philosophy radically different from those of educators and missionaries in the Russian period.

Orthodox mission proceeds from a belief that all things are fulfilled in Christ, not *replaced* by Christ. Thus, traditional cultures are "baptized" into a "newness of life," not discarded and replaced by alien cultures. If all persons share in the image and imprint of Divinity, then each person is most fully Christian and most fully the image of God when he or she dedicates his or her energies, personality, and culture to Christ rather than discarding them and trying to become the image of someone

else. The old person is reborn, not replaced by a substitute. In contrast, some groups in Western Protestant Christianity called for eradication of Native language, culture, and religion, and replacement by American language, culture, and religion. This was the irreconcilable conflict initiated into Alaska Native life in the American period.

In the early 1880s, Protestants in Philadelphia partitioned Alaska into mutually respected spheres of influence. Generally, the Methodists got Unalaska and the Aleutians; the Baptists, Kodiak; the Presbyterians, the

PEG CALENDAR. Introduced by the Russians for keeping track of Orthodox religious holidays, the calendar took many shapes and was made of wood, bone, or ivory by the Alaska Native converts. Whether round or rectangular, they always contained twelve months divided into twenty-eight, thirty, or thirty-one days, with the holidays marked by a cross or a circle in red. Pegs were moved daily.

Sitka National Historical Park.

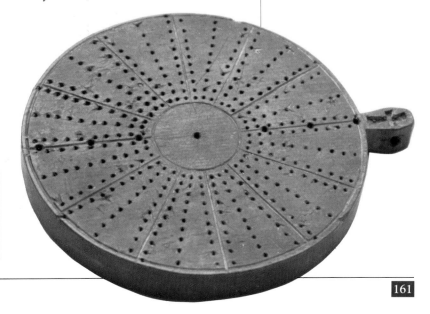

Southeast and the Arctic; the Moravians, the Kuskokwim; and the Episcopalians, the upper Yukon and Interior. It is interesting that the Lutheran church was not included, being the only Protestant church previously active in Russian America, with pastors and a congregation in Sitka, 1840-65. The Catholic church was not included in the meeting, but eventually got the mid and lower Yukon.

Conspicuously absent from this ecclesiastical nonaggression pact were the Orthodox, and Protestant churches and boarding schools were established in traditionally Orthodox areas. The impact was not purely "religious" in the conventional sense, but cultural as well. In these areas traditional Native world view and Orthodox Christianity conflicted head-on with American secularism. Unfortunately for the Orthodox, and, I believe, for the Native people as a whole, the new world view had the force of law. Thus, the

American government could and did close Orthodox church schools by force, and public use of Alaska Native languages could be and was in fact outlawed as a punishable offense. Records of the 1890s and 1900s indicate considerable tension between these conflicting visions. The Native people did in fact protest. Also, there was considerable hostility between the Orthodox and Protestant clergy. All of this is documented in correspondence, newspapers, and journal accounts of the late nineteenth and early twentieth centuries.

Sheldon Jackson himself had no use whatsoever for Orthodoxy, and he is quoted as having predicted its early demise in Alaska. A growing body of evidence further suggests that he actively worked toward that goal, envisioning eradication of Orthodoxy as well as Alaska Native language and culture as vestiges of a pre-American past. It was probably not by accident that in Sitka, Unalaska, and Kodiak, Protestant missions were established less than half a mile from traditional centers of Orthodoxy, and vested with legal power to remove Native children from home and community. But this must wait for another and more detailed paper on that period. This article has documented some aspects of education in Russian America, and noted that bilingual education—despite the legal and pedagogical battles of the 1970s and 1980s—is not new in Alaska, but was standard in its first century. Sheldon Jackson was a product of his age and culture, as were the Russians, and we should not judge him unfairly.

I believe it is not only fair but also imperative to judge an educational system by the people it produces, and the community mental health it creates. In both respects we find the Russian period admirable, and the American period wanting. The reality of educational achievement in Russian America

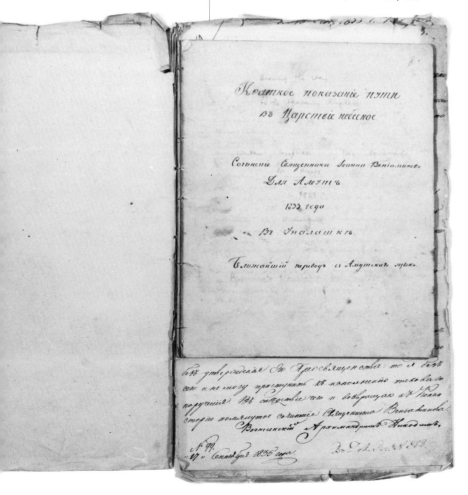

contradicts the stereotypes of brutality and incompetence all too often recycled in our popular history books. The battle for full implementation of the new monolingual and monocultural American policies started after one hundred years of Russian education with a different cultural, spiritual, and pedagogical base. The battle is far from over, and is still being waged legally, pedagogically, and emotionally in our classrooms today.

Richard L. Dauenhauer is Program Director, Language and Cultural Studies, Sealaska Heritage Foundation, Juneau.

For Further Reading

Afonsky, Bishop Gregory. *History of the Orthodox Church in Alaska (1794-1917).* Kodiak: St. Herman's Seminary Press, 1977.

Black, Lydia. "The Curious Case of the Unalaska Icons." *Alaska Journal* 12, no. 2 (Spring 1982).

_____. "Ivan Pan'kov, An Architect of Aleut Literacy." *Arctic Anthropology* 14, no. 1 (1977), pp. 94-107.

_____, trans. *The Journals of Iakov Netsvetov. The Atkha Years, 1828-1844.* Kingston, Ontario: Limestone Press, 1980. *The Yukon Years, 1845-1863.* Ed. Richard A. Pierce. Kingston, Ontario: Limestone Press, 1984.

Dauenhauer, Richard L. *Conflicting Visions in Alaskan Education,* Occasional Paper No. 3. Fairbanks: University of Alaska, Center for Cross-Cultural Studies, 1982.

_____. "The Spiritual Epiphany of Aleut." *Orthodox Alaska* 8, no. 1 (January 1979), pp. 13-42.

_____. "Two Missions to Alaska." *The Pacific Historian* 26, no. 1 (Spring 1982), pp. 29-41.

_____ **and Michael Oleksa.** "Education in Russian America." *Education in Alaska's Past: Conference Proceedings.* Anchorage: Alaska Historical Society, 1983.

Garrett, Paul D. *St. Innocent: Apostle to America.* Crestwood, New York: St. Vladimir's Seminary Press, 1979.

Krauss, Michael. *Alaska Native Languages: Past, Present, and Future,* Research Papers, No. 4. Fairbanks: Alaska Native Language Center, 1980.

_____. "Iazyki korennogo naseleniia Aliaski: proshloe, nastoiashchee i buduschee." V. P. Alekseev et al. *Traditsionnye Kul'tury Severnoi Sibiri i Severnoi Ameriki.* Moskva: Academiia nauk SSSR, 1981.

_____ **and Mary Jane McGary.** *Alaska Native Languages: A Bibliographical Catalogue. Part One: Indian Languages,* Research Papers, No 3. Fairbanks: Alaska Native Language Center, 1980.

Miyoka, Osahito. "Alaska Native Languages in Transition." *Alaska Native Culture and History.* Ed. Y. Kotani and W. B. Workman. Senri Ethnological Studies, No. 4. Osaka: National Museum of Ethnology, 1980.

Oleksa, Michael. *Alaskan Missionary Spirituality.* New York: Paulist Press, 1987.

_____. "The Alaskan Orthodox Mission and the Evolution of the Aleut Identity among the Indigenous Peoples of Southwestern Alaska." Ph.D. dissertation. Prague: Orthodox Theological Faculty, 1988.

_____. "The Creoles and their Contributions to the Development of Alaska," *Russian America: The Forgotten Frontier* (this volume).

_____. "On Orthodox Witness." In Gerald Anderson, *Witnessing to the Kingdom: Melbourne and Beyond.* Maryknoll, New York: Orbis Books, 1982, pp. 77-94.

_____. *Orthodox Alaska.* Crestwood, New York: St. Vladimir's Seminary Press (in press).

_____. "The Orthodox Mission and Aleut Culture." *St. Vladimir's Seminary Quarterly* (forthcoming).

_____. "The Orthodox Mission and Native Alaskan Languages." *Orthodox Alaska* 8, no. 1 (January 1979), pp. 1-12.

_____. "Orthodoxy in Alaska: The Spiritual History of the Kodiak Aleut People." *St. Vladimir's Theological Quarterly* 25, no. 1, pp. 3-19.

_____. *Three Saints Bay and the Evolution of the Aleut Identity.* Unpublished manuscript 1982 subsumed in "The Alaskan Orthodox Mission" and *Orthodox Alaska.*

Smith, Barbara. "Cathedral on the Yukon." *Alaska Journal* 12, no. 2 (Spring 1982).

Starr, J. Lincoln. *Education in Russian America.* Juneau: Alaska State Library Historical Monographs, No. 2, 1972.

Veniaminov, Ioann. *Notes on the Islands of the Unalashka District.* Trans. and ed. Lydia Black and R. H. Geoghegan, ed. Richard Pierce. 1840; Kingston, Ontario: Limestone Press, 1984.

Notes

Richard Dauenhauer wrote the original version of this paper with Fr. Michael Oleksa for the Education in Alaska's Past Conference, Valdez, Alaska, October 7-10, 1982, and published it in 1983. This revision is Dauenhauer's alone, but Oleksa's subsequent contributions to the intellectual history of Alaska are noted in the suggestions for further reading following this article. For reasons of space and uniformity of style, portions of this paper have been condensed. Readers are directed to the works listed in "For Further Reading" for references to the extensive scholarly literature underlying this article.

Sitka

by Joan M. Antonson

When the United States purchased Alaska from Russia in 1867, only two settlements in the territory could be considered towns: Sitka and Kodiak. The latter served as the Russian-American Company headquarters from 1799 until 1808, when Sitka became the colonial capital. In 1816, the Russian Orthodox mission center also moved from Kodiak to Sitka. Kodiak continued to be an important location for the company's economic activities, including the fur trade, brickmaking, and later the ice industry. After the administrative offices moved, however, new buildings were put up in the town to meet immediate economic needs. The Russian-American Company focused its attention on the Sitka settlement. At its zenith, the southeast Alaska community boasted schools for boys and girls, a hospital, an officers' club, a cathedral, a ballroom in the governor's house, a library and museum, and an observatory. Over half of the Russians in America lived at Sitka, and it had large Creole and Aleut populations as well. Approximately one thousand Tlingits lived outside the fortified walls of the town. For sixty years, Sitka was the cultural and commercial center for the Russians in America. There is no better way to tell Sitka's story than through the eyes of the many visitors who described the town during its heyday.

For sixty years, Sitka was the cultural and commercial center for the Russians in America.

Establishment

After visiting the Sitka Sound area in 1794, Alexander Baranov, then chief manager of the Shelikhov-Golikov Company, decided to build a fur-trading post there. Baranov hoped to discourage British and American penetration of Alaska. In addition, since sea otters could still be found in southeast Alaska waters, a post would facilitate longer periods of hunting there by reducing the number and length of voyages between Kodiak and southeast Alaska.

Although he preferred the present site of Sitka, in July 1799 Baranov purchased a tract of land six miles to the north from the local Tlingit chief. Construction began on St. Archangel Michael's Redoubt. The next year Baranov returned to Kodiak. During his absence, area Tlingits attacked the post, killed all but a handful of the Russian and Aleut inhabitants, and burned the fort in June 1802.

When he learned of the attack, Baranov resolved to re-establish the post. He returned to Sitka Sound in 1804. Supported by a warship, the *Neva*, under the command of Captain Iurii F. Lisianskii, the Russians bombarded the Native village at what would be called Castle Hill. When the Tlingits moved to a nearby fort, a battle ensued in which several Russians and Tlingits were killed and some were wounded, including Baranov. After four days, the Indians abandoned the fort and left the area; the Russians burned the fort, destroyed the Tlingit village around Castle Hill, and began constructing New Archangel, also known as Sitka, the Tlingit name for the island.

WATERCOLOR OF Sitka by Captain Iurii F. Lisianskii, drawn during his visit to Sitka in 1804-05. This scene shows the settlement within a year of its establishment in 1804. Lisianskii was captain of the Russian vessel Neva, which assisted Baranov in seizing the site from a hostile Tlingit force.

From Lisianskii's Voyage around the World, 1803-1806 *(St. Petersburg, 1812); photograph courtesy of Anchorage Museum of History and Art.*

Sitka, 1805-1820

Sitka in 1805 was a frontier fortress. When Georg von Langsdorf visited the outpost in that year, he wrote:

> *The settlement of New Archangel was at our arrival quite in its infancy. Under such circumstances, nothing like the conveniences of life could be expected: the habitations were for the greater part unfinished and consisted of small chambers without stoves, with so thin a thatch, that the rains, which we had continually, often came through. The Promuschleniks [promyshlenniki] were kept constantly hard at work upon the barracks, warehouses, and other buildings, which were so exceedingly wanted.[1]*

When Lisianskii returned to Sitka in the fall of 1805, a Russian-American Company clerk, Nikolai Korobitsyn, wrote:

> *The New Archangel fort is situated on a high promontory which, projecting out from the coastline into the sea, presents a pleasant view; and considering its situation, is fairly safe from any kind of foe. Its*

> *fortification consists, because the settlement is new, of a gabion around the entire fort, interspersed with twenty cannons.... Inside the fort is the Manager's residence with his office and kitchen...[and] a house, consisting of four rooms, for the officers and ship captains of the Company's maritime fleet. In the middle of the fort is a square, measuring 20 sazhen long and 10 sazhen wide [140 by 70 feet]. In the center of the latter stands a flagstaff on which the Company flag is hoisted on festival and ceremonial days, as well as upon the entry of vessels into the harbor.[2]*

Another visitor that first year was Nikolai Rezanov, Shelikhov's son-in-law and high chamberlain to the tsar. He traveled to Russian America in 1805 to study the operations of the new Russian-American Company. He emphasized the military and economic aspects of Sitka, and also described the new settlement:

> *The site of the fort is a high rock, or kekur, on a peninsula projecting into the inlet. On the left side, on a hill located on the same kind of peninsula that adjoins the kekur, is an enormous barrack with two booths or small towers for defending the place. The*

building is almost entirely of mast timber set on a larch log foundation reinforced with cobblestones, with cellars built inside it, extending down the slope of the hill all the way to the water. Beside it is a building consisting of two shops, a storeroom for provisions, and two cellars. To the side of this building stands a large shed on posts for storing foodstuffs; beneath the entire shed is a barnlike structure for processing the Company's wares. On the side opposite the fort is an enormous shed for storing cargo, with a log storehouse on the water side and a wharf between it and the fort. On the right side, at the foot of the hill, is a chamber building containing a kitchen, bath, and several compartments for housing Company workers; along the shore is a large building complex nine sazhens long and five sazhens wide [sixty-three by forty-five feet], in the center of which is a large smithy with three furnaces and with compartments for workshops along the sides. A cattleyard is located to one side.

In addition to the above buildings, there is also a bath house, and another bath house with a light room below the fort.[3]

In August 1808 the Russian-American Company moved its headquarters from Kodiak to Sitka and began the fort's transformation into a town. New buildings, including sixty houses, spread out below the fort. They were enclosed by a wooden wall with lookouts sited about every twenty yards, where people were on watch twenty-four hours. A small Russian Orthodox chapel, built in the traditional Russian octagonal style, was constructed in 1813. Icons salvaged from the *Neva*, wrecked in 1813 on Kruzof Island, were placed there. The center of activity became the shipyard, where, over the years, ships from a number of countries were repaired and several ships, including the *Politkofsky*, a steam vessel, were built. The townscape included numerous vegetable gardens.

SITKA, LOOKING toward the governor's residence and palisade on the kekur (high rock) overlooking Sitka Bay. An engraving by Freidrich H. von Kittlitz, expedition artist on the Seniavin.

From the F. P. Litke Atlas, Alaska and Polar Regions Dept., Elmer E. Rasmuson Library, University of Alaska, Fairbanks.

The 1820s-1830s

The tsar renewed the Russian-American Company's charter for twenty years in 1821. Prior to replacing Baranov as chief manager in 1818, the company thoroughly investigated its operations in North America. In the accounting prepared at that time, Kyrill T. Khlebnikov, who was second-in-command in the colony from 1817 until 1832, observed:

Buildings were at first entered without a value, but subsequently, so that accounts might be put in order, they were appraised. However, at the time Baranov was replaced, only one large warehouse, out of the entire complex of buildings, was of any value. In general, the rest of the buildings were worthless. The barracks had no heat, were empty, and on the verge of collapse; thus there were no living quarters for personnel. A few of the promyshlenniks *had built five small dwellings behind the fortress.*[4]

As part of the review in 1818, company administrators debated abandoning Sitka, but instead decided to make Sitka the chief port and the place where the chief administrators lived. Subsequently, a major building program was undertaken.

Captain Frederic P. Litke, on a round-the-world expedition in the sloop *Seniavin,* was at Sitka for a month in the summer of 1827, at the conclusion of the construction undertaken during the administration of Governor Matfei I. Murav'ev (1820-1825). According to Litke, the Russians, Creoles, and Aleuts at Sitka totaled eight hundred people. He noted that the settlement was built in concentric circles. The center was the fortress that enclosed the governor's two-story house on the hill. A palisade without cannon surrounded the next ring and included barracks for the workers, houses of employees, a hospital, baths, storehouses, commissaries, and workshops. A church, gardens, and about twenty-five other buildings were outside the fortress.

Under the leadership of Ferdinand P. von Wrangell, governor of the colonies from 1830 to 1835, the building program at Sitka continued. Baroness von Wrangell, the first wife of a governor to live at Sitka, had a profound impact on the community. She visited the sick, encouraged education, and entertained frequently.

Writing in early 1840, Lavrentii A. Zagoskin, an officer of the Russian-American Company, noted Sitka's carpentry, coppersmith, locksmith, and blacksmith shops (the latter with three forges), gristmill, and covered shipyard. He remarked that the log buildings with their steep hipped plank roofs predominated everywhere that Russians chose to settle. But he also noted the effect of the Baroness and other changes:

With the spread of enlightenment came heightened luxury: silk-lace dresses and satin bonnets were ordered from Petersburg

CATHEDRAL OF St. Michael the Archangel, ca. 1900. Designed by Bishop Innocent and built 1844-48, the cathedral is in the center of Sitka, Lincoln Street flowing around it. It has three altars and a richly decorated interior. The original building was in use until 1966, when it was destroyed by fire. Already designated a National Historic Landmark, it was rebuilt by private and public funds using documents of the original building, developed by the Historic American Buildings Survey, and reconsecrated in 1976.

Photograph courtesy of Collections of Alaska State Library, Juneau.

A VIEW OF rural Sitka that illustrates the basic blockwork design and notched corners of Russian log structures. An engraving by Freidrich H. von Kittlitz, who visited Sitka in 1828.

From the F. P. Litke Atlas, *Alaska and Polar Regions Dept., Elmer E. Rasmuson Library, University of Alaska, Fairbanks.*

for the Creole girls and in these they used to go barefoot to fetch water....[5]

The company began to view Sitka more as a community than as a frontier outpost.

The 1840s-1850s

In 1841 Tsar Nicholas I renewed the company's charter a second time. Again, the company undertook major construction projects at Sitka.

A new home for the governor of the Russian-American Company, a two-story mansion on the hill overlooking the harbor where the fort originally stood, was completed in the early 1840s. Known as Baranov's Castle—although the first governor of Russian America never saw it—the mansion included among its furnishings mirrors and full-length portraits of the tsar and his family. The company library, established in 1805 and increased annually, a cabinet of nautical maps and instruments, a museum collection of birds and animals found in Russian America and the costumes of all the Native peoples of the Northwest coast of America, and a school were all housed in Baranov's Castle. Above the roof was a belvedere with a light that served as a lighthouse.

In addition to the governor's mansion, the company constructed a number of other significant buildings in Sitka during the 1840s. They began to build an observatory on Japonski Island in 1841. That same year the Russian Orthodox church appointed a Bishop of Kamchatka, the Kuriles, and the Aleutian Islands. The first bishop, Innocent (Veniaminov), established his headquarters at Sitka. Construction of a home for the new bishop, with offices, classrooms, and a chapel, began in 1841 and was completed the next year. The cornerstone for St. Michael's Cathedral was laid in 1844, and the church was dedicated on November 20, 1848.

During the 1840s company officials also placed importance on education. The first

FOREST ON SITKA Island, an engraving by Alexander F. Postels, an expedition artist on the Seniavin, which stopped at Sitka on its round-the-world voyage, 1826-28. The dense forests and islands of southeastern Alaska provided ample food and timber for the establishment of a new colonial capital, but also concealed the hostile Tlingits, who never fully accepted the Russians.

From the F. P. Litke Atlas, *Alaska and Polar Regions Dept., Elmer E. Rasmuson Library, University of Alaska, Fairbanks.*

school at Sitka had opened around 1810. The company assigned *promyshlenniki* to teach the Aleuts and Creoles the commandments, Russian language, arithmetic, and navigational science. Zagoskin observed this new emphasis on education in his diary in 1840:

> *During this past autumn, nine boys were chosen from the latter group [older pupils] to be taught the science of navigation. Following the suggestion of the present Commander-in-Chief, a teacher has been sent out from the Commercial Pilot's School to take charge of these boys. Formerly the pupils who were destined for a naval career had no special instructor and were consequently trained by ships' captains who only had time to give them a few practical instructions while at sea.[6]*

In 1839 a school for girls opened at Sitka that continued to operate into the 1860s.

Economic conditions could not sustain construction on such a lavish scale. Following the discovery of gold in California in the late 1840s, the Russians began to ship ice cut from lakes in the Sitka and Kodiak areas to California. Although it was profitable, other new economic ventures were not, and the fur trade profits declined.

The 1860s

With the imperial government inclined to discontinue the charter that was to be renewed in 1862, the Russian-American Company assessed its operations. The board of directors commissioned Petr A. Tikhmenev to compile a company history. He completed his comprehensive

two-volume work in 1863. Because Tikhmenev was a company employee, some considered his work biased. The Naval Ministry published several earlier reports and one prepared by Lt. Capt. Pavel N. Golovin in 1862 on the Russian-American Company and the colonies. The Naval Ministry sent Golovin to Russian America in 1860 to accompany Sergei Kostlivtsov, who was dispatched by the Ministry of Finance. Golovin had separate instructions to conduct an independent investigation of company affairs. In addition to his official report, his letters to his family during his trip were published after his death in the mid 1860s.

Golovin reported that Sitka had facilities for the repair, outfitting, loading, and construction of ships. In addition, it had two sawmills, a machine shop for repairing nautical instruments, metalwork, blacksmith, carpentry, cooperage, tannery, ropewalk, paint, lathe, sailmakers, and copper, iron, and zinc casting shops. Golovin noted that "every shop has several young creole apprentices," and "thus the Company is constantly training new master craftsmen; in exchange for their education they are required to serve the Company at a set salary for 15 years, beginning at the age of 17." Golovin went on to note that "All of the shops are located in quite rundown buildings, except for the foundry; although that building is new, it was built in a careless manner from blocks and boards."[7] He also described the flour mill, the public laundry, and the place where furs were processed at Sitka.

A chapter in Golovin's report is devoted to educational facilities. On November 15, 1860, an All-Colonial School opened at Sitka. All children of persons employed in the colonies could attend the five-year program provided they could pass annual examinations. The curriculum included biblical scripture, church history, Russian language, geometry, geography, Russian history, penmanship, drawing, and ecclesiastical training sufficient for students planning to enter a seminary. Graduates whose expenses were paid by the company were required to serve the company for ten years. Golovin said that if the school could be kept "from falling into disrepair as has been the case in the past" it would help provide trained workers for the company.[8]

Golovin's personal letters were more descriptive. About the governor's house he wrote:

The building is a large, ugly two-story wooden structure with many annexes. The whole is painted yellow, and is surrounded by a wooden wall in which there are cannon embrasures and gun batteries.... At the base of the cliff on which the fortress stands, along the shore, there are the harbor facilities, warehouses, et cetera. Then to one side there is the settlement which consists of small wooden houses where the service personnel and Company officials, prikaschiks and lower ranks live. Farther on there is a wooden cathedral, the club, the Bishop's residence, and the infirmary. The street, the only one in the settlement, is narrow; since it rains all the time it is quite impassable because of the mud for at least three-quarters of the year. Consequently, boards have been laid all along the middle of the street. On the other side of the fort, partway up the hill, there are some workshops; beyond them there is a wooden wall which separates the Russian settlement from the Kolosh.[9]

Golovin also found that the Sitka settlement had a museum with portraits and drawings from the Academy of Arts at St. Petersburg, sketches of ships drawn by Naval Minister P. V. Chichagov, a prayer book, cartographic materials, and scientific instruments. He enjoyed evenings at the officers' club, where he played billiards, dinners with the gover-

PRINCESS MARIA *Alexandrovich Maksutova, second wife of the last governor of Russian America. The princess was one of several "first ladies" of the Russian-American Company who brought gaiety, fashion, and culture to the capital of Russian America, earning it the somewhat tongue-in-cheek epithet, "Paris on the Pacific." The princess was nineteen upon her arrival in Sitka in 1864.*

Dimitrii P. Maksutov Collection, Alaska State Library, Juneau.

BARONESS ELIZABETH von Wrangell, wife of Governor Ferdinand P. von Wrangell, who served in Sitka from 1830 to 1835. The baroness was the first wife of a governor to accompany her husband to Russian America. Only twenty years old when she arrived in the capital, she quickly inspired admiration and devotion from colonials and Tlingits alike with her gaiety, friendliness, and grace. The old bachelor's castle was transformed by her hand into a gracious home with frequent balls and formal dinners.

Photograph courtesy of Richard A. Pierce.

nor, and a ball he and Kostlivtsov hosted in their rooms at the castle.

With all of its amenities, Sitka was far away from Europe. Zagoskin wrote:

One has to stay at Sitka for a while to appreciate the suspense of nearly 1,000 men who are waiting for the arrival of the Okhotsk boat on which, once a year, official papers, newspapers, and letters arrive from Europe at the American colonies.[10]

Although Sitka had many more buildings and offered more cultural diversions than other Russian posts in Alaska, the community was a company town. All of the buildings were company property. The predominant interest of the Russians in Alaska was the fur trade. When that economic activity ceased to be profitable—along with development of the fur trade in Siberia's Amur River valley and the outcome of the Crimean War—the tsar opted not to renew the company's imperial charter for a third time and to sell the territory. The company's board of directors voted to endorse the sale, with the provision that the North American holdings not be sold to Great Britain. Negotiations with the United States, suggested in the 1850s, resumed in the mid-

1860s following the American Civil War. Representatives of the two governments drafted the treaty in March 1867, and it was ratified over the next several months. Russia sold its North American holdings to the United States for $7.2 million.

On October 18, 1867, the Russians lowered their flag and the Americans raised theirs, signaling the end of an era. Although it was the capital of the District of Alaska until 1906, Sitka stagnated during the generation following the sale. Most of the Russian buildings, constructed predominantly of wood, deteriorated, burned, or were destroyed. The governor's house burned in 1894. A warehouse at the foot of Lincoln Street that became the Sitka Trading Company was torn down in the 1920s. A road was put through the Russian cemetery. The wooden Cathedral of St. Michael the Archangel survived until 1966, when it burned.

Only two Russian buildings remain standing in Sitka today, the Bishop's House and Building No. 29 (Tilson Building). The former has been restored by the National Park Service. The second floor re-creates Bishop Innocent's surroundings in 1853, and the first floor has museum exhibits about Russian Alaska. A reconstruction of St. Michael's Cathedral stands on the site of the one that burned in 1966. The residents of Sitka saved all but one of the church's icons. The Sitka Historical Society maintains several Russian-American exhibits. The Alaska Division of Parks and Outdoor Recreation has interpretive signs at the Old Sitka site (the 1799 post site) and Castle Hill, and the National Park Service has interpretive information at the Tlingits' Indian River fort site. All interpret the Russians in North America, and particularly life at its colonial capital, Sitka.

Joan M. Antonson is State Historian, Office of History and Archaeology, Alaska Division of Parks and Outdoor Recreation, State of Alaska.

For Further Reading

Colonial Russian America: Kyrill T. Khlebnikov's Reports, 1817-1832. Trans. Basil Dmytryshyn and E. A. P. Crownhart-Vaughan. Portland: Oregon Historical Society, 1976.

Golovin, Pavel N. *The End of Russian America. Captain P. N. Golovin's Last Report, 1862.* Trans. Basil Dmytryshyn and E. A. P. Crownhart-Vaughan. Portland: Oregon Historical Society, 1979.

_____. *Civil and Savage Encounters: The Worldly Travel Letters of an Imperial Russian Naval Officer 1860-1861.* Ed. Basil Dmytryshyn and E. A. P. Crownhart-Vaughan. Portland: Oregon Historical Society, 1983.

Lieutenant Zagoskin's Travels in Russian America, 1842-1844. Ed. Henry N. Michael. Toronto: Arctic Institute of North America, 1967.

Litke, Frederic. *A Voyage Round the World 1826-1829.* Ed. R. A. Pierce. Kingston, Ontario: Limestone Press, 1987.

Okladnikova, E. A. "Science and Education in Russian America." *Russia's American Colony.* Ed. S. Frederick Starr. Durham, North Carolina: Duke University Press, 1987.

Pierce, Richard A. "Reconstructing 'Baranov's Castle.'" *Alaska History* 4, no. 1 (Spring 1989), p. 33.

Senkevitch, Anatole, Jr. "The Early Architecture and Settlements of Russian America." *Russia's American Colony.* Ed. S. Frederick Starr. Durham, North Carolina: Duke University Press, 1987, pp. 147-195.

Tikhmenev, P. A. *A History of the Russian-American Company.* Ed. and trans. R. A. Pierce and A. S. Donnelly. Seattle: University of Washington Press, 1978.

Notes

1. Georg H. von Langsdorf, *Voyage and Travels in Various Parts of the World during the Years 1803-06,* 2 vols. (London, 1814), II, p. 87.

2. Anatole Senkevitch, Jr., "The Early Architecture and Settlements of Russian America," *Russia's American Colony,* ed. S. Frederick Starr (Durham, North Carolina: Duke University Press, 1987), p. 182.

3. P. A. Tikhmenev, *A History of the Russian-American Company,* ed. and trans. R. A. Pierce and A. S. Donnelly (Seattle: University of Washington Press, 1978).

4. *Colonial Russian America, Kyrill T. Khlebnikov's Reports, 1817-1832,* trans. Basil Dmytryshyn and E. A. P. Crownhart-Vaughan (Portland: Oregon Historical Society, 1976), p. 18.

5. *Lieutenant Zagoskin's Travels in Russian America, 1842-1844,* ed. Henry N. Michael (Toronto: Arctic Institute of North America, 1967), pp. 68-69.

6. Ibid., p. 70.

7. *The End of Russian America: Captain P. N. Golovin's Last Report, 1862,* trans. Basil Dmytryshyn and E. A. P. Crownhart-Vaughan (Portland: Oregon Historical Society, 1979), p. 50.

8. Ibid., p. 59.

9. Pavel N. Golovin, *Civil and Savage Encounters: The Worldly Travel Letters of an Imperial Russian Navy Officer, 1860-1861,* trans. Basil Dmytryshyn and E. A. P. Crownhart-Vaughan (Portland: Oregon Historical Society, 1983), p. 81.

10. Zagoskin, *Travels,* p. 67.

RUSSIANS AND NATIVE AMERICANS

Perspectives *on* Aleut Culture Change *during the* Russian Period

by Douglas W. Veltre

Of all Alaska Native peoples, Aleuts[1] have the distinction of experiencing the longest and harshest history of contact with non-Natives, beginning with the Russian *promyshlenniki,* or fur hunters. This paper examines some of the consequences of Russian expansion into the Aleutian Islands to the people of that region, and it encourages a broader, more culturally balanced view of Russian-Aleut interaction than has often been afforded this topic.

For the most part, discussion of the Russian contact period in the Aleutian Islands, and in Alaska as a whole, has been historical: the focus has been on significant events, places, and individuals. For example, the effects on Aleuts of Russian contact have largely been characterized in terms such as the number of Aleuts who died from disease, accidents, and atrocities; the number of foreign ships plying Aleutian waters and the value of their cargoes; the famous and infamous Russian personalities responsible for various deeds; the Aleuts who emerged as notable leaders, skilled artisans, or clergy; and the introduction of new material goods such as metal and beads, and of Western foodstuffs such as cattle, flour, and tea. Few studies of the contact period in the Aleutians, however, have asked fundamental anthropological questions about how Aleut culture *as a whole* actually responded to the pressures brought upon it during the Russian years.

This essay proceeds from the basic and not at all revolutionary assumption that Aleut culture, like that of most precontact indigenous societies, was in a state of long-term balance, or equilibrium, with its natural and cultural environment. It also assumes that Aleut culture was a complex entity operating in a systemic manner: its various components, however we may wish to define them, functioned interdependently to maintain cultural adaptation, with change in any one component likely affecting to some degree other components of the cultural system. We should likewise assume that Aleut culture change during the Russian era was a complex phenomenon, understandable not in simple historical terms, but only through analysis of all major aspects of Aleut society and the Russian presence.

Cultural and Historical Overview

Upon its "rediscovery" by Russia in the middle 1700s, Alaska was peopled by perhaps seventy-five thousand Native inhabitants living in some nineteen major linguistic and cultural groups. They were the descendants of the original discoverers of the North American continent, some of whom traveled across the Bering Land Bridge fifteen millennia ago during the last ice age.

The sole occupants of the Aleutian Islands, an archipelago of two hundred volcanic islands stretching over a thousand miles from the tip of the Alaska Peninsula westward toward Kamchatka, were the Aleut people. Culturally, biologically, and linguistically

Most areas of Aleut life changed drastically during the Russian period. Aleut population decline was the single most drastic change because of its direct relationship to virtually all facets of culture.

distinct from the neighboring Eskimos to the east on the Alaska Peninsula and the coast of the mainland, Aleuts had lived in the islands for between four thousand and nine thousand years.

Aleuts were superbly adapted to their marine environment. The diversity and

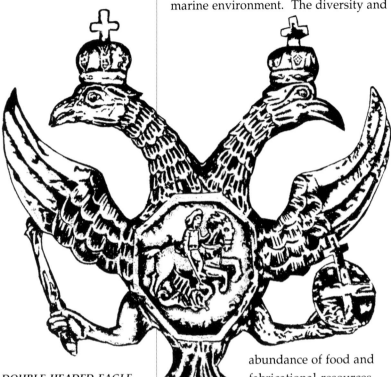

DOUBLE-HEADED-EAGLE imperial crest. One of only two such crests to survive, this superb piece belonged for many years to a Tlingit family. Family tradition held that the crest had been given to a chief by Governor Baranov after the establishment of Sitka, both as a gesture of amity and of Russian dominance. The Tlingits themselves prized the crest, viewing it as a capture of the Russian totemic symbol. Russian explorers were given a number of such crests to display prominently as evidence of Russian authority over the land. Only this one has survived in Alaska, the other having been found in Oregon, probably after entering the Northwest coast trade routes.

Alaska State Museum, Juneau.

abundance of food and fabricational resources, combined with the ability of almost all members of an Aleut community to contribute to their families' food supplies, resulted in a large and dense population occupying most habitable portions of the coastline.

Food resources fell into five broad groups: marine animals (including harbor seals, sea lions, sea otters, fur seals, and whales), marine invertebrates (including sea urchins, mussels, clams, and octopus), eggs and birds (such as murres, cormorants, ducks, and geese), fish (including ocean species like cod and halibut and anadromous species such as Dolly Varden and several species of salmon), and plant foods (such as crowberries, wild celery, and wild rice). Fabricational materials included such things as driftwood, stone,

and grasses, as well as the bones, teeth, skins, and other parts of the animals used for food.

Aleut settlements consisted of both large, relatively stable villages and small seasonal subsistence camps. Houses were semisubterranean *barabaras* constructed of stones, driftwood, and whalebone, and were occupied by several families, likely linked by ties of matrilineal kinship.

Traditional ideology included fundamental beliefs in the existence of spirits for humans, animals, and inanimate objects. Success in hunting or warfare, for example, depended on proper ritual observances. Shamans functioned as intermediaries between the everyday and spirit worlds, and their services were engaged to ensure successful hunting, cure the sick, bring bad luck to enemies, and so on.

To briefly summarize the well-known story: Russian contact began in 1741 with the voyages of Bering and Chirikov. Within the next three decades, dozens of fur-hunting expeditions had been made in the Aleutians, the *promyshlenniki* pushing eastward in their pursuit of the sometimes elusive, and ever-fewer, sea otters. These voyages were usually of several years' duration. The Russian hunters collected *iasak*, or tribute, from the Aleuts, usually in the form of sea otter skins, and, to insure good relations with the Natives, the *promyshlenniki* took hostages from among the Aleuts.

The *promyshlenniki* quickly learned that to further their own economic pursuits they needed the knowledge and skill of the Aleut hunters. Aleut men, expert at hunting sea mammals of all types, were soon forced to turn a large portion of their energies to procuring sea otters for the various independent fur-trading companies. Later they performed compulsory labor for the monopolistic Russian-American Company.

By 1799, the Russian-American

Company had monopolistic rights to all hunting activities north of 50° north latitude. As with earlier fur-hunting enterprises, the Russian-American Company's success was based on the availability of Aleut labor (and other indigenous labor elsewhere in Alaska). There was a chronic shortage of Russians to undertake hunting pursuits (there were usually fewer than six hundred Russians in the whole of Alaska at any one time), but there were a number of Aleuts who knew how to hunt. A Russian naval officer observed in 1820:

If the [Russian-American] company should somehow lose the Aleuts, then it will completely forfeit the hunting of sea animals, because not one Russian knows how to hunt the animals, and none of our settlers has learned how in all the time that the company has had its possessions here.[2]

Such exploitation of Aleut labor was repeated in the Pribilof Islands, which were uninhabited when discovered by the Russians in 1786. The vast fur seal herds that summered on the Pribilofs were a new source of wealth, since these animals could more easily be killed on land than at sea, and by the early 1800s the Russians took some Aleuts from their home islands in the Aleutians and made them permanent residents of St. George and St. Paul. To a greater extent than Alaska Natives elsewhere, they were virtual slaves of the Russian-American Company, their lives controlled by the Russian managers.

The Aleut Response to Contact

Most areas of Aleut life changed drastically during the Russian period. Aleut population decline was the single most significant change because of its direct relationship to virtually all facets of culture. Important as are the causes and size of loss, this chapter focuses on the cultural effects of the loss, along with the related changes that occurred in patterns of settlement.

While the Aleut population of the later Russian period is documented to have been approximately two thousand, the population at initial contact has been much more difficult to determine. Because accurate Russian censuses were not taken until substantial loss of life had occurred, there is uncertainty over the actual contact population. Estimates have

INHABITANTS of Unalaska with Their Canoes, *an engraving by Freidrich H. von Kittlitz, 1828. The Aleuts were skillful hunters in their lithe but sturdy bidarkas, and much admired by the Russians, who impressed them into service to gain the benefit of this adaptation to marine life.*

From the F. P. Litke Atlas, *Alaska and Polar Regions Dept., Elmer E. Rasmuson Library, University of Alaska, Fairbanks.*

ranged widely, though most have favored figures close to the range of twelve to fifteen thousand.[3] Therefore, it appears that approximately 80 percent of the Aleut population was lost during the first half of the Russian period (1741 to about 1800).

Concomitant with this severe population loss was population resettlement. Villages became fewer in number, frequently consolidating with others. Especially in the central and western Aleutians, entire islands and island groups became deserted. Whole Aleut villages (or remnants thereof) and occasionally entire island populations were sometimes resettled at the discretion of the Russians. By the end of the Russian period, population loss and resettlement had left only a handful of Aleut villages in existence.

Household settlement patterns changed as well during the Russian period. From the precontact multifamily *barabara,* a semisubterranean structure built with driftwood, stones, and whalebone and covered—except for the entryway in the roof—with a layer of grassy sod, houses

took on a variety of forms following contact. Some were quite large, measuring at times over one hundred feet in length and having attached rooms along their sides. Others were smaller and housed fewer people. By the 1820s, some Aleut houses were built mostly above ground and had windows, side entries, interior metal stoves, and other modern trappings.

What do these things say, then, about Aleut culture change? They suggest that the precise magnitude and, to a lesser extent, the relative importance of the various causes of the population loss are not especially significant. Few reliable quantitative data exist about the relative importance of Russian-Aleut conflicts, Russian atrocities, the devastating effects of introduced diseases, and increased accidental death rates.[4] What is important is that Aleuts suffered a massive population loss and a Russian presence they could only have loathed. It is immaterial that there were some well-meaning, kind Russian fur hunters; what is important is that Aleut culture was devastated.

INTERIOR OF a House in Unalaska, *engraving by John Webber, 1778. Webber was expedition artist with Captain James Cook, the English explorer whose third voyage, 1776-79, brought him into contact with Russians in the Aleutians. The Aleuts developed housing that was admirably suited to the treeless islands.*

Anchorage Museum of History and Art.

Furthermore, the possible cultural implications of population loss go beyond the obvious, though most have not been investigated for the Aleut situation. For example, not only were villages and households moved, but so too were individuals. Able-bodied men were often away from home for long periods of time, many of them compelled to pursue the ever-decreasing sea otters or to labor at other tasks. If mostly males are lost (either through death or labor away from home), how is the subsistence economy affected? The subsistence lifestyle of those left at home—mainly women, children, and elderly—likely shifted to resources obtainable without their male hunters present, such as fish, marine invertebrates, eggs, and imported Russian foodstuffs.

One example of research into these kinds of questions is that of Christy G. Turner II, who conducted ethnohistoric and archaeological work on Akun Island, in the eastern Aleutians. He states that "...contact appears to have initiated a wide number of disadvantageous changes [in Aleut culture] that resulted on the whole in a higher expenditure of energy by the Aleuts to gain the same ends, namely reproduction and eating." Turner also adds the following:

> Two seemingly very significant changes that we feel came about were a disruption of the seasonally sensitive Aleut birth cycle and a severe reduction in summer whale and other migratory sea mammal hunting.... Taking the Aleut males away [to hunt for the Russians] not only had a limiting effect on the conception rate during the early summer, it also clearly reduced the amount of sea mammal meat, blubber, and fabricational bone, skin, and gut that would be normally procured during the summer months....[5]

In a similar manner, Leda C. Milan has provided an excellent analysis of the changes that occurred in Aleut health and disease from precontact to modern times, including the roles of population loss and Russian oppression. The Russian period, she states,

> ...was not a period of "selective assimilation" of new traits, but one of destruction and exploitation and intense disruption of Aleut cultural growth accompanied by an overwhelming loss of human life.

In terms of health and disease, Milan claims:

> What murders and atrocities did not accomplish during the first 80 years of Russian reign, disease accomplished through the rest of Russian rule. Syphilis, tuberculosis, influenza, pneumonia, measles, smallpox, scurvy, all made their appearance and reached immense proportions.[6]

Traditional Aleut social organization—including their kinship system, marriage and family structure, and leadership patterns—also changed under Russian

A TLINGIT button blanket, from Wrangell, late nineteenth century. The bifurcated head of this totemic eagle design suggests Russian influence, a borrowing of the double-headed-eagle imperial crest. Rather than being purely decorative, the use of an enemy's crest suggested power, even defeat, of the enemy.

Denver Art Museum.

dominance. The traditional kinship and leadership patterns yielded to forms instituted by the Russians, further eroding the fabric of Aleut society. Multiple-spouse marriages and household-based leadership, for example, were replaced by monogamous, church-sanctioned marriages and a formalized system of village chiefs. When Russian managers used local village leaders to recruit laborers, those leaders and their families were exempt from compulsory work. It is likely that precontact distinctions based on leadership, rank, and wealth were accentuated, with Aleut leaders of the Russian period acting more and more as middlemen, or brokers, between the two cultures. Ivan Pan'kov (whose role in Aleut literacy is discussed below), for example, was both an Aleut chief *and* a representative of the Russian-American Company.

Many other questions may be asked relating to population loss and resettlement. To what extent did diseases preclude people from participating in subsistence pursuits, thus placing additional (and perhaps impossible) burdens on healthy members of a community? Did the old and infirm, possibly including the tradition-bearing elders of a community, suffer higher mortality from stress or disease, thereby resulting in disproportionate loss of certain cultural knowledge? Did population resettlement bring together people from previously unallied Aleut communities? Were resettled Aleut hunters able to provide as well for their families in unfamiliar waters? How did the emotional trauma of those who survived, each of whom must have personally experienced the loss of several friends and family members, affect the cultural vitality of Aleuts as a whole?

In the late 1790s, Russian Orthodoxy became a prominent feature in the lives of Aleuts and Eskimos of southwestern Alaska with the arrival of the first missionaries and the eventual establishment of churches in most communities and traveling priests to serve them. The Russian Orthodox church, a forceful agent of change for the Natives of Alaska, brought about some benefits, including schooling and literacy for limited numbers of Aleuts, Koniags, and Tlingits. Eventually, the church replaced most, if not all, of the precontact religious foundations of the Native cultures, although the Russian Orthodox church, specifically, never gained as firm a foundation among the Tlingits as later missionary efforts by other denominations. While some authors have attempted to explain Aleut acceptance of Russian Orthodoxy by noting similarities between it and aspects of traditional Aleut spiritualism,[7] it seems more reasonable to view the spread of Orthodoxy from the perspective of the acceptance of a new religious order by

TLINGIT BATTLE helmet worn at the Battle of Sitka in 1802, when the Tlingits destroyed the first Russian base on Sitka (now Baranof) Island. The Tlingits never lost their essential hostility to the Russians, and an uneasy truce existed throughout Russia's tenure in southeastern Alaska.

John H. Hauberg Collection, Seattle.

decimated, demoralized, exploited, and powerless Native peoples yielding to the social and economic pressures of the dominant Russian presence.

The Two Russian Eras

By the end of the 1700s, Aleuts were no longer in control of their own lives. Aleuts' precontact adaptive mechanisms for coping with changing conditions were wholly inadequate for handling the kind and magnitude of changes forced upon them by the Russian fur hunters. Imposed new social forms, religious institutions, and material culture had changed nearly the entire fabric of Aleut life. However, because the logistics and costs of foreign supply of foodstuffs to the Aleutians were prohibitive, the necessity of turning to the sea for the bulk of subsistence resources continued. To this day, the subsistence economy, especially in terms of the kinds of foods and resources utilized, the importance of cooperation and sharing, and the use of seasonal subsistence camps, remains the Aleuts' strongest tie to their pre-Russian past.

In explaining processes of culture change, it is of little value to focus extensively on famous or infamous personalities, on the worst atrocities, or on those events that happened to get recorded in historical accounts. This approach, which can become merely anecdotal, focuses on things that are only a small part of the much larger, and mostly unwritten, history of what happened during the contact period in the Aleutians. Knowing that one particular Aleut was educated in Russia and became a skilled craftsman, for example, is but one small step in our effort to understand how Aleuts lived and adapted day to day during the Russian period.

More attention must be placed on the years from 1741 to about 1800, roughly the first half of the Russian era. That was the period during which Aleuts experienced their greatest population and cultural

losses, most settlements were relocated, the pattern of forced labor of Aleuts became set, and Russian Orthodoxy began to take hold.

The overemphasis by some writers on the events of the second half of the Russian period, however, has served to de-emphasize that much more significant earlier period. The earlier years of Russian contact are too frequently glossed over in order to focus on the "achievements" of the Russian-American Company and the Russian Orthodox church in areas of education, religion, and literacy. Following is an example of this perspective, from a work that ignores the magnitude of Aleut population loss: "The story of the evolution of the Aleut culture, beginning with Vitus Bering's first visit in 1741, ...is an exciting and inspiring one."[8]

MAN AND WOMAN of Unalaska, *engraving by W. Alexander from a sketch of Martin Sauer, secretary to Joseph Billings of the Billings-Sarychev expedition of 1790-92.*

From M. Sauer's An Account of a Geographical and Astronomical Expedition to the Northern Parts of Russia *(London, 1802). Washington State Historical Society, Tacoma.*

In a similar fashion, a series of publications and papers over the last twelve years have suggested that Aleuts became a literate people in the early 1800s as a result of the accomplishments of notable Aleut leaders working with Russian Orthodox priests. Such claims are obviously appealing, in part because they point to an apparently positive outcome of an often-described bleak period in Aleut history, and in part because the Russian Orthodox church is a vital feature of Aleut identity today, evoking ready praise for its past accomplishments.

The essence of the claim for literacy lies in the efforts of Father Ioann Veniaminov, priest in Unalaska from 1824 to 1834, to publish the church liturgy in the Aleut language. Assisting him was a remarkable Aleut man, Ivan Pan'kov, chief of Tigalda Island, in the eastern Aleutian Islands. Together, these men produced Aleut-language versions of scripture and liturgy. The following statement by Lydia Black summarizes her view of this period:

Soon after Russian entry into the Aleut area, the Aleuts became converted to Orthodox Christianity. The Orthodox Church became a vehicle for maintenance of group identity and group solidarity, replacing the aboriginal religion. Less well known is the fact that literacy was a concomitant introduction: Aleuts became literate in their own language.[9]

Although valid, claims of Aleut literacy have not been placed in proper cultural and historical context, including the devastation of Aleut population and traditional culture in the 1700s. The first Aleut texts were published ninety-nine years after the first Russians came to the Aleutian Islands. Even the opportunity for literacy was not achieved until quite *late* in the Russian period.

A related difficulty is that scholars who assert "Aleut literacy" nowhere demonstrate that ordinary Aleuts—the bulk of the Aleut population, many living in villages remote from the commercial and religious centers of Unalaska and the Pribilofs—could actually read and write the Aleut (or Russian) language. Yet, popular ability to read and write is the essence of literacy, not whether someone translated church texts into Aleut.

The ways of life of all Alaska Natives who came into contact with Russians were unavoidably and, in most cases, purposefully changed, but nowhere was this more extreme than for the Aleuts of the Aleutian Islands. The maintenance of precontact Aleut cultural traditions was at best a secondary consideration both to the Russian fur hunters, whose primary purpose in coming to Alaska was to exploit the natural and human resources of the region, and to the clergy of the Russian Orthodox church, whose fundamental goal was to instill a new religion.

Both the first and second halves of the Russian period are crucial to understanding the changes that occurred in Aleut culture and, along with knowledge of the American period, to a full appreciation of Aleuts today. However, just as the events of the period from 1741 to 1800 cannot properly be understood without knowledge of the immediate precontact Aleut

CAPTAIN'S HARBOR, Unalaska Island, with the Aleut Village of Illiliuk, *an engraving by Luka Voronin, ca. 1790-91. The Aleuts' semi-subterranean housing was adopted by the Russians until wood could be imported from Kamchatka or Sitka. The ship in the background is the* Slava Rossii (Glory of Russia), *under command of Gavriil Sarychev.*

From Gavriil Sarychev's Atlas, Alaska and Polar Regions Dept., Elmer E. Rasmuson Library, University of Alaska, Fairbanks.

culture, neither can the Russian period from 1800 to 1867 be understood without a more complete appreciation of the devastation wrought upon Aleut culture in the eighteenth century.

Douglas W. Veltre is Professor of Anthropology, University of Alaska, Anchorage.

For Further Reading

Black, Lydia T. "Ivan Pan'kov—An Architect of Aleut Literacy." _Arctic Anthropology_ 14, no. 1 (1977), pp. 94-107.

Dauenhauer, Richard. _The Spiritual Epiphany of Aleut._ Anchorage: Alaska Native Foundation, Center for Equality of Opportunity in Schooling, 1978.

Fedorova, Svetlana G. _The Russian Population in Alaska and California, Late 18th Century - 1867._ Trans. and ed. Richard Pierce and Alton Donnelly. Kingston, Ontario: Limestone Press, 1973.

Gibson, James R. _Imperial Russia in Frontier America._ New York: Oxford University Press, 1976.

Lantis, Margaret. "The Aleut Social System, 1750-1810, from Early Historical Sources." _Ethnohistory in Southwestern Alaska and the Southern Yukon: Method and Content._ Lexington: University of Kentucky Press, 1970.

_____. "Aleut." _Handbook of North American Indians_, vol. 5. Washington, D.C.: Smithsonian Institution, 1984, pp. 161-184.

Laughlin, William S. _Aleuts: Survivors of the Bering Land Bridge._ New York: Holt, Rinehart and Winston, 1980.

Makarova, R. V. _Russians on the Pacific, 1743-1799._ Trans. and ed. Richard Pierce and Alton Donnelly. Kingston, Ontario: Limestone Press, 1975.

Milan, Leda C. "Ethnohistory of Disease and Medical Care among the Aleut." _Anthropological Papers of the University of Alaska_ 16, no. 2 (1974), pp. 15-20.

Oleksa, Michael. _Alaska Missionary Spirituality._ New York: Paulist Press, 1987.

Tikhmenev, P. A. _A History of the Russian-American Company._ Trans. and ed. Richard Pierce and Alton Donnelly. 1861-63; Seattle: University of Washington Press, 1978.

Turner, Christy G., II. "Russian Influence on Aleut Ecology, Culture, and Physical Anthropology." _National Geographic Society Research Reports_ 13 (1981), pp. 623-633.

Veltre, Douglas W. and Mary J. Veltre. _A Preliminary Baseline Study of Subsistence Resource Utilization in the Pribilof Islands, Alaska._ Technical Paper, No. 27. Juneau: Alaska Department of Fish and Game, Division of Subsistence, 1981.

_____. _Resource Utilization in Unalaska, Aleutian Islands, Alaska._ Technical Paper, No. 58. Juneau: Alaska Department of Fish and Game, Division of Subsistence, 1982.

_____. _Resource Utilization in Atka, Aleutian Islands, Alaska._ Technical Paper, No. 88. Juneau: Alaska Department of Fish and Game, Division of Subsistence, 1983.

Veniaminov, Ioann. _Notes on the Islands of the Unalashka District._ Trans. and ed. Lydia Black and R. H. Geoghegan, ed. Richard Pierce. 1840; Kingston, Ontario: Limestone Press, 1984.

Notes

1. Following contemporary anthropological and linguistic usage, in this paper "Aleut" refers to the precontact Native population of the Aleutian Islands and the western tip of the Alaska Peninsula.

2. Quoted in James R. Gibson, _Imperial Russia in Frontier America_ (New York: Oxford University Press, 1976), p. 8.

3. Margaret Lantis, "The Aleut Social System, 1750-1810, from Early Historical Sources," in _Ethnohistory in Southwestern Alaska and the Southern Yukon: Method and Content_ (Lexington: University of Kentucky Press, 1970), pp. 139-311; Lantis, "Aleut," in _Handbook of North American Indians_, vol. 5 (Washington, D.C.: Smithsonian Institution, 1984), pp. 161-184; William S. Laughlin, _Aleuts: Survivors of the Bering Land Bridge_ (New York: Holt, Rinehart and Winston, 1980), p. 15.

4. Lydia Black ("Early History," in "The Aleutians," _Alaska Geographic_ 7, no. 3, p. 105; and in Ioann Veniaminov, _Notes on the Islands of the Unalashka District_, trans. and ed. Lydia Black and R. H. Geoghegan, ed. Richard Pierce ([1840; Kingston, Ontario: Limestone Press, 1984], p. 256n) has cast doubt on the high number of Aleut deaths attributable to Russian conflict and atrocities, while Michael Oleksa, for example, ("Note," _Alaska Journal_ 10, no. 2, 1980, pp. 78-79) discusses Russian-period culture change without even a mention of the magnitude of Aleut population loss.

5. Christy G. Turner II, "Russian Influence on Aleut Ecology, Culture, and Physical Anthropology," _National Geographic Society Research Reports_ 13 (1981), pp. 629, 630.

6. Leda C. Milan, "Ethnohistory of Disease and Medical Care among the Aleut," _Anthropological Papers of the University of Alaska_ 16, 2 (1974), pp. 19, 20.

7. Richard Dauenhauer, _The Spiritual Epiphany of Aleut_ (Anchorage: Alaska Native Foundation, Center for Equality of Opportunity in Schooling, 1978), passim; Michael Oleksa, _Alaska Missionary Spirituality_ (New York: Paulist Press, 1987), pp. 3-35.

8. Ibid., p. 4.

9. Lydia T. Black, "Ivan Pan'kov—An Architect of Aleut Literacy," _Arctic Anthropology_ 14, no. 1 (1977), p. 94.

The Creoles *and* *their* Contributions *to the* Development *of* Alaska

by Archpriest Michael J. Oleksa

Of all the groups that have made significant contributions to the development of Alaskan culture and society, none have been overlooked or slandered as much as those designated officially as "Creole" in the Russian colonial censuses. Because many, if not most, "Creoles" were of mixed Native Alaskan and Siberian/Slavic ancestry, they have often been classified with the "Russians," which, especially during the Cold War era, meant that their accomplishments would be minimized or ignored. The Creoles without Russian ancestors, who were Creole by virtue of their residence in one of the major settlements and were therefore "townsmen," often retained their Native Alaskan names, and were usually dismissed as "only Natives." Often ridiculed by both Slavs and indigenous Americans, the Creoles were caught in the middle, between two worlds. But their creative response to their social and racial status resulted in many Creoles playing an important role in the exploration, mapping, economic and commercial development, evangelization, and later acculturation of Alaska.

What, then, is a Creole? Initially, the offspring of Native Alaskan women and Siberian *promyshlenniki* (frontiersmen) were granted this special classification as a way of guaranteeing them certain basic civil rights. After the establishment of the Russian-American Company, the government required the monopoly to educate and hire Creoles, in part because the tsarist regime felt it had a moral obligation to provide for the welfare of this new racially mixed category of citizens. But after 1821, all Native Alaskans who pledged their political allegiance to the tsar and became thereby "naturalized citizens" were considered "Creoles." Thus the class included two distinct genetic groups: Native Alaskans and those of mixed Slavic/Siberian-Native Alaskan parentage or ancestry. Creoles combined elements of two cultures, often spoke two languages, and later could read and write two or more, but were not necessarily biologically "mixed." To be Creole was more a matter of the spirit, a state of mind, a question of self-identity.

The First Creoles

Soon after Vitus Bering's voyages, Siberian traders and trappers ventured across the Pacific. Their letters and diaries indicate that getting rich was not their exclusive aim, though they certainly sought to obtain sea otter pelts for the lucrative China trade. These adventurers enjoyed the rigors and dangers of the expedition to the Aleutian archipelago as much as any rubles they might earn. Most voyages failed to make a profit, and one in five never returned. Those that did succeed resulted in handsome dividends for the investors and participants, who often, in gratitude to God, made substantial donations to a local Siberian parish or monastery, celebrated lavishly all winter in a port city, usually Okhotsk, and volunteered for the next trip east, back to Alaska. Some men made a dozen such voyages during the heyday of the sea otter trade, 1741 to 1784.

The Creoles... attempted to create a society in which whatever was valuable or beautiful from the ancient culture was affirmed and cultivated.

ELEVATION OF the Cross Orthodox Church, Russian Mission, on the Yukon River, 1907. The first Orthodox mission in interior Alaska was established in 1845 by a Creole, Rev. Iakov Netsvetov, of Aleut descent. Educated at the seminary in Irkutsk, Netsvetov also established the first church on Atka Island and collaborated with Rev. Ioann Veniaminov on a number of translations of Russian texts into the new Aleut orthography.

J. T. White Collection, Alaska and Polar Regions Dept., Elmer E. Rasmuson Library, University of Alaska, Fairbanks.

Expeditions of this sort characteristically remained in the Aleutians several months, some for a year or more. Each captain had trading partners with whom he regularly did business. The supposed violence and genocidal treatment of the Unangan Aleuts during this era, it seems, have been much exaggerated. The Siberians were always greatly outnumbered by local warriors, and they enjoyed little or no technological advantage over the Alaskans. Few firearms were available in eastern Siberia during this time, and as single-shot muzzle-loading muskets were the state of the art, a Slav with a gun was no greater threat than a Native with a spear or bow and arrow.

Stories of massacres have circulated for decades, and there was certainly conflict and bloodshed during these initial years of contact. However, the entire period cannot be characterized as a continual bloodbath: the depletion of the Aleut population more probably occurred during the reign of Alexander Baranov (1790-1818), especially after the government granted him virtual dictatorial powers following the incorporation of the Russian-American Company. During the earlier period of free-market capitalism,

each trading company needed to maintain cordial relations with its Native partners or risk losing its share of the fur trade. A crew might forcibly seize pelts from a particular village one time, but could hardly make a habit of piracy.

During these first four decades of contact, individual frontiersmen "defected" to Alaska, finding local brides and moving into their *barabaras*.[1] This is evidenced by the founding of several Orthodox prayer chapels in the Aleutians during this time. The Siberians taught their religion to their spouses and children, baptizing them themselves in the absence of ordained clergy. The first generation of Creoles, though not yet recognized as such by any legal sanction, were already young adults by the time Grigorii Shelikhov founded the first permanent Russian settlement in Alaska at Three Saints Bay on Kodiak Island in August 1784.

From Shelikhov's account, it is known that bilingual Native Alaskans were available to serve as translators for the Russian speakers and their Kodiak (Sugpiaq/Alutiiq) counterparts. Seven years after Shelikhov's arrival, the Billings Expedition, circumnavigating the globe, visited the Three Saints Bay village, and the chaplain aboard ship, Father Sivtsov, was kept busy solemnizing marriages and baptizing babies and young children. Thus, by 1800, there was a growing Creole population, though not yet designated as such, in the Aleutian Islands and on Kodiak. Within another twenty years, Creoles would be rising to positions of responsibility and leadership within the colonial administration and the Orthodox church's missions and schools.

Creole/Native Education

The recruiting and training of Creoles and Native Alaskans for service in the Russian-American Company's middle and upper management structure was the responsibility of the Orthodox mission. The original mission, which arrived at Kodiak on September 24, 1794, petitioned its headquarters in Irkutsk to organize a school there rather than send promising students to Russia. Removal from familiar settings and homeland, the monks argued, had proved detrimental to recruits in the past, and a local primary school, given sufficient support, could reach a larger constituency. In 1800, Hieromonk Gideon was sent to Kodiak precisely for the purpose of founding such a school, and within two years, nearly one hundred Aleut and Creole children were attending classes, some of which were conducted in the local (Alutiiq) language.

While Father Gideon's school was short-lived, its initial success encouraged company and church officials to continue to experiment elsewhere. Father Ioann Veniaminov (later Bishop Innocent) and, simultaneously, the first Creole priest, Father James (Iakov) Netsvetov, organized primary schools at Unalaska and Atka, respectively, in the late 1820s. Father Herman, a member of the original missionary team of 1794, conducted classes near Kodiak at the same time. During the

1840s, Veniaminov opened the "All-Colonial School" at Sitka, in the building now called Russian Bishop's House. These schools spawned a score of less known and less well supported local efforts at educating the Creole and indigenous populations throughout the colony. Through its educational efforts, therefore, the Orthodox mission played the central role in the formation of Creole/Aleut culture. The contributions and achievements of the alumni of these schools have been largely overlooked, however, for several reasons.

In past decades there has been, it seems, some reluctance to admit that Russian colonial policy could differ in any significant way from European or American attitudes toward Native Americans. From the very beginning, however, the situations were considerably different. Anglo-Saxon colonialization

A CREOLE AT SITKA, 1827, pencil sketch by Pavel Mikhailov, expedition artist aboard the Moller, which circumnavigated the world in 1826-28. This young man is in the uniform of a navigator. Creoles were obligated to serve the company for ten years if they were educated at company expense, but then were free to live where and as they chose.

Original in the State Russian Museum, Leningrad; photograph courtesy of Alaska and Polar Regions Dept., Elmer E. Rasmuson Library, University of Alaska, Fairbanks.

meant immigration of entire families and communities to the New World, while Russian (and in Canada, very often French) colonialism meant the coming of frontiersmen and adventurers without family ties or ideological commitments. French trappers and traders intermarried with Indians, producing the métis of Canada. Russian *promyshlenniki* found Aleut brides, giving rise to the first generations of Creole Alaskans. As these Alaskans of mixed ancestry married other Native Alaskans, their numbers swelled. They were joined by others, without any Slavic or Siberian ancestry, who, having attended one of the various mission schools and become literate in one or two languages, trained in a mechanical skill, a navigational science, or clerical vocation, and assumed the Creole identity. To be "Creole" came to mean that one had adopted certain Slavic-European attitudes and traits, had been trained to some extent in a Western-type school, and thereby qualified for a position in the middle or upper management of the colony. Creoles were not necessarily of mixed racial stock and did not necessarily abandon much of their heritage as Native Alaskans. They thought of themselves as having the best of two worlds, rather than as victims caught tragically between them.

The Creole Contribution

As self-confident, productive citizens of the Empire, Creoles contributed to the expansion and development of their homeland in several important fields. Creole missionaries brought literacy and Christianity to their own and to neighboring tribes, developing writing systems and undertaking the work of translation into heretofore unwritten languages. They founded schools and produced the textbooks. They operated such schools without outside support after the sale of Alaska in 1867, in some communities for as long as a century after the transfer, demonstrating their commitment to

bilingual education for a hundred years before the United States government recognized the need for it. They explored and mapped large areas of Alaska. They navigated Russian-American Company ships between the Siberian coast and Alaska, visiting California frequently with cargoes of fur and ice. They participated in around-the-world voyages, explored uncharted islands, and visited exotic and remote lands. They painted portraits and icons, became proficient musicians and artisans, and published bilingual periodicals. They ran the shops, offices, mines, and trading posts throughout Russian America. They fought the battles, maintained the forts, and packed the churches.

Creole Clergy

The Creole/Aleut attachment to the Orthodox church has religious but also historical/sociological roots. Because the church played such a pivotal role in the development of Creole/Aleut culture and society, the contributions of Creole Orthodox clergy need special recognition.

Consider Father Iakov Netsvetov, whose diaries have made available in English a full record of his forty years of heroic activity. The first resident pastor at Atka, in the central Aleutians, Father Iakov was trained at the seminary in Irkutsk, Siberia, apparently at his Russian father's personal expense (since none of the Netsvetov sons seems to have owed the Russian-American Company any money or obligatory service after returning from school). He married his Russian wife while in Irkutsk and served as deacon there for two years before being assigned to Atka, where he arrived on June 15, 1829. Initially, Netsvetov set up a tent chapel, but began construction of a church building as soon as he had unpacked his belongings and settled into his house. It was at times impossible to conduct services in the tent because of the legendary winds that sweep the archipelago.

Netsvetov's district included Amchitka Island, where about fifty "free" Aleuts, not in the employ of the company, maintained their traditional way of life, trading their furs with a company agent; and Attu, where about 120 Aleuts, all baptized by 1830 when Netsvetov visited, were governed by their traditional chief. Besides these scattered communities, Father Iakov was obliged to visit Bering Island, where seventy-five Russians, Creoles, and a few Aleuts hunted and trapped fur-bearing animals for the company, and the Kurile Islands, just north of Japan. It was always a great relief to complete one circuit of such a far-flung "empire."

In November 1830, the chapel at Atka was consecrated. That year Netsvetov recorded thirty-two births, eleven weddings, and twenty-four deaths at Atka and Amlia, and a total of nine births, two hundred chrismations (confirmations of those who had been previously baptized by laymen), thirty marriages, and six deaths in the other communities under his pastoral care.

In early 1831 the newly appointed governor, Baron von Wrangell, entrusted Netsvetov with the task of organizing the Atka school, and assigned John Galaktionov, a Creole medical student, to assist him. Netsvetov constructed a two-room schoolhouse and began classes on October 26 with twenty Aleut and Creole boarding students. Netsvetov taught catechism, ethics, and Biblical studies twice a week, while Galaktionov served as reading instructor.

During the next decade, Netsvetov began work on his translations of the New Testament into the Atkan language. This was a very tedious and time-consuming project and Father Iakov felt increasingly isolated and alone. His wife died of cancer in March 1836, and in June of that year his house burned as well. He petitioned to be transferred elsewhere. While the bishop in Irkutsk approved, he required him to remain at his post until a

replacement could be recruited. Netsvetov waited seven more years.

Encouraged by Bishop Innocent (Veniaminov), Netsvetov applied himself to the work of compiling an alternate translation of the former's translation of the Gospel according to St. Matthew in the Atkan dialect, which differs considerably from the Unalaskan dialect in Veniaminov's published volume. It seems probable that Netsvetov also compiled the largest Atkan dictionary produced during these years. In 1841 he recorded in his daily journal the curing of a woman reputedly "possessed" at Amlia, stating that after he read some prayers (possibly exorcisms) she returned to normal. He took her with him to Atka, however, until he was convinced that she had been completely and permanently cured.

Beginning in 1842, Unangan (Aleut) was used in worship in both the Atka and Amlia churches, using translations Netsvetov had prepared. By this time the school at Atka, with the help of Ioann Ladygin and Lavrentii Salomatov, had graduated dozens of Aleut and Creole students, who were productive members of the local company management and staff, keeping the books, charting the coasts, and sailing around the world.

Explorers

After graduating from the Baltic Fleet Pilot School in Kronstadt, Afanasii Klimovskii served as interpreter for the 1818-19 exploratory expedition led by Peter Korsakovskii, which traveled along the Bering Sea coast in kayaks from Kodiak to the Kuskokwim. He also sailed with Avinov in 1821 from Cape Newenham to Norton Sound, and on to Kamchatka.

Fedor Kolmakov, an associate of Baranov's, was one of the first Russians to penetrate the Yup'ik Eskimo region and survive. In 1820 he founded a trading post at Nushagak that he named Fort Alexander, in honor of the ruling tsar. It was here that Veniaminov encountered his first Eskimo converts, baptizing them in the river, which became, he reported, "a new Jordan for them." Kolmakov continued this process, baptizing others who came to him for instruction and this sacrament. Later, Governor von Wrangell permitted him to establish another post, this time on the Kuskokwim River. He named it for himself in 1832. Having married a local Native woman, Kolmakov fathered several Creole sons, who grew up on the Alaskan frontier and became thoroughly familiar with its geography and inhabitants.

Semen Lukin, educated at Kodiak, was assigned to assist Kolmakov at his Kuskokwim trading post, which he managed after the founder's death in 1840. Lt. Lavrentii Zagoskin visited Lukin's operation there and left a very positive account of his visit at Kolmakovsky Redoubt. Lukin himself explored the territory on his various trading expeditions, and his son Ivan traveled the length of the Yukon, at one time being sent in disguise to Fort Yukon to spy on the British there in 1863, and continuing upstream all the way to Dawson before heading home. Lukin's other Creole son, Constantine,

Netsvetov's primary assistant and friend during his twenty-year sojourn in the Yukon-Kuskokwim Delta (1844-63), saved the missionary and the entire settlement from starvation on at least one occasion.

Seamen

Dozens of Creoles and Aleuts were trained to serve aboard company ships as navigators, officers, and crewmen, and as craftsmen and merchants in the towns. The foundries, shops, shipyards, and mines of the colony were manned by Creoles. Creole musicians performed at the governor's mansion in Sitka. Creoles served the religious needs of their own people and brought Christianity to neighboring tribes. By 1860, there were schools in all the larger settlements offering classes in the "four R's"—reading, 'riting, 'rithmetic, and religion—conducted in the local Native language and in Russian as well.

The Netsvetov family produced an "independent" sea captain, Iakov's brother Anton. Another remarkable graduate of the Kronstadt academy, the Creole Ilarion Archimandritov, devoted much of his life to sailing company ships between St. Michael, on the Bering Sea coast, and Sitka, and mapping most of south-central Alaska's rugged coastline.

Perhaps the most remarkable of the Creole seamen was Alexander Kashevarov. Born in Kodiak in 1809, this Creole son of the local schoolteacher and his Kodiak Alutiiq wife probably grew up bilingual and became biliterate. After graduating from the Kronstadt naval academy at the age of nineteen, he returned to Alaska via the Cape of Good Hope, mapping some of the Marshall Islands in May 1828. His brilliant career in the service of Russian America continued in 1831 with a voyage that touched at Copenhagen, England, Brazil, Australia, the Gilbert and Marshall islands, Petropavlovsk, on the Siberian coast, and Sitka. Kashevarov's name translates as

Vasi
accurat
Unalas
him, "I
two or
that pe
coverii
expres
Krii
The fa
closely
script
the icc
Unang
Pan'ke
Georg
the di
in his
ments
and se
transf
its life
Aleut
Kriuk
dral c
Unala

"Cook," and the continuation of his voyage would have done the British explorer Captain James Cook honor: January 1833 in San Francisco, then to Rio via Cape Horn, Copenhagen again, and St. Petersburg in September 1833.

Five years later, in July 1838, Kashevarov was sent to the Arctic coast of Alaska to map the area. Aboard the brig *Polifem,* with a crew of thirteen Russians and Creoles and ten Aleuts, and accompanied by another ship under the command of Creole Nicolai Chernov, he sailed to Cape Lisburne, where they transferred to a large skin boat propelled by twenty-one oarsmen. They paddled along the shore, mapping the coast as they went, until ice made it impossible to continue. They then got into even smaller, three-man bidarkas and proceeded beyond Point Barrow. The Inupiaq Eskimo residents gathered twenty kayaks there to oppose the intruders, and Kashevarov decided not to risk battle with them. He returned to his ship in Kotzebue Sound and sailed back to Sitka.

For the next twenty years, Alexander Kashevarov served the company in various capacities. He sailed the *Aleut* between Siberia and Kodiak, and by 1840 was first mate on the *Okhotsk,* surveying the Asian coastline. In 1850 some of his maps, together with Archimandritov's, were published in Tebenkov's *Atlas of the Eastern Ocean.* The same year, Kashevarov was promoted to lieutenant captain and appointed commander of the port of Ayan, on the Siberian coast. At the end of the decade he retired to St. Petersburg, a brigadier general in the military service, a respected member of the nobility with a distinguished and colorful career of service to his country. During the continuing debate about the future of Alaska, he published several articles opposing the renewal of the Russian-American Company charter. The board of directors, of course, tried to present the growth of their corporation in the most positive light, but Kashevarov contradicted them, writing:

Are we who were born in Russian America really supposed to consider forever the best interests of the Russian-American Company, as we have been taught from our earliest years, and to smother within

***ORTHODOX CHURCH** at Attu on the western tip of the Aleutian Islands, ca. 1900. Built of driftwood and sod, the church illustrates the adaptation of Russian tradition to the treeless terrain of the islands.*

Collections of the Alaska State Library.

A CA
the la
Islan
Russi
1847.
alpha
Nati
orde
with
teac
high
Russ
by th

Alexai
State I

these manuscripts was published: Salomatov's Gospel according to St. Mark appeared in Norwegian linguist Knut Bergsland's 1959 orthography.

Father Andrei Lodochnikov translated Orthodox prayers and hymns into Unangan for a booklet the Diocese of Alaska printed in 1898. This publication served as a model for other collections of Orthodox prayers and hymns in Yup'ik Eskimo and Tlingit during the next ten years. The Aleut people collected the money to finance the cost of printing these and other books in their own language.

On Kodiak Island and in Prince William Sound Creoles perpetuated this cultural and religious tradition for over a century after the sale of Alaska. The Alutiiq-speaking population continued to translate Orthodox hymns and prayers, but these were never compiled or published. Rather, following a much more traditional pattern, these circulated orally, with translations passing from one village to another through traveling readers and singers. Many Chugach Alutiiq, despite the relatively great difference between their dialect and Kodiak's, became familiar with translations developed on the island and faithfully preserved them.

Tikhon Sheratine completed studies at the Orthodox seminary in San Francisco early in this century and returned to Afognak, where he served as choir leader and reader for many years. His nephew, Sergei, continued his uncle's work for the next fifty years at Afognak and later Port Lions. Innokenty Inga performed a similar function at Old Harbor, gathering the village children for "Aleut" or "Russian" school in the church after the end of classes at the public "American" school each weekday. This uniquely Alutiiq tradition was also especially vital in Perryville and English Bay, on the mainland. The fact that none of this translation or educational work was published does

not minimize its importance. Certainly well into the 1960s, Alutiiq children were still attending classes in Slavonic and Alutiiq. The church bell summoned them to reading lessons in the Cyrillic alphabet, and parents insisted that their children attend. Vladimir Melovedoff at Kaguyak and later Akhiok; Father Nicolai Moonin, and later his sons, at English Bay; Emil Kosbruck at Perryville, all worked to preserve this heritage in their communities long before federal or state funds were available to support such efforts.

Nikolski, on Umnak Island, also became a center for the Unangan literary tradition with Afenogin Ermelov, a very talented writer who composed secular as well as religious articles. In 1932 the *Alaskan Sportsman* monthly magazine printed some of Ermelov's stories. His journal, in Unangan Aleut, was copied by the local schoolteacher and linguist Jay Ransom, and survives today.

Father Gregory Kochergin, originally from Nikolski, translated and composed texts in Russian, Aleut, and Yup'ik. In fact, trilingualism was not uncommon by the beginning of this century, for Aleut culture was adaptive and flexible enough to include several languages. The Creole "mind" was, it seems, always ready to become even more inclusive. Kochergin served as storekeeper, manager, and government representative at Nushagak, and traveled throughout the region by kayak and dogsled, in the tradition of Netsvetov, until his death in 1948. By mastering English, he became, in fact, quadrilingual. As recently as 1945, an article in *American Anthropology* stated:

The ability to write their native language has injected into the family of almost every native [Aleut] an atmosphere of study and delight in the realm of the mind. Although his reading must be more or less restricted to the printed volumes of religious material, his writing may conform to anything passing through his thoughts, and what one can write will directly affect the reading of some other person.[5]

Space does not permit the examination of many other fascinating lives. My *Alaskan Missionary Spirituality* lists nearly seventy-five Native Alaskan/Creole churchmen and clergy who became the mainstay of the Orthodox church in the decades following the sale of the Alaskan colony to the United States. By continuing the mission of the Orthodox church, these local leaders served as tradition bearers for the whole Creole/Aleut culture. This volume, *Russian America: The Forgotten Frontier*, itself is a part of the Creole cultural tradition, indirectly because it rests on the scholarly contributions of such present-day Orthodox clergy as Archpriest Paul Merculief among the Unangan-speaking Aleuts and Archpriest Vasily Epchook and Priest Martin Nicolai among the Yup'ik; and directly because the author of this chapter and the tonsured reader Richard John Dauenhauer among the Tlingits represent the continuation of nearly two hundred years of cultural as well as spiritual involvement in the development of Alaskan Native society.

The Creole "state of mind," seeking to embrace the best of two worlds, survives today. In fact, the "Creole Vision," if it can be named such, seems to have particular relevance to the present generation of Alaska Natives, who, together with indigenous peoples worldwide, are seeking an identity in the modern world. The Creoles, regardless of their ancestry, attempted to create a society in which whatever was valuable or beautiful from the ancient culture was affirmed and cultivated, while each person was free to adopt whatever seemed useful or attractive from the new ways without feeling guilty or apologetic about doing so. This openness to both old and new, this "healthy adaptability," was and remains the hallmark of Aleut culture. It provides a model for others to consider today.

Archpriest Michael J. Oleksa received his doctoral degree from the Orthodox Theological Faculty of Czechoslovakia and is currently acting rector of St. Nicholas Church and instructor in Alaska Native Literature and Cross-Cultural Communication at the University of Alaska, Juneau.

For Further Reading

Afonsky, Bishop Gregory. *A History of the Orthodox Church in Alaska, 1794-1917.* Kodiak: St. Herman's Theological Seminary, 1977.

Dauenhauer, Richard John. "The Spiritual Epiphany of Aleut." *Orthodox Alaska* 8, no. 1, 1979.

The End of Russian America; Captain P. N. Golovin's Last Report, 1862. Portland: Oregon Historical Society, 1979.

Fedorova, Svetlana G. *The Russian Population in Alaska and California, Late 18th Century - 1867.* Kingston, Ontario: Limestone Press, 1973.

Ivashintsov, N. A. *Russian Round-the-World Voyages, 1803-1849.* Kingston, Ontario: Limestone Press, 1980.

Netsvetov, Iakov (Archpriest). *Journals,* 2 vol. Trans. Lydia Black. Kingston, Ontario: Limestone Press, 1980, 1984.

Oleksa, Michael J. (Archpriest). *Alaskan Missionary Spirituality.* Mahwah, N. J.: Paulist Press, 1987.

The Russian Orthodox Mission to America, 1794-1837. Ed. Richard A. Pierce, trans. Colin Bearne. Kingston, Ontario: Limestone Press, 1978.

Shelikhov, Grigorii. *A Voyage to America, 1783-1786.* Kingston, Ontario: Limestone Press, 1981.

Tikhmenev, Petr A. *A History of the Russian-American Company.* 1860-63; Seattle: University of Washington Press, 1978.

Veniaminov, Ioann. *Notes on the Islands of the Unalashka District.* Trans. and ed. Lydia Black and R. H. Geoghegan, ed. Richard A. Pierce. 1840; Kingston, Ontario: Limestone Press, 1984.

Notes

1. Svetlana G. Fedorova, *The Russian Population in Alaska and California, Late 18th Century - 1867* (Kingston, Ontario: Limestone Press, 1973), pp. 111-112.

2. A. F. Kashevarov, "Otvet g. Ianovskomu na ego zametku o materialakh dlia istorii Rossiisko-Amerikanskoi Kompanii," *Morskoi sbornik* 44 (54?), no. 7, section S mes, pp. 18-20.

3. Ioann Veniaminov, *Notes on the Islands of the Unalashka District*, trans. and ed. Lydia T. Black and R. H. Geoghegan, ed. Richard A. Pierce (1840; Kingston, Ontario: Limestone Press, 1984), p. 238.

4. Ibid., p. 164.

5. Quoted in Richard J. Dauenhauer, "The Spiritual Epiphany of Aleut," *Orthodox Alaska* 8, no. 1 (1979), p. 24.

Native Artists
of Russian America

by Lydia T. Black

...Native artists blend their own and Russian America's traditions into a new and beautiful and moving whole....

In the last stages of European transcontinental expansion, toward the end of the Age of Exploration, trained artists usually accompanied major seafaring expeditions. They were to record in as much visual detail as possible the new landscape, plants, and animals, and the way of life of the people the Europeans encountered. At that time, the artist was, so to speak, an equivalent of today's camera. Such was the work of John Webber, staff artist on Captain James Cook's third voyage (in Alaska, 1778), which is world famous. Pictorial records made on the Spanish voyages and during the voyage of the French navigator La Pérouse are also well known. Recently, the work of the Russian artists who accompanied the nineteenth-century circumnavigating voyages of the Russian navy has been brought to the attention of the American public. The magnificent drawings by Luka Voronin, in Alaska with the Billings/Sarychev expedition in 1790-92, are one such example. Masterpieces by Mikhail Tikhanov, in Alaska with Golovnin in 1818, are represented in the exhibit connected with this volume. The work of Louis Choris, with Kotzebue aboard the *Riurik,* done at about the same time, and Pavel Mikhailov, in Alaska with Frederic P. Litke and Staniukovich in 1827-28, is relatively well known.

In that day the art of pictorial representation was widely taught. An educated European was expected to be able to draw and paint. The watercolor technique was stressed. Thus, a number of Russians who came to Alaska were able to record their observations in pictorial form. Naturalists aboard the navy ships drew in minute detail flora and fauna of the region and occasionally scenes of Native life. So did the sailors of the time. Our earliest pictorial record of Alaska comes from members of the expedition commanded by Vitus Bering in 1741: Sven Waxell, Safron Khitrovo, and Georg Wilhelm Steller. Captain Mikhail Levashev, who wintered at Unalaska, in 1768-69, left a priceless record of the Aleut culture in the form of watercolors depicting their houses, clothing, and tools. Nameless navigators who served with the fur-trading companies in the eighteenth century also drew their impressions on the navigational charts. A splendid example of such a pictorial record is the chart compiled in 1775 in Okhotsk by or for Captain Timofei Shmalev. It shows a whale, a school of dolphins, pods of killer whales, sea lions, seals, and sea otters cavorting in the seas surrounding the Aleutian archipelago. Aleuts are pictured in ritual hats, drumming and dancing, their wives and daughters singing at a ritual feast. Aleut men are shown hunting sea lions and sea otters, or simply paddling their kayaks. An Aleut *baidara* (large, open boat) is shown, as is a Russian one, sporting a sail, and a Russian merchant vessel is contrasted with a navy one.

Representational Art Introduced to Aleuts

We do know that the practice of pictorial representation of everyday life spread to the Native Alaskans. There is circumstantial evidence to suggest that some Russian notions about pictorial representations were introduced to the Aleuts of the Aleutian archipelago quite early after contact. It is also certain that some Russian fur hunters taught young

Aleuts, living in their encampments as hostages or captives or sometimes as godsons, to read and write. It is also conceivable that the drawing of objects and persons was introduced at that time. Such introduction would have found fertile ground, as Aleuts had a well-established tradition of flat polychrome art, known to us primarily through the magnificent painted sea-mammal-hunting or war hats and visors. Somewhat later the new techniques and materials spread to the Tlingits, who also were masters of flat art on wooden objects. Evidence for this survives in the form of an undated watercolor of Sitka harbor by an unknown artist, and a representation of a Tlingit initiation ceremony, painted for I. G.

VASILII KRIUKOV, a young Aleut, is referred to by Rev. Ioann Veniaminov in his journal as a gifted artist, particularly of the human form. The four icons pictured on these two pages and the next are among seven known to have been in the Church of the Holy Ascension of Our Lord, the first church at Unalaska, and are believed to have been painted by Kriukov, ca. 1825. This is the icon of the Archangel Gabriel of the Annunciation.

Photograph courtesy of Lydia T. Black.

Voznesenskii by an unnamed Sitka Tlingit sometime in the early 1840s. It is tempting to speculate that perhaps Mikhail Levashev taught drawing and the art of watercolor painting to the three young Aleuts who lived in his camp, particularly the sixteen-year-old Russian-speaking Semeon, from Akutan, who asked to accompany Levashev to Kamchatka. Later on, when the first Russian schools were established, music and art formed part of the curriculum.

Aleuts became acquainted with religious art and traditional Russian iconography very early in the contact period. All Russian fur-trading ships carried icons on board. Chapels, either house chapels in the corners of communal barracks, or special structures, were built at many a camp. Such a house chapel existed at Unalaska by 1778 and on Kodiak after 1785 or 1786.[1]

When the religious mission arrived on Kodiak in 1794, the school was transferred to their jurisdiction. Church music was taught there, as was art beginning in 1804. The first man who taught art to the young Kodiak Islanders was a former navy officer, Borisov. He arrived in Alaska aboard the *Elizaveta,* one of several men seconded to Alaska to skipper the Russian-American Company's growing fleet. In 1806, Hieromonk Gideon attempted to have Borisov appointed permanently as a teacher, to teach arithmetic, geography, and art (*risoval'noe iskusstvo*). From Gideon we learn that Borisov "with great diligence and willingness has taken this task upon himself, out of love for and the benefit of the local youth. His success in teaching two boys he had previously taken on, and the procedure he followed, served both as the reason for his appointment and a guarantee of his success." Unfortunately, the names of Borisov's two students have not been preserved.[2]

We know that by the 1840s, in the seminary established in Sitka under the guidance of Bishop Innocent (Veniaminov), church music and iconography were taught. However, the two Native iconographers Kriukov and Petukhov, whose work can be documented, were self-taught.

Vasilii Kriukov

The first iconographer of whom we have definite information is Vasilii Stepanovich Kriukov (ca. 1814-1880) of Unalaska Island. He was the grandson of Ivan Kriukov, a Russian settler and, for a few years, manager of the Unalaska District of the Russian-American Company. The elder Kriukov produced eloquent accounts of life in the Aleutian Islands that incited Ioann Veniaminov to volunteer for service in the colonies. A year after Veniaminov's arrival on Unalaska as the first parish priest in 1824, he began the construction of a new church to replace the small, decaying octagonal chapel built in 1808. He engaged Aleut woodcarvers to beautify the church and was especially proud of the *iconostas* (altar screen), intricately carved by the Aleut craftsmen and

decorated with icons painted by Vasilii Kriukov, then only sixteen years old.

Part of this *iconostas* survives today. When I first reported on the surviving art of Vasilii Kriukov, I believed that it was represented by six icons from the Royal Gate (the central or priest's gate in the altar screen) now hung separately in the chapel of St. Innocent of Irkutsk, one of two side chapels in the modern Cathedral of the Holy Ascension of Our Lord in Unalaska. There are also several icons, possibly painted by Kriukov, in the main

THIS ICON of St. Andrew, which reveals an iconographically unconventional background that bears a resemblance to Unalaska's terrain.

Photograph courtesy of Lydia T. Black.

THE ICON of the Theotokos (Mother of God) at the Annunciation.

Photograph courtesy of Lydia T. Black.

body of the cathedral. Further research revealed that the entire Royal Gate from the church built by Veniaminov in 1825-26 survives, forming part of the *iconostas* in the Chapel of St. Sergius of Radonezh, the second side chapel in the cathedral. The icons there remain in place.

Though there are certain differences between the icons originally identified as Kriukov's work and those on the ancient Royal Gate now in the chapel of St. Sergius of Radonezh, the similarities are very strong and the common authorship of both sets can hardly be doubted. The differences in style are slight. The differences in color may be accounted for by the fact that the set of icons now in the chapel of St. Innocent of Irkutsk was painted much later, in the 1850s, when the original church building was replaced during the tenure of the first Aleut parish priest of Unalaska, Father Innokentii Shaiashnikov. This *iconostas* was later replaced by another one, but the icons were preserved. Apparently, different paints were used.

In addition to his iconographic work, Kriukov was also famous, even as a young man, for his portraits. Veniaminov tells us that he made "excellent water-color portraits. It was enough for him to see a person two or three times and he would bring that person's image alive on paper, covering the whole gamut of facial

THE ICON of St. Mark the Evangelist. Both icons are thought to have been painted by Aleut artist Ivan Kriukov, ca. 1825.

Photograph courtesy of Lydia T. Black.

expressions."[3] Unfortunately, no portrait by Kriukov is known to survive.

Grigorii Petukhov

The work of the second Aleut iconographer, Grigorii Petukhov, was not known until very recently. He was born in 1828 at Unalaska and died at the age of thirty in Sitka. As he was the iconographer who painted the icons for the Tlingit Church of the Holy Resurrection in Sitka (no longer in existence), he was buried near the entry to this church.

The present location of the icons from the Church of the Holy Resurrection in Sitka is difficult, if not impossible, to ascertain, as they were widely dispersed after the church was dismantled. In 1986, going over an old inventory of the church on the island of St. George, I came across a reference to two icons by Grigorii Petukhov "of Sitka period" having been placed in the church. These icons are not in the Church of St. George at present. The collection of old dilapidated icons removed to the basement could not be examined at the time. In 1988, however, while preparing an inventory of the church in Kenai, Barbara Sweetland Smith came across a documented icon painted by

Grigorii Petukhov, according to nine-teenth-century church records. Two other icons were also found in the Kenai church. To judge by the style, Petukhov, like Kriukov, was self-taught. Characteristic is the inept treatment of hands, creating an odd contrast with the rest of the image. It is possible, on the basis of style and the treatment of hands, to postulate that a set of icons representing the twelve major Feasts of the Church (not all surviving) now in the church in Juneau, sent there in the late 1880s from Sitka, is by Petukhov, originally painted for the Sitka Church of the Holy Resurrection. No works by Petukhov have been located so far at Unalaska, where icons painted in his early, pre-Sitka period are likely to have been placed.

Other Native Artists

There were other Native artists in Russian America, secular painters as well as iconographers. Two of the former are known, but only a single work by one of them survives. This is a view of Sitka painted in 1837 by Aleksandr Vasil'evich Ol'gin (1810-1860). The original is located in the Navy Archives of the USSR.[4] The work of the second Native secular artist, "the Aleut Smirennikov," does not survive to my knowledge, though it is possible that it may come to light if a specific search is made in the Navy Archives of the USSR. Smirennikov was assigned as staff artist to the Russian-American Company vessel *Promysel,* which was sailing to the Polar Sea in 1849.

The absence of later secular Native artists owes much to the suppression of Russian education for Natives after Americans took possession of Alaska in 1867. Russian schools had taught art, as well as literature and music; American schools for Natives were more likely to teach crafts like shoemaking. Conse-quently, twentieth-century Native artists have lacked formal schooling. Self-taught village artists met communal needs, and those were religious—to decorate a new

HAND-CARVED wooden box for use at baptisms, created by Victor Nick, an Eskimo artist living in Kwethluk, 1987. The scene is of the Baptism of Christ by John, with three angels in attendance.

St. Herman's Theological Seminary, Kodiak.

ICONS OF THE archangels Gabriel (left) and Michael (right), written by the Aleut iconographer Grigorii Petukhov. The artist worked out of Sitka and probably was attached to the cathedral or the seminary. Only a few of his works are known. Both of these hang in the Church of the Holy Assumption of the Virgin in Kenai.

Courtesy of Icon Preservation Task Force, Alaska Association for Historic Preservation, Anchorage.

church, to adorn an old one further. No patrons commissioned them to produce landscapes. The nineteenth-century secular artists Ol'gin and Smirennikov both attended school at Sitka; when its curriculum became unavailable to Natives, Natives by and large stopped producing secular art.

Iakov Netsvetov

Equally unfortunate is the loss of icons and ecclesiastical sculpture by Father Iakov Netsvetov, the first Native Alaskan to become an Orthodox priest. In 1829 he became the parish priest for the Central and Western Aleutians and supervised the construction of the church at the Russian settlement on his mother's native island of Atka, on Korovin Bay. Soon thereafter he assisted in building the chapel in the Aleut settlement on the neighboring island of Amlia. When the Amlia settlement was abandoned in the late 1860s and early 1870s, the chapel was moved to the church in the new settlement on Nazan Bay, where the modern village of Atka is located. The icons in this chapel and the *iconostas* were the work of Iakov Netsvetov. Presumably, they perished in 1942, when the church and the village were burned at the orders of the local U.S.

Navy commander prior to evacuation of the Aleuts from Atka.

In 1845 Iakov Netsvetov went to the Yukon, where he established the first Orthodox church among the Yup'ik at Ikogmiut, now known as Russian Mission. The original Church of the Elevation of the Holy Cross had the *iconostas* carved by Father Netsvetov and a number of icons that he had painted. Reportedly, he also carved ritual vessels for the altar, notably the paten, in ivory. The original church is long since gone and a disastrous fire may have destroyed many of the church's treasures.

Alaskan Artistic Traditions

In general, many Alaskans whose names are not known to us contributed their artistic skills to the beautification of their churches. The practice continues to this day. As in the past, they utilize their own artistic traditions and native materials to express their devotion to the new faith.

When Veniaminov returned to Alaska as its first bishop, the women of Unalaska presented him with a set of *orlitsy*, round rugs decorated with images of eagles on which a bishop stands at certain times during the service. These *orlitsy* were of grass, woven in the same traditional manner that Aleut women have used for centuries. Today, Bishop Gregory of Sitka and Alaska proudly speaks of a *panagiia* (worn by a bishop on his chest) woven for him by a master Aleut weaver. Several priests in Alaska treasure pectoral crosses woven for them by their parishioners out of beach grass. Others are proud to wear pectoral crosses carved for them by Native wood-carvers. An Aleut self-taught artist, the late Agafangel Stepetin, painted icons. Victor Nick of Kwethluk, in the Kuskokwim river basin, carves icons, altar utensils, and crosses in wood and ivory. His work, represented in this exhibit, is exquisite. Recently, he completed the carving of the *iconostas,* notably the Royal Gate and the two Deacon's Gates, for the village church of Kwethluk. Other Yup'ik icon carvers are Father Nikolai Larsen of Napaiskak and Vasilii Epchuk.

In other areas, Native artists make beaded Bible covers and altar crosses, or priestly vestments. A splendid example of the latter is the work of Mrs. Emma Marks (now of Juneau), who made a complete set of beaded vestments for the Cathedral of St. Innocent of Irkutsk in Anchorage, on display in this exhibit. The secular paintings by the Yup'ik artist Xenia Oleksa have the feeling of Orthodox icons. All are focused on the village churches and the parishioners' faith, be it the cemetery at the Athabaskan village of Eklutna or the procession with the Star set against the church in the village of Old Harbor, on Kodiak. In this grass-roots church art, Native artists blend their own and Russian America's traditions into a new and beautiful and moving whole—hallmark of a true art.

Lydia T. Black is Professor of Anthropology, University of Alaska, Fairbanks.

For Further Reading

Black, Lydia T. "The Curious Case of the Unalaska Icons." *Alaska Journal* 12, no. 2 (1982), pp. 7-11.

_____, trans. *The Round the World Voyage of Hieromonk Gideon, 1803-1809.* Kingston, Ontario: Limestone Press, 1989.

Documents on the History of the Russian-American Company. Ed. Richard A. Pierce, trans. Marina Ramsey. Kingston, Ontario: Limestone Press, 1976.

Fedorova, Svetlana G. *The Russian Population in Alaska and California Late 18th Century - 1867.* 1921; Kingston, Ontario: Limestone Press, 1973.

Fitzhugh, William W. and A. Crowell. *Crossroads of Continents: Cultures of Siberia and Alaska.* Washington, D.C.: Smithsonian Institution, 1988.

Henry, John Frazier. *Early Maritime Artists of the Pacific Northwest Coast, 1741-1841.* Seattle and London: University of Washington Press, 1984.

John Ledyard's Journal of Captain Cook's Last Voyage. Ed. James K. Munford. Corvallis, Oregon: Oregon State University Press, 1963.

Shur, Leonid A. and R. A. Pierce. "Artists in Russian America: Mikhail Tikhanov." *Alaska Journal* 6, no. 1 (1976), pp. 40-49.

_____. "Artists in Russian America: Pavel Mikhailov." *Alaska Journal* 8, no. 4 (1978), pp. 360-363.

Smith, Barbara S. "Cathedral on the Yukon." *Alaska Journal* 12, no. 2 (1982), pp. 4-6, 50-55.

Veniaminov, Ioann. *Notes on the Islands of the Unalashka District.* Trans. and ed. Lydia T. Black and R. M. Geoghegan, ed. Richard A. Pierce. 1840; Kingston, Ontario: Limestone Press, 1984.

Notes

1. *John Ledyard's Journal of Captain Cook's Last Voyage,* ed. James K. Munford (Corvallis, Oregon: Oregon State University Press, 1963), p. 95. Also see Katrina H. Moore, "Spain Claims Alaska," *The Sea in Alaska's Past Conference Proceedings* (Anchorage Office of History and Archaeology, Alaska Division of Parks, History and Archaeology Series No. 25, 1979), p. 68.

2. *The Round the World Voyage of Hieromonk Gideon, 1803-1809,* trans. and introduction Lydia T. Black (Kingston, Ontario: Limestone Press, 1989), p. 96.

3. Ioann Veniaminov, *Notes on the Islands of the Unalashka District,* trans. and ed. Lydia T. Black and R. H. Geoghegan, ed. Richard A. Pierce (1840; Kingston, Ontario: Limestone Press, 1984), pp. 164-165.

4. S. G. Fedorova, *The Russian Population in Alaska and California Late 18th Century - 1867* (originally published in Russian, Moscow, 1921; Kingston, Ontario: Limestone Press, 1973), Fig. 14.

Alaska Native Languages *in* Russian America

by Michael E. Krauss

During the 120-odd years that the Russians dominated Alaska, the position of Alaska Native language was not at all weakened, and in several cases considerably strengthened. However the Russians' effect on other aspects of Alaskan Native life and cultural heritage may be assessed, they did only good for the heritage of our Native languages.

Those of us who work for the preservation and promotion of this rich, unique Alaskan heritage of Native languages, academically at the university, educationally in the bilingual programs at the schools, and to some extent also in the churches, are very thankful for the Russian period: for the documentary work done by many Russians, but even more for the precedent they set in their use and cultivation of Alaska Native languages in their churches and schools. Although this was replaced by an American pattern quite opposed to it, like other aspects of the Russian legacy in Alaska, its good effect has not been forgotten and is now again contributing to Alaska's cultural future.

We shall now look more closely at this Russian period. The first forty years of it, the 1740s to the 1780s, mainly saw the visitation of the *promyshlenniki* to the Aleutian Islands. However harmful to the people and the sea otter, their activity was limited essentially to the Aleutian Islands. These Russians cared little one way or the other about Aleut language or culture. Toward the end of this period a Russian headquarters of sorts developed at Unalaska, and the first short Aleut word lists, showing the interest in the language typical of explorers and scientists, appear in the 1770s and 1780s. Before that, in the 1740s, '50s, and '60s, we have only the Aleut names of islands and a few persons.

By the 1780s, the Russians began to feel that other European powers threatened their control of the area. They also felt the need to move farther east for sea otters as the Aleutian supply dwindled. It was time to organize and establish a more substantial headquarters to the east, on Kodiak. That, in turn, was soon moved even farther east to Sitka by 1808. We shall, for our purposes, designate this second forty-year period, 1780s to 1820s, as one of rapid expansion of Russian domination: into the Gulf of Alaska and most of Southeastern (though with considerable Tlingit resistance), and north into Norton Sound and into the Yup'ik and Athabaskan interior. Also colonized (with Aleuts) were two pairs of islands hitherto uninhabited, the Pribilofs and Commanders (Komandorskis). Even the Kurile Islands, near Japan, and Ross Colony in California were temporarily colonized (with Koniags and Aleuts).

During the first decade of this period, there was a considerable increase in attention to and documentation of the Native languages, especially by scientists on expeditions, Russian and others, such as Merck and Robeck with Billings, 1790-91. Russian knowledge of Alaskan language distribution is nicely summed up in what may be the first Alaska Native language map,[1] compiled for Grigorii Shelikhov in 1796, clearly designating six language areas in the part of Alaska then well known to the Russians: Aleut, Koniagi

...The precedent of Native language use and support in Russian America is an important part of the force that keeps this heritage alive.

(including Bristol Bay), Kenaitsi (Tanaina), Chugachi, Ugaliakhmiuti (Eyak!), and Koliuzhi (Tlingit). This is more than the Americans understood (especially concerning Eyak) over a hundred years later.

The Clergy Arrive

In 1794 Kodiak received the first group of clergy somewhat reluctantly, for they were potential whistle-blowers on company treatment of Natives. Taking a far stronger interest in the nonmaterial, they soon established at Kodiak the first Russian Orthodox church-school and, in 1805, we have reports of the first educational work in an Alaska Native language, associated with the arrival of Chamberlain Nikolai Rezanov and Hieromonk Gideon. Rezanov, himself very interested in Alaska Native languages, spent what must have been several weeks working in Sitka on a remarkable dictionary of Alaska Native languages, about twelve hundred words in each of six parallel columns— one for each of the language areas recognized on Grigorii Shelikhov's 1796 map. This amazing work has never been published as such, and Rezanov probably only increased his unpopularity with his countrymen in Alaska by pointing out in his letters that the priests were not paying sufficient attention to these languages in their work, and that he was writing the dictionary to get them started.

A most significant exception was Hieromonk Gideon at the Kodiak school, who documented some Koniag poetry in his reports, and had a senior student, Paramon Chumovitskii, compile a dictionary of Koniag, and a student of grammar, Aleksei Kotel'nikov, work under teachers Kodiak Ivan and Khristofor Prianishnikov, with a view toward the use of Koniag translation for religious purposes. The results of this work have been lost, and the effort may have lasted only for the three years that Gideon remained at Kodiak. Nevertheless, the basic principle that Native language is important, worthy of scientific documentation, and can and should be used in spoken and written form in the church schools was clearly proposed as a policy for that system.

Ioann Veniaminov

This second period was to continue for nearly another twenty years without real development of that system, ending finally with the arrival of the most outstanding cultural figure in the history of Russian America, Father Ioann Veniaminov. This young priest from Siberia was the only applicant for the long-unfilled job as priest to the Aleutians, where he arrived in 1824. A man of great energy and leadership, Veniaminov had many talents and interests, including linguistics for Alaska Native languages, both for science and for religious education and cultural development. He was also able to gain the very effective cooperation of Aleut leaders for this work, the first of whom was Ivan Pan'kov, Chief of Tigalda. The first catechism translation, in 1826, was rejected because the Church had meanwhile issued a new catechism. This turned out for the better, though, because for the next version the authors revised the orthography, having by then achieved some very fundamental insights into the Aleut sound system.

Aleut is quite different from Russian, especially in having not one but two kinds of *k* sounds, *g* sounds, and *x* (German *ch*) sounds, one kind pronounced farther back in the mouth. For the sounds made farther back in the mouth, they invented special letters by putting a cross-mark on the *k* and a loop over the *g* and *x*. In addition, for the *ng* sound, absent in Russian, they invented a new symbol combining the *n* and the *g,* and for voiceless *hl* they wrote *l* with a loop over it. This was a brilliant achievement for its time, to recognize the different sounds (no doubt insisted upon by Pan'kov!), and then to understand that special symbols could and should be consistently assigned to them. That they did not correctly recognize the distinction between long and short vowels was evidently a minor fault. This brilliant and very powerful achievement was to provide a firm basis for the development of Aleut literature and literacy, and for Koniag and Central Yup'ik as well, since these same special sound distinctions are crucial to all Eskimo-Aleut languages. The Veniaminov-Pan'kov writing system was the first to recognize these distinctions fully, well ahead of the Danes, who had by then worked with Greenlandic for over a century.

By 1830 Veniaminov and Pan'kov had finished the new catechism in the new orthography. This was printed in St. Petersburg in 1834, the first book published in an Alaska Native language. The book was typeset without anyone who knew the language to supervise. When Veniaminov received the copies, he found them so riddled with errors that he decided not to release them. He may have destroyed them, as no surviving copy of this first Alaska Native language book has yet been found. It is known about only from reports.

Veniaminov determined then to oversee the typesetting of any further work personally in St. Petersburg. This he did finally in 1840, by which time he had published a primer, catechism, and sacred history (usually together in one volume, xxiii, 24, 51, and 104 pages), and what is apparently an original work, written in 1833, *The Way to the Kingdom of Heaven* (120 pages). Though the latter went through many editions as an important work in Russian, it was actually first published in Aleut. Veniaminov's *Notes on the Islands of the Unalaska District*, published in 1840, also includes much of importance for Aleut language.

By 1836 Veniaminov was also working with the Atkan Creole priest Iakov Netsvetov, another very able and dedicated man. Netsvetov provided an Atkan

MAP FROM Shelikhov's own account of his journey of 1783-86.

From Grigorii Shelikhov's Travels in 1783 from Okhotsk through the Eastern Ocean to the American Shore (*in Russian, 1791*). Alaska and Polar Regions Dept., Elmer E. Rasmuson Library, University of Alaska, Fairbanks.

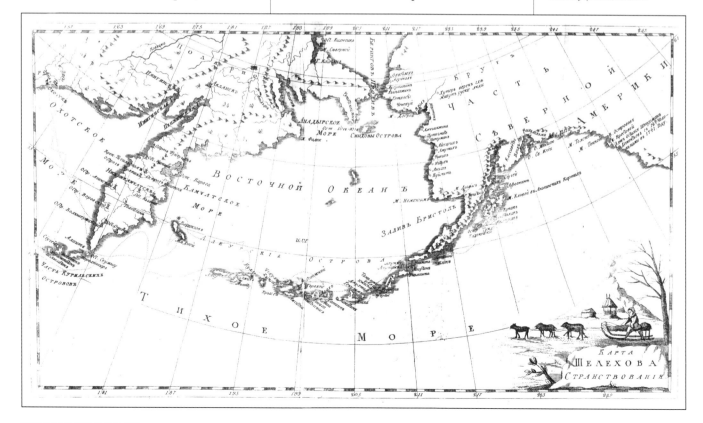

ALEUT IN a bidarka, drawn by Sven Waxell on his chart of Bering's voyage of 1741. This is the first recorded image of an Aleut.

From Golder's Bering's Voyages (1922). Photograph courtesy of Anchorage Museum of History and Art.

(Western Aleut dialect) introduction, and, throughout, Atkan footnotes to the primer-catechism-history printed in 1840. In 1846 Veniaminov had printed a revised primer, with new notes by Netsvetov. That same year he also published a grammar and dictionary of Aleut that he had finished in 1834. For many years it remained the best-known such work on any Alaskan language (and is still sold in an English translation by Richard Geoghegan, published in 1944). Finally, in 1848, Veniaminov published a complete translation of the Gospel of Matthew into Eastern Aleut, including Atkan introduction, appendices, and footnotes throughout by Netsvetov.

These publications, together with the missionary and educational zeal of Veniaminov and his able colleagues, laid the foundation for the conversion of Aleut society into an essentially literate nation. Literacy was, for thousands of years, until the invention of the phonograph and electronic transmission, the only technology for the empowerment of a people's spoken word over time and space, for both information and entertainment. Literacy

thus flowered in Aleut society of the past century, adding great strength to Aleut language and culture, which it would sorely need for what was later in store.

Two other important contributors to Aleut literature emerged in the 1850s: the priest Lavrentii Salomatov (Netsvetov's successor at Atka), who wrote an Atkan primer, and translated a catechism and the Gospels of Mark, Luke, and John into Atkan; and the Unalaska priest and leader Innokentii Shaiashnikov, even more prolific, who translated all four Gospels and the Acts of the Apostles, besides a new primer and a sermon. Their extensive work remained unpublished throughout the Russian period, however, and was only partly published much later. To this we shall return in the epilogue.

During the 1840s, Veniaminov also expanded this movement to the two neighboring Yup'ik languages, Koniag Alutiiq and Central Yup'ik. For these, one could use fundamentally the same writing system as for Aleut, especially with the addition of the fourth vowel (written *e* in the modern systems), for which Slavonic ъ was appropriately chosen. Veniaminov himself composed a brief grammatical sketch of Koniag, published in 1846, including portions of the Gospel of John translated by a Koniag, Grigorii Terent'ev. Again, Veniaminov picked capable men for furthering the task.

On Kodiak he had the priest Elias Tyzhnev working with the Koniag specialists Gerasim Zyrianov and Kosma Uchilishchev to produce a Koniag primer (both monolingual and bilingual versions) and Koniag translations of the catechism and sacred history, and of the Gospel of Matthew. These were printed in 1847 and 1848.

In the case of Central Yup'ik, Veniaminov expanded the effort in a rather different way, by sending the Atkan priest Netsvetov to the distant post of Ikogmiut (Russian Mission) on the Yukon, so boldly far beyond the already missionized Bristol Bay sector that to this day it constitutes a somewhat separate northerly Russian Orthodox enclave within Central Yup'ik. This strategy must certainly have been based on the accurate perspective of Central Yup'ik as a single language. It must have been a difficult new assignment for the veteran Aleut scholar, sent so far, to work in a new language (at first accompanied, incidentally, by the young Innokentii Shaiashnikov). Netsvetov remained there for seventeen years, all but the last two years of his life, much of them in a rather miserable state, a poor reward for his labors in the foundation of literature and literacy in two Alaskan languages. Whatever his output at Ikogmiut, little of it survives, and none was published during his time. Other clergy, particularly Zakharii Bel'kov and Ioann Orlov, also became involved in the translation of prayers into Central Yup'ik, but like Netsvetov's, none were published until still later. Again, to this we shall return in the epilogue.

MAP OF ALASKA'S Native languages devised by the Alaska Native Language Center, University of Alaska, Fairbanks (copyright 1982). Russian officials took an early interest in linguistics, with the first dictionary compiled in 1805 by Nikolai Rezanov. Russian policy also encouraged the use of Native language in school and home.

Map from Alaska's Native People, *a publication of* Alaska Geographic.

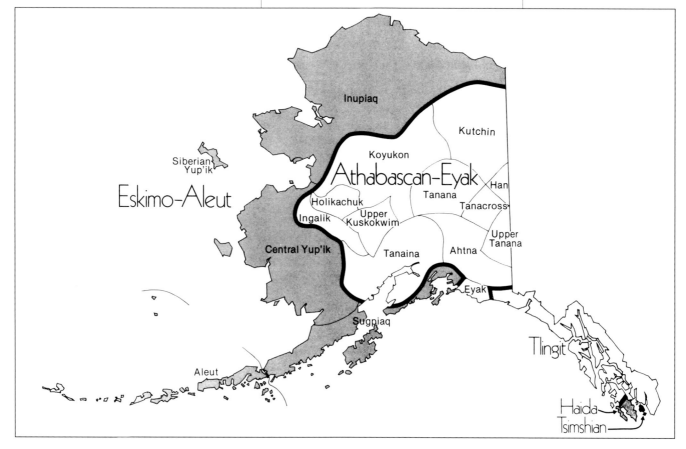

The Koniag books had a considerable effect. We even have record of their use in the Kuriles. They certainly made their contribution to the emerging Orthodox Alutiiq identity, strong to this day. Alutiiq literacy must have grown throughout the language area, though not so powerfully as the Aleutian Aleut. In the case of Central Yup'ik during the Russian period, the spread of Orthodox literacy must have been still more limited, as nothing was printed.

The other Alaskan language with which the Russians had major contact was Tlingit, a very different kind of language and people. Veniaminov tried his hand at that, too, but with less success. One reason was technical: The Tlingit sound system is still more different from Aleut than anything a Russian ear was accustomed to, for instance, in having not just two types of *k*, but six, three of each type (plain, aspirate, and glottalized, which we now write *g g̲ k k̲ k' k̲'*, respectively), not to mention many other sounds that must have been equally perplexing. Though Veniaminov had managed, with Pan'kov's help, to recognize the two Aleut *k*'s, six was too much. In addition to the technical difficulties, there were the social. There

was no Tlingit Pan'kov to help. Russian-Tlingit contact came at a time and place where the struggle between exploitation and Native resistance was less uneven. The Tlingits generally firmly resisted Russian influence on more intimate aspects of their culture and language, so were not easily interested in Russian religious writing in their language. The Russian priest Ivan Nadezhdin made efforts in the 1850s; we have, for example, a manuscript translation of the Gospel of Matthew, but in a hardly readable, slavishly literal translation, and with a writing system so faulty that the spread of literacy would have been severely impeded even if there had been good translations and interest in them. Veniaminov himself had published, in 1846, together with his brief sketch of Koniag grammar, a sketch of Tlingit grammar and vocabulary almost as long as Rezanov's, but no religious work was published in Tlingit until well after the Russian period.

Other Alaskan languages either had little or no direct contact with the Russians or rather late marginal contact, e.g., Inupiaq Eskimo, or Koyukon and Ahtna Athabaskan. That leaves only two of the

ALEUTS, a watercolor by Louis Choris, 1818. Choris was expedition artist on the Riurik, 1815-18, which explored the North Pacific and particularly the northwest coast of Alaska under the command of Otto von Kotzebue.

Anchorage Museum of History and Art.

habitans des îles Aléoutiennes.

languages already recognized on Grigorii Shelikhov's map and in Rezanov's dictionary, Tanaina and Eyak, for which we do not know of any Russian attempt at establishing a literature, though both groups are Russian Orthodox. Both have the formidable Indian consonant system, including, for example, the six *k's*, and the reputation of being unpronounceable, and were much smaller groups than Tlingit, Koniag, Central Yup'ik, or Aleut, the four for which a literature was begun.

To sum up, for the third forty years of the Russian period, the Orthodox clergy under Veniaminov began a written literature in all four of the major contacted languages, printing significant publications during the 1840s in two of them, Aleutian Aleut and Koniag Alutiiq. Much remained unpublished, as writing spread at least somewhat in Central Yup'ik, more in Alutiiq, and most of all in Aleut.

I have concentrated on the remarkable development of this religious literature during this last forty-year period of Russian America at the expense of the significant scientific work. I may cite here, for example, Netsvetov's six-thousand-entry Atkan dictionary (unpublished), or Leopold Radloff's work with a Tlingit speaker for some months in St. Petersburg (including a vocabulary file of eight thousand cards, according to a report from Soviet archives, not yet seen), 1861-62; the Tlingit speaker was Tikhontin, taken to St. Petersburg for these purposes. It was to be a full century before American interest and work in Alaskan languages reached a similar level.

This last forty years of Russian America, after the arrival of Veniaminov, I have called a "Golden Age" for Alaskan languages, at least in comparison to what preceded, and especially in comparison to what followed.

Epilogue

During the first twenty "neglectful" years of the American period, as mentioned, writing in these languages continued. In Aleut it grew far beyond religious use into everyday life, making Aleut an essentially literate culture. In Alutiiq it began to grow somewhat beyond religious use, and in Central Yup'ik it continued at least in religious use. In Tlingit, too, in the work of Donskoi and Sinkiel, religious literature began to develop—now that the Russians were gone. Orthodoxy no longer represented the intrusive power, but rather served to resist the intrusion of the new power, the American. This was led by Protestant missionary schools under Sheldon Jackson, who forcefully opposed the Russian pattern of Native language use, and also would no doubt have preferred to encounter heathens rather than faithful adherents to the despised "Greek Church."

The pattern of American education led by Jackson began in the 1880s at Wrangell and Sitka, and soon spread widely. Also in the 1880s, Moravians and Roman Catholics, who did believe in writing Native language, began missions and schools in the Central Yup'ik area. Thus, the Orthodox church was moved to significant new publishing activity, as it was now threatened by the Americanization of the schools, relentlessly suppressing the language in the Tlingit, Alutiiq, and Aleut areas, and by the Catholic and Moravian competition in Central Yup'ik, beginning themselves to prepare religious materials for publication. In fact, the Church published more Native language material during this period than during the period of Russian America (seven or eight books in Aleut and Alutiiq in the 1840s, but fifteen in the period from 1893 to 1903—nine in Aleut, four in Tlingit, and two in Central Yup'ik).

Thus, in the 1890s all the Aleut books from the 1840s were republished in St. Petersburg, with funds supplied by the

Aleut people themselves, and new books were printed in New York: Lodochnikov's liturgy translation in 1898, and finally, about forty years after they were done, Shaiashnikov's Luke, John, Acts, and sermon, in 1902. A valiant stand. Though the last Aleut religious schools, at Unalaska, were closed, forcibly, in 1912, these works remain a meaningful source of strength in Aleut heritage.

For some reason the Koniag books were never reprinted, nor was any new material printed in Alutiiq during this initial period of confrontation between the old order and the new. Whether this was due to lesser strength or greater opposition, or both, is not yet clear. In the case of Tlingit and Central Yup'ik during this period, Russian Orthodox publications finally appeared. Printed in New York, 1895-1901, in Tlingit, were a small booklet of translated prayers from Nadezhdin and the later work by Donskoi and Sinkiel: a booklet of prayers and hymns, their translation of the catechism and sacred history, and now also Veniaminov's *The Way to the Kingdom of Heaven*, translated by Sergei Kostromitonov. Finally, in Central Yup'ik, two liturgical booklets of translations, one by Netsvetov and Bel'kov for Yukon-Kuskokwim and one by Bel'kov and Orlov for Kuskokwim-Bristol Bay, were published in 1896 in New York and San Francisco.

Though this later publication program lasted only from 1893 to 1903, the Russian Orthodox tradition of writing continued strong into recent memory. At least in Aleut, and even in Alutiiq, there may still be a few elders with some traditional knowledge of it. In all four languages, however, it is more than a memory: it is a symbolically significant part of the culture in the Orthodox community of today, even though the younger generations do not know their ancestral language. More important still, for all of Alaska, the precedent of Native language use and support in Russian America is an important part of the force that keeps this heritage alive.

Russian America did not end in 1867. For one thing, the Orthodox church itself remained, as a new kind of American institution, with its roots firmly planted in Alaska. Because of the church's historical support of Native languages, these languages now have a significant position in the spiritual domain of church life, as liturgical languages of song and prayer, even though they may be replaced by English otherwise.

In another interesting way, the impact of Russian culture on Alaskan languages may be measured in the number of words of Russian origin incorporated and still used in them. (To keep this number in perspective, however, we should note at the outset that all Alaskan languages, even Aleut, the most affected, with perhaps 10 percent of its modern vocabulary from Russian, are still 90 percent "pure." They remain vastly more so than English, for example, which has only 20 percent of its modern vocabulary from Anglo-Saxon, and all the rest from French, Latin, Greek, Dutch, Dakota, Mandingo, and dozens of other languages with which it has come in contact, absorbing words from them quite promiscuously.)

The Russian loanwords in Alaskan languages are mostly nouns, for new concepts, especially new items of trade. A few of the most widespread are: tea, coffee, flour, sugar, butter, soup, beer, money, playing cards, table, matches, skillet, clock, and key. The Russian sounds (sometimes also the meanings) are generally more or less adapted to the Native systems, as in Central Yup'ik's *Alussistuaq*, "Christmas," from the Russian *rozhdestvó*; or the Tlingit *gíwa*, "beer," and the Ingalik *miyoq*, "homebrew," (through Yup'ik *piivaq*), from the Russian *pívo*, "beer"; or Iliamna Tanaina's *gazashchik*, "second chief," from the Russian *zakazchik,* to take only a very few examples. The language with the largest number of such Russian loans is, of course, Aleut, with about seven hundred; next Alutiiq, with about six hundred; then Tanaina, with about five hundred. Central Yup'ik, however, has only about two hundred, and Koyukon and Ahtna perhaps one hundred. The rest of the languages with such loans have most or all directly through their neighbors: Upper Kuskokwim, about seventy; Ingalik, sixty; Holikachuk and Tanana, forty (but Chena dialect, thirty; Salcha dialect, twenty); Tanacross and Upper Tanana, about five; Eyak, thirty; Inupiaq has about twenty, especially on Seward Peninsula; and St. Lawrence Island, only about ten (including the garbled *kurugak,* "pig," from the Russian *koróva,* "cow"). The rest have none (Kutchin and Han, which have some words from French through "Slavey Jargon"; Haida and Tsimshian). The Tlingits are perhaps the most interesting: the Russian capital was in their territory, but they borrowed only about ten words from the Russians (for example, *lekwa,* from the Russian *khleb,* "bread," meaning "host at communion," probably borrowed only after 1867), strong testimony to the Tlingit spirit of resistance.

Though adapted and adopted into these Alaskan languages, this Russian element is still rather distinctive and felt as such. So, in this intimate way, speakers of Alaskan languages are still daily reminded of the Russian legacy.

Michael E. Krauss is Professor of Linguistics, University of Alaska, Fairbanks.

For Further Reading

Black, Lydia T. "Ivan Pan'kov: An Architect of Aleut Literacy." *Arctic Anthropology* 14, no. 1 (1977), pp. 94-107.

Blomkvist, E. E. "Istoriia izucheniia v Rossii iazykov severo-amerikanskikh indeitsev (iz arkhiva) ["History of the Study in Russia of North American Indian Languages (from the Archives)"]." *Sbornik Museiia Antropologii i etnografii, Institut Etnografiia, AN-SSSR [Journal of the Museum of Anthropology and Ethnography, Institute of Ethnography, Academy of Sciences, USSR],* no. 31 (1975), pp. 94-117.

Dauenhauer, Richard L. *Conflicting Visions in Alaskan Education.* Occasional Paper No. 3. Fairbanks: University of Alaska, Center for Cross-Cultural Studies, 1982.

_____. "The Spiritual Epiphany of Aleut." *Orthodox Alaska* 8, no. 1 (January 1979), pp. 13-42.

Krauss, Michael. *Alaska Native Languages: Past, Present and Future.,* Research Papers, no. 4. Fairbanks: Alaska Native Language Center, 1980.

Ransom, J. Ellis. "Writing as a Means of Acculturation among the Aleut." *Southwestern Journal of Anthropology* 1 (1945), pp. 333-344.

Notes

1. Original mss. perhaps in color, at Central State Military-Historical Archives, Moscow (TSVGIA), f. VUA, d. 23461, published in A. V. Efimov, ed., *Atlas of Geographical Discoveries in Siberia and in Northwest America XVII-XVIII Centuries* (Moscow, 1964), map no. 184.

RUSSIA'S LEGACY IN NORTH AMERICA

The Architectural Legacy *of* Russian America

by Kathleen Lidfors and Steven M. Peterson

RUSSIAN AMERICA

"The houses were all of logs, but painted a dull yellow, the metal roofs were red and with the emerald green spire of the church, projected against the dark evergreen of the adjacent hills, presented an extremely picturesque appearance. It was quite unlike anything else in America, and seemed to belong to a world of its own."[1]

So William Dall described Sitka, the capital of Russian America, as it appeared in 1865, two years before Tsar Alexander II authorized sale of the colonies to the United States.

Eighty-one years had passed since Siberian fur traders, or *promyshlenniki*, established the first permanent Russian settlement in America on the island of Unalaska in the Aleutian archipelago. This settlement, like those that followed at Kodiak, Sitka, Yakutat, and other coastal sites, was strategically located to serve the North Pacific fur trade. Proximity to fur-bearing animal populations, safe harbors, access to food and fresh water supply, and an effective position for defenses against attack were the primary considerations in determining where the Russians would settle. Relationships with the Native people were also a paramount concern. At Unalaska, the Russians settled close to the Aleuts, who were impressed into service as hunters on the seas, while at Sitka they chose a promontory rock for security in the face of hostile Tlingits.

Although the first buildings at Unalaska were made of driftwood and sod in the Aleut manner, subsequent outposts and colony centers were constructed entirely of wood with methods and building types stemming from medieval northern Europe and from the farmsteads and fortifications of Siberia. The chief merchant whose company organized Russian settlement, Grigorii Shelikhov, intended the new colonies to look like proper Russian towns. His instructions to Alexander Baranov for the new settlement of Slavo-Rossii called for a plan laid out in squares with wide streets, symmetrical arrangement of houses, public buildings that were distinguished from other structures, and amenities that included obelisks raised in honor of Russian patriots. The dwellings, modeled on the eastern Siberian "connected house," were to be "well built white cottages" that incorporated outbuildings, such as storage areas and barns, into adjoining wings, "taking care that they appear clean and attractive from the streets."[2]

Shelikhov's plans for well-designed settlements erected under the professional guidance of an engineer did not come to fruition. Even Pavlovsk Harbor (Kodiak) and New Archangel (Sitka), which served in turn as administrative centers for Russian America, lacked distinction in plan and architecture. Most settlements were simple trading outposts that typically comprised a Russian Orthodox church or chapel, dwellings for the *promyshlenniki*, storage buildings, and huts for Native hunters. A wooden stockade provided fortification. Lavrentii Zagoskin described the settlements he encountered in Alaska during 1842 to 1844 as "semi-martial," though he noted that "a Russian person is everywhere the same. No

"...A Russian person is everywhere the same. No matter where he chooses to live...he everywhere puts up his national log cabin, cook-house, and bath house, and provides himself with a housekeeper."

(Lavrentii Zagoskin, 1842-44)

CHAPTER 18

A VIEW OF the Russian capital, 1827, an engraving by Freidrich H. von Kittlitz. The composition shows the high-pitched roofs and log construction of the rustic capital, with the elaborate Church of St. Michael the Archangel in the right background. This is one of the few images of the first church in Sitka. Built in 1813, it was replaced in 1834 by another church, and in 1848 by a cathedral.

From the F. P. Litke Atlas, Alaska and Polar Regions Dept., Elmer E. Rasmuson Library, University of Alaska, Fairbanks.

unit of each building was a "blockwork" frame formed of logs laid horizontally in the shape of a rectangle or octagon and fit together at the corners by interlocking notches. The logs were hollowed slightly on the bottom side so that one frame would fit snugly over the one below. The frames, or *venets,* were then placed on top of one another to the desired height, with moss or oakum packed between as insulation. These simple geometric units were sturdy and weatherproof and, as in the churches, could be combined in a variety of expressive building forms.

Typically, Russian-American Company buildings were one to three stories, constructed of logs, and covered with steeply pitched hipped roofs, and they often exhibited elements of Russian neoclassical style, such as front gables with fanlights, colonnaded porches, and lighted cupolas. Since company life was communal, buildings were large to accom-modate multiple living quarters and corporate kitchen, bakery, laundry, and storage facilities. Massive round logs were used for warehouses and common residences. However, the more important administrative buildings and officers' residences were hewn "so as to leave no crevices, with the internal and external logs so well dressed as to be suitable for painting or papering."[5]

The few buildings remaining from Russian America, though varying in function and in some aspects of form, all belong to the Russian wooden architec-tural tradition. Further, each building represents a distinct and significant function of colonial life.

The oldest of these original colony buildings is the *magazin* built in Kodiak between 1804 and 1808 to provide water-front storage space for furs awaiting ship-ment. Positioned on a low bluff above a channel between Kodiak and Near islands, the *magazin* stands above a rock seawall

that remains from a Russian-American Company dock and warehouse built in the 1860s.

The two-story rectangular building was constructed of horizontal courses of logs in the Russian manner. Built to store furs, the *magazin* is more crudely constructed than other structures from the Russian American period. The logs are not carefully matched, the hewing is rough, and squaring is only sufficient to provide

modern Kodiak landscape. The physical evidence still speaks of the two prongs of Russian colonial activity: the primary reason for the settlement, the harvest of marine mammal furs, is represented by the wharf and warehouse, while the presence of the church, whose evangelizing efforts followed close after the *promyshlenniki,* is evident in the large open space of the churchyard and the twentieth-century Orthodox church built in the traditional style.

a reasonably flush surface. But the moss insulation, evidence of previous interior canvas wall covering, and the absence of an interior passage between the two main rooms on the first floor, are typical of Russian construction.

The building has experienced some important modifications, including additions and changes to the roof and facade. On the interior, the second floor has been greatly altered, although the Kodiak Historical Society has restored the basic configuration of the first floor. The society operates the building as an office and museum.

Almost as important as the basic log frame of the *magazin* is its setting. With the remnant dock in front and the historic Russian church behind, an important core of the old settlement is still visible in the

Bishop's House

The Sitka residence of the first Bishop of Kamchatka and Alaska (Russian Bishop's House National Historic Landmark) is the only colonial-period building remaining as evidence of the church's active role in the colonizing effort. Built by the Russian-American Company during 1841-42 under directives from the newly consecrated Bishop Innocent (Veniaminov), the large two-story log structure served as Bishop's residence, chapel, school, and administrative headquarters for the church in America.

The building is a type commonly seen in Siberia, although it lacks the decoratively carved wooden window surrounds so characteristic of houses in Irkutsk and other Siberian towns. The long facade is divided into nine bays, each seven feet (one Russian *sazhen*) wide with a multiple-light casement window and transom. The

DRAWING OF St. Paul Harbor, Kodiak Island, ca. 1794. The image shows typical Russian "blockwork" buildings constructed of log units in rectangle, octagonal, and ogee shapes.

From A. V. Efimov's Atlas of Geographical Discoveries in Siberia and Northwest America, XVII-XVIII Centuries *(Moscow, 1963). Alaska and Polar Regions Dept., Elmer E. Rasmuson Library, University of Alaska, Fairbanks.*

hipped roof is covered with sheet iron painted red, while the front and side walls are sheathed in weatherboard. The exterior is painted with yellow ocher. Attached to the east and west ends of the building are subordinate shed-roofed structures known as galleries. Framed in heavy timber, they traditionally housed stairways, storage, latrines, and entryways.

The floor plan is an *enfilade,* or a sequence of adjoining rooms that open into each other rather than being connected by passageways. Interior walls and ceilings are covered with canvas, or painted. The floors are wide-hewn planks supported on half-logs with spaces between joists filled with sand for insulation. Although these features are typically Russian, certain characteristics of the building, such as the raised thresholds, suggest construction by shipwrights. Some details of the carpentry have prompted a view that the residence was built by Finnish carpenters brought to

CATHEDRAL OF St. Michael, Sitka, ca. 1900. The essential features of classical Russian church architecture are evident in this striking winter scene of the side of the cathedral, revealing the sanctuary (left), the dome over the nave, and the bell tower over the entry.

Historical Society of Seattle and King County.

CHURCH OF THE Holy Protection, St. Michael, 1906-08. This church was completed in 1884, built by Zacharii Bel'kov, an Aleut who lived at Russian Mission from 1845 and had resided for a time in Sitka.

Anchorage Museum of History and Art.

the colony by General Manager Etholen in the 1840s.[6]

The 1867 agreement transferring the Russian American colonies to the United States allowed the Russian Orthodox church to retain its lands and property. Thus, the old bishop's residence remained in use by the church until 1973, when its condition had deteriorated to the point where the church could no longer maintain it. The National Park Service purchased the building as an addition to Sitka National Historical Park and has subsequently restored it to its 1843-53 appearance. The building was opened to the public in 1988 with exhibits on the first floor and the restored and refurnished bishop's quarters and private chapel on the second floor.

Fort Ross

Fort Ross, on the Sonoma coast north of San Francisco, is an important complex of buildings representing the Russian-American Company's efforts to extend its reach along the coast to new sea otter hunting grounds and to establish a viable agricultural base for colony food supplies. Although the fort is almost entirely a re-construction, with only one building remaining from the colonial period, it is the only representation of an entire Russian settlement on American soil.

Built in 1812, the California fort, with its wooden stockade and polygonal log blockhouses, looked as if it had been transported from Siberia or Alaska. By the 1820s the stronghold contained a commandant's house, barracks for officials, quarters for Russian employees, storehouses and other secondary structures, and a chapel. A new commandant's house, erected in 1836, remains today, partially reconstructed. Outside the stockade were the dwellings of the Aleuts (brought south to hunt sea otters), a number of Russians, and the Kashaya Pomo Indians, as well as a windmill, farm buildings, granaries, cattle yards, a tannery, workshops, and gardens.

In 1906 the state of California designated Fort Ross a state historic site. By this time the fort had undergone many modifications and was in part quite dilapidated. Shortly thereafter the great earthquake struck, resulting in further damage to the fort. Nonetheless, several decades of reconstruction and interpretive efforts

ELEVATION OF the Holy Cross Church at Russian Mission, on the Yukon River, 1898. With its dome and multilevel roofline, this "cathedral of the Yukon" bears a striking resemblance to the cathedral in Sitka. It was designed and built by Rev. Zacharii Bel'kov.

Historical Society of Seattle and King County.

by the state have borne fruit. The buildings today closely approximate the original design and materials, while the site as a whole reflects the character and scale of the historic settlement.

Building No. 29

The last building remaining from the Russian period is a company residence in Sitka (identified as Building No. 29 on the 1867 transfer map), probably built in the 1850s. The two-story building is three bays wide, with a side gallery covering entrances and second-story staircase. The construction reveals fine craftsmanship, with logs hewn flush inside and out and each log incised with a log and course number. Although in the 1880s the roof was redesigned and the building enlarged, the original structure was virtually intact until the mid 1980s, encased by additions and newer finishes. In recent years, however, the private owner has modified the building in ways that have seriously undermined its historic integrity.

Nonetheless, Building No. 29 is an important element in Sitka's historic townscape. Located a few doors from St.

Michael's Cathedral on what was the main street of New Archangel, this last Russian-American Company building in Sitka has a height and bulk that provide a visual link with the commercial life of the colonial town. It is, as well, the only extant structure representing the domestic life of Russian-American Company employees.

Churches

The architectural legacy of Russian America, however, is not limited to colonial-period buildings. The footprint of the original fortified Russian settlement is still visible in many Alaskan villages and towns in their orientation, street plans, patterns of development, and especially in their Russian Orthodox churches.

Because of their maritime orientation, Russian-American Company settlements were located at what are still remote sites on far-flung islands and coasts or on rivers leading to the interior of Alaska. Typically, settlements grew from the waterfront, where fortifications and trade were concentrated, with dwellings, secondary buildings, and gardens spreading out from this core. The church, on its own reserved land and often at a higher elevation, was usually set apart from the main activity areas. As in a typical Russian village, the church was the most highly designed building in a settlement, expressing in its domes and spires the aspirations and identity of its people.

Although no churches remain from the colonial period, second- and third-generation structures have been built on the original church reservations, often incorporating elements from the first structures, such as the *iconostas* (altar screen), into subsequent buildings. Numerous icons and liturgical objects from the Russian period, carefully protected by the Orthodox faithful, remain in present churches.

The architecture of the newer churches also retains many traditional elements. A typical wooden Russian church from the seventeenth or eighteenth century would be constructed of logs in three separate blockwork units, each with its own roofline: the *trapeznaya* or *predvor*, which is a public space often used for secular as well as religious gatherings, through which one passes into the main body of

the church, or nave (*naos*), which is separated from the sanctuary or altar area (*bema*) by the *iconostas*. A *kryltso*, or covered entrance porch, with dual staircase leading to the main door, was part of all but the simplest churches or chapels. The buildings were strongly vertical, with steeply pitched roofs carrying blockwork towers crowned by ogee or bulbous domes, which, in turn, were surmounted by crosses.

The three-part plan is unchanged in the Alaskan churches, although not always architecturally expressed in three contiguous structures. The strong vertical emphasis also remains, as do the traditional domes. The Church of the Holy Assumption in Kenai, a National Historic Landmark, is an outstanding example of the Russian tradition in Alaska, with its log tripartite construction and vertical mass. The perimeters of the original church reservation are intact, containing priest's residence, cemetery, and the small log chapel of St. Nicholas.

TWO ORTHODOX crosses top buildings on the hill above Russian Mission on the Yukon River, ca. 1900. The larger structure is the "Cathedral on the Yukon," the Church of the Elevation of the Cross, built in 1896 by Zakharii Bel'kov. Connected to it by a walkway is the chapel built on the site of the first church on the Yukon, which was erected in 1845 by missionary Rev. Iakov Netsvetov. The summer log homes of the Yup'ik Eskimos line the riverbank behind giant stacks of wood, fuel for the steamship traffic to the goldfields in the north.

R. K. Woods Collection, Alaska and Polar Regions Dept., Elmer E. Rasmuson Library, University of Alaska, Fairbanks.

ORTHODOX CHURCH *of St. George the Victorious, St. George Island, Pribilof Group, 1986. Constructed in 1936, this church is part of the Seal Islands National Historic Landmark.*

National Park Service, Alaska Region, Anchorage.

The Church of the Holy Ascension of Our Lord in Unalaska, the first Alaskan parish of Bishop Innocent (Veniaminov) is architecturally noteworthy; it also contains many of the earliest icons, books, and liturgical items to arrive in Alaska, including items that belonged to Veniaminov, now canonized as an Orthodox saint. Many other parishes, from the hexagonal church at Juneau to the reconstruction of St. Michael's Cathedral at Sitka and the small log churches at Angoon and Nondalton, retain important elements of the Russian tradition. The historical and architectural significance of thirty-seven of Alaska's Orthodox churches have been recognized by their listings in the National Register of Historic Places.

The relatively gradual encroachment of modern development in remote areas of Alaska and the strong persistence of the Orthodox faith among Alaska Natives have worked to preserve both historic landscape elements of the Russian-American outposts and an architectural tradition that began in medieval Russia and found its easternmost expression in Alaska's churches. Today, however, many of the sites and buildings that embody this tradition are jeopardized by the ravages of time and weather and the inevitable pressures of economic development in Alaska's coastal communities. Both public agencies and private groups are responding to this challenge with research and documentation programs, preservation planning, and restoration efforts to keep alive the unique heritage of the Russian Empire on American soil.

Kathleen Lidfors is Regional Historian with the National Park Service, Anchorage.

Steven M. Peterson is Regional Historical Architect with the National Park Service, Anchorage.

For Further Reading

Bartenev, Igor Aleksandrovich. *North Russian Architecture.* Moscow: Progress Press, 1972.

Buxton, David Roden. *Russian Medieval Architecture.* New York: Hacker Art Books, 1975.

Cloyd, Paul C. and Anthony S. Donald. *Historic Structure Report, Administrative and Architectural Data Sections: Russian Bishop's House, Sitka National Historical Park, Alaska.* Denver: Denver Service Center, National Park Service, U.S. Department of the Interior, 1982.

Fedorova, Svetlana G. *The Russian Population in Alaska and California: Late 18th Century - 1867.* Ed. and trans. Richard A. Pierce and Alton S. Donnelly. Kingston, Ontario: Limestone Press, 1973.

Opolovnikov, Alexander and Yelena Opolovnikova. *The Wooden Architecture of Russia: Houses, Fortifications, and Churches.* New York: Harry N. Abrams, Inc., 1989.

Senkevitch, Anatole, Jr. "The Early Architecture and Settlements of Russian America." *Russia's American Colony.* Ed. S. Frederick Starr. Durham, North Carolina: Duke University Press, 1987.

Voyce, Arthur. *The Art and Architecture of Medieval Russia.* Norman, Oklahoma: University of Oklahoma Press, 1967.

The buildings discussed in this chapter are further described in:

Estus, Joaqlin. "Russian Bishop's House." National Register of Historic Places Inventory-Nomination Form, National Park Service, Alaska Region, February 11, 1983.

Fort Ross: Indians, Russians, Americans. Ed. Bickford O'Brien. Jenner, California: Fort Ross Interpretive Association, 1980.

Lidfors, Kathleen. "Building No. 29, Sitka, Alaska." National Register of Historic Places Inventory-Nomination Form, National Park Service, Alaska Region, November 17, 1986.

Smith, Barbara. "Russian-American Company *Magazin*." National Register of Historic Places Inventory-Nomination Form, National Park Service, Alaska Region, November 30, 1986.

Notes

1. William H. Dall, *Alaska and Its Resources* (Boston: Lee and Shepard, 1870), p. 255.

2. *Russkie otkrytiia v Tikom okeane i Severnoi Amerike v XVIII veke: A Collection of Documents*, ed. A. I. Andreev (Moscow, 1948), p. 132. Quoted by S. G. Federova, *The Russian Population in Alaska and California, Late 18th Century-1867*, trans. and ed. Richard A. Pierce and Alton S. Donnelly (Kingston, Ontario: Limestone Press, 1973), p. 216.

3. *Lieutenant Zagoskin's Travels in Russian America, 1842-1844*, ed. Henry N. Michael. Arctic Institute of North America series, *Anthropology of the North: Translations from Russian Sources*, No. 7 (Toronto, Ontario: University of Toronto Press, 1967), p. 185.

4. *Kyrill T. Khlebnikov's Reports, 1817-1832*, trans. Basil Dmytryshyn and E. A. P. Crownhart-Vaughan (Portland: Oregon Historical Society, 1976), p. 73.

5. U.S. Congress, House, *Russian America*, Ex. Doc. No. 177, 40th Cong., 2nd Sess., 1868, p. 69.

6. Paul C. Cloyd and Anthony S. Donald, *Historic Structure Report, Administrative and Architectural Data Sections: Russian Bishop's House, Sitka National Historical Park, Alaska* (Denver: Denver Service Center, National Park Service, U.S. Department of the Interior, 1982), p. 119.

Following *the* Star: From *the* Ukraine *to the* Yukon

by Ann Fienup-Riordan

Anyone who has lived in western Alaska has likely heard about and sometimes been lucky enough to participate in *Selaviq*—the cross-cultural, ethnically diverse, and regionally unique celebration of Russian Orthodox Christmas. Most visitors probably are unprepared for the depth and richness of cultural elaboration that begins on January 6 and continues in full swing for the next ten days. Those unfamiliar with *Selaviq* are often perplexed by its repetitive form and sugar-laden content. Indeed, *Selaviq* makes no sense in terms of the Protestant ethic, which values individuality and moderation over repetition and abundance. Alternately viewed as a squandering of scarce and limited resources or an unnecessarily tedious series of similar meals, the cultural bounty and creativity that *Selaviq* embodies are often lost in translation.

The name *Selaviq* derives from the Russian *slava/slavit*, meaning praise or glory, and is at base a celebration of the birth of Christ through prayer and song. The event is also often referred to as "Starring" because of the large wooden stars carried door-to-door in ceremonial procession. This Starring tradition originated in the Carpathian Mountains of the Ukraine in the sixteenth century as a grass-roots response by Orthodox laity to the forced latinization of the Russian Orthodox church. As originally developed, the Starring songs and customs of the "Little Russians" were unknown in other parts of Russia and helped maintain a separate Orthodox identity in regions of western Russia occupied by Poland into the mid twentieth century. Ironically perhaps, *Selaviq* has placed aspects of this Slavonic folkloric tradition within a framework of Yup'ik interpretation and style to produce an event as central to the maintenance and expression of local identity as was its original.

Selaviq in Western Alaska

Selaviq is celebrated in many Russian Orthodox communities throughout Alaska, including those in the Yukon-Kuskokwim Delta of western Alaska. Russian Orthodoxy is practiced in close to half the communities in the delta region. In the half-dozen predominantly Orthodox villages, the celebration of *Selaviq* marks the single biggest ceremonial event of the entire year, a ritual distribution, community celebration, and religious holiday all rolled into one.

One community in which *Selaviq* is celebrated is Kasigluk, a Yup'ik Eskimo village of just over four hundred people located approximately thirty miles west of Bethel in the tundra region of western Alaska. *Selaviq* has been celebrated in Kasigluk since the people moved from the old village of Nunacuarmiut in the early 1930s and built a Russian Orthodox church at the site. Older villagers remember the introduction of *Selaviq* by Russian Orthodox priests, who brought it down from Russian Mission and the upper Kuskokwim, where it had been introduced somewhat earlier, possibly by Ukrainian-born Father Iakov Korchinskii in the late 1800s or Hieromonk Amphilokhii in the early 1900s.

As a boy, Father Korchinskii had probably participated in the elaborate folk tradition that

In the celebration of Selaviq in Kasigluk today, multiple pasts collide, coexist, and interact. Russian Orthodox, Ukrainian, and indigenous systems of belief and practice all contribute to the event....

CHRISTMAS FESTIVAL star. With an icon of the Nativity in the center, a brightly decorated star is carried aloft through many villages during Orthodox Christmas (January 6) week. This star was made by the Eskimo students at St. Herman's Theological Seminary on Kodiak Island and is held by Lance Gust, a first-year student from New Stuyahok, on the Nushagak River.

Courtesy of St. Herman's Theological Seminary, Kodiak; photograph by Mike Rostad.

attended the celebration of Christmas in his native land. In the Ukraine, a procession of carolers went from house to house carrying a long pole topped by a small star. In the center of the star was an icon of the Nativity illuminated by a candle. This Starring tradition continues to be practiced in some parts of the Ukraine to this day, including the area around Lvov, where the Stalinist suppression of church processionals did not occur.

Like its Alaska counterparts, Starring in the Ukraine varies considerably. In some areas, it is preceded by the Holy Supper on Christmas Eve. This meatless meal marks the end to the fasting that precedes Christmas. As soon as the host sees the first star in the sky, he carries a bowl of boiled wheat around the house three times, reciting prayers. After he returns, he stands in the doorway and calls out to the souls of the ancestors to join the family at supper. When the meal is done, candies are strewn under the table for the children to find. *Kolyadi* (folk carols) are then sung in the home, after which the family goes to church. The next morning the three-day house-to-house caroling begins, during which only *kolyadi* are sung, without church songs.

In western Alaska, the Ukrainian celebration of the Holy Supper did not take root. The Slavonic Starring and caroling traditions, however, were joined to Yup'ik hosting practices embodied in the traditional ceremonial cycle. The traditional Yup'ik ceremonies in their pure form were discouraged by the Orthodox priests. Villagers recall, however, that from the 1930s the priests actively encouraged Starring. In so doing, they prepared the way for its incorporation of Yup'ik ends and means.

In Kasigluk today, preparation for Starring begins during the summer, when salmon are netted and berries are gathered to serve at the *Selaviq* feast. If a hunter takes a moose in the fall, he is careful to put by some of the meat. By the first of January, the ordinarily well-stocked shelves of the village store are all but empty. Families purchase tremendous quantities of rice, tea, sugar, and flour to feed their guests. Small presents are also taken home by the caseload for distribution, including such things as gloves, socks, needles, pens, combs, and bars of soap. No less than thirty thousand dollars' worth of candy is purchased wholesale for the occasion. Each family spends as much as three thousand dollars in preparation for their part of the feasting.

In 1989, *Selaviq* at Kasigluk opened with a two-and-a-half-hour Christmas service held at the church on the morning of January 7. During the Christmas service, Christ and the saints were made present through the icons, and together the human and heavenly community celebrated the glory of Christ's birth. At its close, four young men brought two large five-pointed stars and two icon banners from the sanctuary into the body of the church and presented them to the congregation. The lighted candles of the icon banners were to guide the procession announcing the birth of Christ. Just as the three kings followed the Star of Bethlehem to the place of Jesus' birth, so the *Selaviq* procession followed the ceremonial star during the three days of Russian Christmas. Some people said that the star entering the houses was a symbol of Christ entering the people's homes and being reborn in their souls.

Each star was two and a half feet across and was hung from a thick strap worn around a young man's neck. At the star's center was a painted Nativity scene. Electric Christmas lights had been used to frame the Nativity, requiring the bearer to plug himself in at every house. Throughout the service he kept the star spinning in a counterclockwise direction by regularly pushing a half-dozen heavy metal balls that weighted the star at its back.

As the stars and banners were held facing the congregation, the choir led the people in a series of songs and formal blessings that would be repeated in every household throughout the village during the next ten days. The song service opened with Russian Orthodox hymns sung in both Slavonic and Yup'ik. Along with the hymns were Ukrainian *kolyadi*, of up to ten verses each, sung alternately in Ukrainian and English. The villagers consider both the *kolyadi* and the Orthodox hymns equally "traditional," that is, having to do with the unique oral history of the Yup'ik people. These songs were sung from memory by the members of the choir, who have passed them down orally one to another "from their ancestors."

At the close of the song service, the star- and icon-bearers led the congregation out of the church to the home of the village priest. There the company entered and the song service was repeated. The priest then delivered a short sermon, following which the guests took seats anywhere they could find them, and the host family began a careful and lengthy distribution of candy. In a large house full

*PROCESSION OF the Star during **Selaviq** in the village of Kasigluk, 1989. During three days of Christmas, the entire village follows the star from house to house, being greeted in each home with treats and gifts.*

Photograph by James Barker.

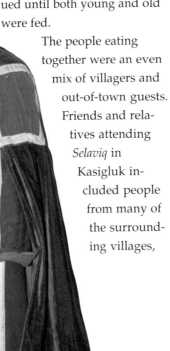

PRIEST'S VESTMENTS, handmade by Rev. Gerasim Schmaltz, priest and monk at Kodiak for many years, until his death in 1969. The priest-monk was Russian-born and came to Alaska in 1918 to care for the grave of the monk Herman (d. 1836) on Spruce Island, near the town of Kodiak. Father Gerasim rose to the rank of archimandrite, allowing him to wear the miter, which he himself also made.

St. Herman's Theological Seminary, Kodiak; photograph by Mike Rostad.

of one hundred people, this could take up to an hour, with each guest receiving a dozen different treats. Other households gave less, but all included a handful of Christmas hard candies, which were, like the Ukrainian carols, considered a "traditional" ingredient of the event.

After the candies had been distributed, the priest blessed the feast and, with the help of his wife and children, began to pass out pieces of dried fish, bowls of moose soup, and plates of *akutaq* (literally "a mixture," including berries, shortening, and sugar). The older men and church readers seated themselves at the table and were served first, followed by the younger men, until all had been served. Only then did the women take their turn. The serving continued until both young and old were fed.

The people eating together were an even mix of villagers and out-of-town guests. Friends and relatives attending *Selaviq* in Kasigluk included people from many of the surrounding villages, both near and far. Not only were out-of-towners welcomed, but non-Orthodox guests were also in abundance. Approximately 80 percent of Kasigluk's residents are Russian Orthodox, yet almost the entire village participated in *Selaviq*. The local priest emphasized that before the arrival of the Moravians at the end of the nineteenth century, all the people living in the area had been Russian Orthodox and, for this reason, all were encouraged to participate in what he called the "traditional Yup'ik Christmas celebration."

When the last of the women finished their tea, the star-bearers and their companions carried the stars and icon banners out of the back room and the people rose to follow the stars out of the house. After this initial three-hour feast, the congregation divided into two groups. The first group walked across the river and continued visiting the houses in the old village. The second group loaded their star into a station wagon and took it to the site of the new village housing project. There they entered the home of the church's first reader and began the service all over again.

As the *Selaviq* procession moved from house to house, the participants enjoyed variations on the theme described above. Finally, ten days and over one hundred feasts later, the congregation returned to the cemetery beside the church, where the song service was repeated one last time. After the service, the stars were returned to the church to be stored until the following year.

Since its introduction in Kasigluk more than fifty years ago, Starring has undergone many changes. In the 1930s, when the population of Kasigluk was less than one hundred, the congregation traveled from house to house as a single group. When there were only a dozen houses, each could be visited by the entire congregation on each of the three nights of Russian Christmas.

As the village grew, so did the magnitude of *Selaviq*. By the early 1960s the number of houses and people in Kasigluk had doubled, as had the time it took to complete the *Selaviq* visitations. As a result, the people divided into two groups following two stars. By dividing the village, the people managed to visit each house three times in three days.

By the 1970s the increasing number of houses made it difficult for participants to complete the full *Selaviq* cycle. One choir member recalled those as trying years. With so many houses and so much food, it was harder and harder to breathe and sing at the same time.

Although *Selaviq* was becoming increasingly unmanageable, the intellectually conservative older generation was willing to change *Selaviq* only enough to allow it to remain the same. In 1983, however, thirty-seven houses were built at the new downriver village site. With twice the number of houses, it became impossible for all the people to visit each house three times in under a week. As a result, the number of visits began to decrease. In 1989, fifty-nine of the village's sixty-seven households were visited once, forty-five of them a second time, and the third visit was eliminated altogether. Also, the amount of time needed to complete the visitations dramatically increased. What had originally been a three-day celebration became a ten-day marathon of singing, feasting, and gift-giving.

Local church leaders are presently considering cutting back *Selaviq* to a single visitation per home. Sentiment is divided, however, as the final rounds customarily involve the most elaborate gifting and feasting. Though cognizant of the apparent impracticality of the full-fledged celebration and the degree to which it has grown out of its original form, villagers

REV. IAKOV Korchinskii was the Orthodox priest at Russian Mission on the Yukon from 1896 to 1901. Of Ukrainian origin, the priest is believed to have introduced his own regional custom of Starring to the Yukon-Kuskokwim region, where it has spread and evolved, even as it has declined in the Ukraine.

James Stephen Collection, Alaska State Library, Juneau.

are equally proud of their capacity to host such a spectacular distribution, the full enactment of which they will only reluctantly relinquish.

Starring and the Yup'ik Ceremonial Cycle

Russian Orthodox priests introduced Starring not only to the Yup'ik Eskimos, but also to their Tlingit, Koniag, and Aleut converts, and it is widely practiced throughout Alaska to this day. Western Alaska, however, is unique in the degree to which Starring has been elaborated. What was it about the original Starring tradition that appealed to the Yup'ik sense of appropriate ritual form? The answer may in part relate to common themes present in Orthodox ritual, Ukrainian custom, and the nineteenth-century Yup'ik view of the world.

The people of Kasigluk explicitly identify *Selaviq* with their past, both Yup'ik and Orthodox. We can, in fact, see striking points of articulation between the celebration of *Selaviq* in western Alaska today and the nineteenth-century Yup'ik ceremonial cycle. Understanding the ways in which this Christian ritual is performed in a decidedly Yup'ik manner can help us better understand how and why Starring has acquired its present regal stature in the contemporary Yup'ik ceremonial cycle.

ICON OF ST. MATTHEW, from an unknown Alaskan church.

Security Pacific Bank, Seattle.

On the most general level, the feasting associated with *Selaviq* requires the same seasonal preparations—fishing, hunting, berry gathering—that were such an important part of the traditional annual round. Although the intensity of the harvesting effort has diminished and the technology employed has been transformed, life in Kasigluk today continues to alternate between seasonal dispersal for harvesting activities and a winter pulling together at a central village site.

Just as *Selaviq* requires continuity in the annual seasonal cycle, it also reflects traditional social distinctions. In the nineteenth century, village space was residentially divided: all men and boys over the age of five lived together in a central house, which was surrounded by individual women's houses. The men's house was the focus of numerous public ceremonies, whereas the women's houses were the focus of private productive activity. Women's activity was believed to directly affect a man's ability to succeed as a hunter, and contact with women was carefully circumscribed.

In Kasigluk, aspects of this division found confirmation in Orthodoxy as originally presented. For example, the first Orthodox priests required men and women to occupy opposite sides of the church. This restriction made sense in terms of the traditional Yup'ik sexual division and is followed to this day during the celebration of *Selaviq*.

Moreover, Russian Orthodoxy as practiced in western Alaska today prohibits women from attending church while they are menstruating and during the forty days after giving birth. These restrictions derive from the Old Testament requirement that no blood be shed in the temple where the "bloodless sacrifice" was offered. This was a relatively minor point in Orthodox church doctrine and is not followed in most contemporary Orthodox congregations. What was minor in the Orthodox canon, however, remains a cardinal tenet of the faith in western Alaska.

A striking parallel also exists between Orthodox and traditional Yup'ik ritual activity in the importance given to the act of circling and the movement from center to periphery. Moving in a circle is an important part of a number of Russian Orthodox rituals. As part of an Orthodox wedding ceremony, for example, the couple walks in a circle around the inside of the church. This circling is always to the right, signifying the sun's rising and Christ's coming. The congregation also circles the church three times to the right on Holy Friday and again on Easter Sunday carrying Christ's shroud.

Formal ceremonial circuits were also an important part of traditional Yup'ik ritual activity and were often tied to spiritual power and visibility of the spirit world. For example, during the nineteenth-century Yup'ik ceremony known as *Qaariitaaq*, village boys had their bodies painted and were led from house to house each night for three to five successive nights, and the women gave them food.

During another ceremony, called *Aaniq*, held directly after *Qaariitaaq*, two older men dressed in gutskin parkas and referred to as "mothers" led a group of boys, who were termed their "dogs," around the village. The men collected newly made bowls filled with *akutaq* from the women, a dramatic reversal of the day-to-day pattern of women bringing cooked meat to their men in the men's house. They were also sometimes given tea to drink in the houses, where the male "mothers" might sing a long song.

During *Selaviq* today, two young men lead villagers on a house-to-house circuit of the village, during which the members of the procession sing songs and feast on *akutaq* in individual homes. Although invested with a new Christian meaning, this house-to-house feasting bears a striking resemblance to the nineteenth-century ceremonial circuit. Although the contemporary division between church and home differs in important respects from that between the traditional men's and women's houses, in *Selaviq*, as in the traditional ceremonies, the profane day-to-day gap is bridged by a sacred ceremonial circuit. As the ritual circuit opened the traditional winter ceremonial season and

perhaps marked the entry into the human community of members of the spirit world, so the Starring procession is said to open people's hearts to the spirit of Christ at the same time that it announces His birth.

Moreover, for both the Yup'ik Eskimos and the Russian Orthodox, the direction as well as the act of circling is significant.

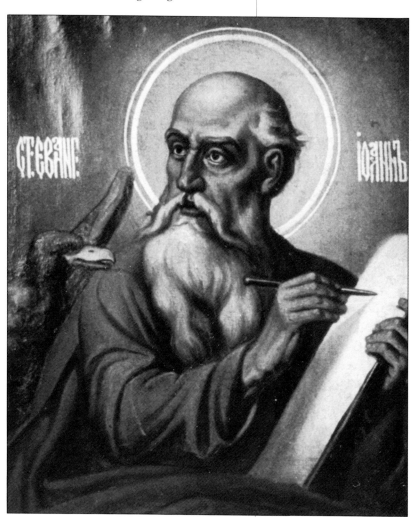

Just as Orthodox ritual requires processions around the altar and church, a number of nineteenth-century Yup'ik ceremonies involved the performance of a ritual circuit in the direction of the sun's course. For example, one of the most important nineteenth-century ceremonies was the Bladder Festival, which was held to host the souls of the animals killed during the year and ensure their return in the future. At the beginning of the

ICON OF ST. JOHN, from an unknown Alaskan church.

Security Pacific Bank, Seattle.

Bladder Festival, young men ran around the village in the direction of the sun's course before entering the men's house bearing bunches of wild celery needed to purify inflated bladders believed to hold the animals' souls.

The spinning of the star during *Selaviq* is likely tied to these traditional ceremonial acts, both Yup'ik and Orthodox. In Eastern Europe, the star was held stationary. It is only in Alaska that the star is kept in motion. The ritual movement of the star around the village to celebrate the birth of Christ, as well as the star's perpetual movement during its ritual circuit, recalls the efficacy of this traditional ritual act. It hardly seems accidental that when the star is put in motion in western Alaska, it is in the direction of the sun's course.

In the celebration of *Selaviq* we see continuity as well as change in the form and meaning of the ritual process. As in the traditional Bladder Festival, a ceremonial circuit ritually "opened" the human community and functioned to connect it to a larger spiritual reality. Both were opportunities for encounter through which the spirit world was made manifest. Just as the Bladder Festival opened the traditional winter ceremonial season, so *Selaviq* is the first major Orthodox ritual, followed by the celebration of Russian New Year, the Epiphany, and finally *Pashka*, or Easter. Also, like the Bladder Festival, *Selaviq* is an enjoyable, festive celebration during which food replaces famine and light replaces dark.

On the last night of the Bladder Festival, the entire village as well as invited guests from nearby villages gathered in the men's house. Parents gave gifts to celebrate their children's accomplishments, and a huge village-wide distribution took place in which large

amounts of frozen and dried fish were given away. The thousands of dollars' worth of gifts and food distributed during the final days of *Selaviq* today in some measure keep this tradition alive. Instead of using money and storing goods in a conservative Western way (i.e., accumulating capital, investing profits), the Yup'ik people annually continue to disperse large quantities of hard-earned goods, transforming material wealth into a statement of community.

The Bladder Festival is not the only nineteenth-century Yup'ik ceremony that has given meaning to the contemporary Yup'ik celebration of *Selaviq*. *Selaviq* also relates to the traditional Yup'ik Feast for the Dead—the public occasion on which the spirits of the human dead were invited into the community to receive the fresh water, food, and clothing they required. During the Feast for the Dead, the feeding and clothing of the namesakes of the deceased were believed to feed and clothe the dead as well. *Selaviq* continues this tradition of honoring children, in whom the ancestors are in some essential way believed to live again.

The Yup'ik belief in spiritual rebirth also ties into a very special aspect of *Selaviq*—the capacity of guests to repeatedly feast, yet never get full. According to Yup'ik tradition, the dead suffer from tremendous hunger and thirst. Even people who no longer hold this belief may still cite it to explain the custom of feasting during *Selaviq*. Today when asked why they never get full during the *Selaviq* feasts, older villagers say that it is because when they eat they are feeding the insatiable spirits of the dead. Moreover, just as the Ukrainians invited their ancestors to partake of the Holy Supper with them, the Yup'ik Eskimos typically leave their windows uncovered during *Selaviq* to admit the spirits of the departed to the feast. Many modern Christian Yup'ik men and women retain their belief in the cycling of souls characteristic of nineteenth-century Yup'ik cosmology. Russian Orthodox ritual symbolism and eschatology (e.g., the belief that the dead are forever present among the community of the living) allowed their converts to become Christians at the same time that they continued to view the world from a pre-Christian Yup'ik point of view.

An Evolving Tradition

In sum, both contemporary *Selaviq* and the traditional Yup'ik ceremonies focus on annual spiritual renewal and rebirth. Both are built around the ritualized dramatization of inherent conflicts of oppositions, including feast-famine, light-dark, birth-rebirth, and center-periphery. The referent has changed, from the renewal of game and seasonal rebirth, to the birth of Christ and the salvation of mankind. Yet, the feasting and gift-giving that attend *Selaviq* do not affirm the dominance of the mission system and its attendant moral and social order over the traditional Yup'ik view of the world—they signify their consenting union. Far from reflecting the primacy of the Christian mission, the historical roots of *Selaviq* are as much Yup'ik as they are Orthodox.

In the celebration of *Selaviq* in Kasigluk today, multiple pasts collide, coexist, and interact. Russian Orthodox, Ukrainian, and indigenous systems of belief and practice all contribute to the event, which the Yup'ik people of western Alaska continue to modify. Many non-Natives consider *Selaviq* to be primarily a Russian Orthodox tradition because of its focus on Christmas and its reliance on Orthodox liturgical and Ukrainian folk traditions. Today in Kasigluk, however, Yup'ik Eskimos understand *Selaviq* as an important part of their own history, which includes but is by no means controlled by their interaction with Russian Orthodox clergy.

Far from a corruption of a Russian tradition or the sign of a secularized or compromised Yup'ik tradition, *Selaviq* enacts the retention of human communion and feasting in a sacred ritual context. For the traditional Yupiit, communal feasting was a spiritually significant act, and in the form of *Selaviq* it continues so to this day.

Ann Fienup-Riordan is an anthropologist in Anchorage who has published numerous books and articles on Yup'ik culture. Research for this article was supported by The National Endowment for the Humanities.

For Further Reading

Fienup-Riordan, Ann. *The Real People and the Children of Thunder.* Norman, Oklahoma: The University of Oklahoma Press, 1990 (in press).

The Journals of Iakov Netsvetov: The Yukon Years, 1845-1863. Ed. Richard A. Pierce, trans. Lydia T. Black. *Alaska History Series* 26. Kingston, Ontario: Limestone Press, 1984.

Oswalt, Wendell H. *Mission of Change in Alaska: Eskimos and Moravians on the Kuskokwim.* San Marino, California: Huntington Library, 1963.

Smith, Barbara S. "Cathedral on the Yukon." *Alaska Journal* 12, no. 2, pp. 4-6, 50-55.

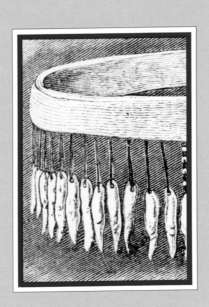

The Russian Legacy
of the Alaska Native Claims

by David S. Case

I n the mid twentieth century, Alaska Natives, like aboriginal residents of other parts of the United States, successfully claimed substantial amounts of land that had passed out of their control. Many assume that the Alaska Native land claims began (and ended) then. Others view them as unique, and certainly the method used for their settlement (the Alaska Native Claims Settlement Act)[1] is distinct in significant respects from the methods used elsewhere in the United States. In fact, the question of aboriginal claims in Alaska, as elsewhere in the Americas, began with the first contact between Europeans and the aboriginal inhabitants. In Alaska, that contact was with tsarist Russia, beginning in the mid eighteenth century. As the Russians came to know the Natives better, their policies evolved. The three charters granted to the Russian-American Company embody that evolution.

The Russian "discovery" of Alaska differs in certain respects from the history of the "discovery" of the rest of the New World. Since it was Russian, it did not necessarily follow the legal principles that attended the Spanish or English occupation of the rest of North and South America. Another distinction was the relatively tenuous, even minimal, role the tsarist government played in the management of the Alaskan discoveries of its merchant princes. There was never a true colonial government in Alaska; instead, the interests of the Russian state were indirectly represented through the imperially chartered Russian-American Company. As time went on, to be sure, the government became more involved in the company's operations. After the Second Charter of 1821, only high-ranking naval officers held the title of Administrator General of the colony. High-ranking members of the tsarist government also invested in the company and sat on its board, and by 1857 all the merchant members of the board had been replaced by government officers. Nevertheless, this governmental involvement was a far cry from the complex web of laws, taxes, treaties, and colonial governments with which the British and the Spanish controlled their discoveries.

From 1799 to 1867, the Russian government promulgated only some fifty-eight laws and decrees related to its affairs in Alaska. Between 1763 and the American Revolution, the British government alone negotiated some sixty-eight separate treaties with individual Indian tribes. Parliament and the colonial legislatures enacted numerous laws on a wide range of topics. This disparity in formal government involvement with colonial affairs is no doubt due in large part to several obvious but important facts.

The first is that the Russian discovery of Alaska occurred nearly three centuries after the earliest voyages of discovery of the other European powers. Another is that Alaska's northern latitude made it a generally harsh and inhospitable place to colonize. The result was a sparse non-Native population and little pressure to resolve the land claims of Alaska's first inhabitants. A third factor may have been the tsarist government's desire to avoid conflict with the British and American governments by not appearing too "imperial."

It is somewhat peculiar that the tsarist policies of the Russian Empire should in several respects seem more favorable in their treatment of Alaskan Natives than the policies of its democratic successor.

OIL PORTRAIT of Nicholas I, Tsar of Russia, 1825-55. The third and final charter of the Russian-American Company was granted by Tsar Nicholas in 1844. It further refined the categories of Native population, serving as the basis for the description of the status of Alaska Natives immediately before the Treaty of Purchase in 1867.

Sitka National Historical Park.

INUIT bone drawings.

From William H. Dall's Alaska and Its Resources (Boston, 1870).

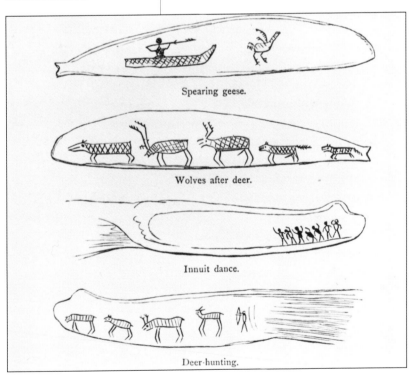

Spearing geese.

Wolves after deer.

Innuit dance.

Deer-hunting.

In this vacuum, the Russians never attempted any resolution of Native claims. The cumulative interpretation of the three charters of the Russian-American Company and later American judicial opinions is that the Russians divided the residents of Alaska into several distinct classes or "estates," but did not attempt to resolve Native land claims.[2] Some courts and commentators have suggested that the Russian classification of Natives has some bearing on their claims, but neither the courts nor Congress has considered the status of Natives under Russian rule significant in resolving those claims.[3]

The First Charter (1799-1821)

The First Russian-American Charter of 1799 merely encouraged the company to "sponsor the conversion of the newly discovered people into the Christian religion and the making of them into subjects of His Imperial Majesty." The same section expressed the intention "to treat the Americans and the Islanders amicably." The actual policies implemented these vague promises extremely loosely. The first administrator of the Russian-American Company, Alexander Baranov, was known for his often ruthless exploitation of the Natives as he developed the fur trade and extended the company's influence from Kodiak to Sitka and, for a time, as far as Hawaii and California.

Overland travel through Siberia was difficult, so the tsarist government maintained tenuous supervision of its Alaskan domain with occasional visits by the Imperial Navy. Naval reports in the early nineteenth century confirmed the persistent maltreatment of the Natives. Lieutenant Captain Golovnin's report in 1818 led both to Baranov's discharge and provisions in the company's 1821 Second Charter better defining the status and treatment to be accorded the Natives.

The Second Charter (1821-1844)

The 1821 Charter placed the Alaskan Natives in three pragmatic, but not very clear, categories. The "Creoles" and "Islanders" were all Russian subjects, although each had unique rights, privileges, immunities, and obligations. The "Tribes inhabiting the coasts" were described in terms indicating that they were considered independent of Russian administration.

The Creoles were defined as people of mixed Russian and Native blood, and in 1821 amounted to only about three hundred people. Under the terms of the Second Charter, they were to constitute a "special estate" as Russian subjects with the rank of "commoners," unless by merit or for special cause they obtained a higher rank. As Russian subjects, they were entitled to protection by the government, but as Creoles they were not taxed and the Administrator General of the colonies was required specifically to "take care of them and their property." Creoles could also enter the service of the company and on the company's discretion be admitted to the privileges accorded those who entered the company's service as commoners. If educated at company expense as physicians, military officers, or civil servants, they could be required to serve at least ten years in the colonies, but were then free to go elsewhere. Many Creoles rose to high positions in the company and the professions. In general, the Russians do not seem to have practiced racial discrimination against either the Creoles or Natives, as became all too common under later American administration.

The Islanders were those Native tribes inhabiting the Kurile, Aleutian, and other islands administered by the company as well as the Kenai, Chugach, and other tribes "living on the American coast." The description seems pragmatically vague and calculated to include those tribes clearly within the company's sphere of influence as well as those the company might wish were or that might later come within it. The Islanders were also Russian subjects and therefore protected by and expected to conform to the "general laws of the Empire," although they were not subject to any tax or tribute, except as described below.

Unlike the Creoles, up to half the male population of the Islanders between the ages of eighteen and fifty could be required to hunt sea mammals for the company. For this they were supplied with proper clothes, food, and boats, and were required to be paid "not less than one fifth of the pay received by Russians" for the animals they caught. They could not be forced to this labor for more than three years. While this was not exactly slavery, it was a form of serfdom with which there were parallels under tsarist law.

Even though they were Russian subjects, the Islanders were not subject solely to Russian law. Section 47 of the Second Charter also said that the "Islanders are governed by their *toiens* (chiefs, nobles) under the supervision of superintendents appointed by the colonial authorities from among the best Russian employees of the Company." The chiefs and the superintendents were required to "look after the Natives in their jurisdiction, settle their mutual disputes and take care of their needs." The company was also required to "leave at the disposal of the Islanders as much land as is necessary for all their needs, at the places where they are settled or will be settled."

The Russian policy under the Second Charter was not to extend the company's activities to new areas without the consent of the aboriginal inhabitants. Specifically, the company was to avoid "anything which might create in these people suspicion of the intention to violate their independence." The aboriginal inhabitants of new areas could, however, voluntarily move into the Russian colonies, in which case they would be classed with the Islanders and have the same rights and privileges.

The contrast between the First and Second charters was significant. Where the First Charter had spoken vaguely of

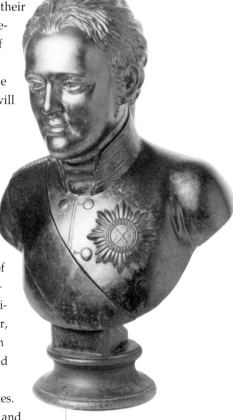

BUST OF Alexander I, Tsar of Russia, 1801-25. This metal statue was brought to Kodiak by the tsar's chamberlain, Nikolai Rezanov, in 1805, and stood on a pedestal near the chief manager's office. Alexander granted a second charter to the Russian-American Company in 1821 that placed all Natives in three categories: "Creoles," "Islanders," and "Tribes Inhabiting the Coast." Creoles were given special status, enjoying the protection due a Russian subject but exempt from taxation and military service.

Collection of William Lamme, Anchorage.

TLINGIT spoon handle.

From William H. Dall's Alaska and Its
Resources (Boston, 1870).

"newly discovered peoples," the Second Charter described a three-group social system (four groups, counting the Russians), each with distinct rights and duties. This system of social classification was no doubt alien to nineteenth-century American democratic principles. Above all, the classification of the Creoles as "commoners" had real rather than ceremonial meaning only in a monarchical system of government. The Islanders' serfdom is another example of the tsarist system treating Natives differently (but perhaps not much worse) than analogous American law, which of course recognized and regulated slavery. On the other hand, some elements of the Islanders' treatment—particularly the relationship between the hereditary chiefs and company superintendents in matters of tribal government and land allocations—are reminiscent of the control the Bureau of Indian Affairs exercised over tribal matters in mid-nineteenth-century America.

The Third Charter (1844-1867)

The policies of the Second Charter were repeated, elaborated, and refined in the Third Charter of 1844. Although the Third Charter expired five years before the American purchase in 1867, it is the basis for the description of the status of the Alaska Natives under the tsarist regime immediately prior to the 1867 Treaty of Cession. The Charter appears to divide the population of Alaska into six distinct categories: (1) people employed on contract, (2) colonists, (3) Creoles, (4) settled tribes, (5) not wholly dependent tribes, and (6) independent tribes. The categories overlap in some respects. Creoles, for example, could also be employed on contract, and if they followed an "independent means of livelihood," were to be regarded as "colonists."

The colonists were those Russian subjects who had the right to leave the colony but chose to remain. After

terminating their contracts with the company, they were to be "assigned to settlements along the Kenai shore of America" or other locations approved by the Administrator General. In allotting land to the colonists, the company was specifically required to "bear in mind that the natives are not to be embarrassed." The colonists were also required to support themselves "by their own labor, without any burden on the natives."

The mixed-blood children of colonists were to be regarded as Creoles, and were specifically allowed to be employed by the company at established rates of pay. In general, the Creoles appear to have had the same rights as under the Second Charter. They were Russian subjects with the rank of commoner, but were also protected by a "special guardianship" over them and their property. They were still exempt from "any governmental tax or dues."

The major refinement in the Third Charter was the designation of the "settled tribes." These were clearly the "Islanders" of the Second Charter, and included the inhabitants of the Kurile Islands, the Aleutians, Kodiak, the Alaska Peninsula, and the "natives living on the shores of America, such as the Kenai natives, the Chugach, etc." As under the Second Charter, up to half the male population of the settled tribes between the ages of eighteen and fifty could be required to give three years of service to the company. Unlike the Second Charter, the Third Charter protected families in a small way by requiring that enough male workers be left in each family "to provide for the women, children, and the disabled" and that no man could be separated from his family for more than two of the three years. The description of the localities is more detailed and accurate than under the Second Charter, probably reflecting a better understanding of Alaskan geography.

Additionally, the Third Charter seemed to place the settled tribes under tighter governmental control. Like its predecessor, the Third Charter acknowledged that settled tribes were "governed by their chiefs under the supervision of the superintendents." The chief's appointment was to be "confirmed" by the colonial Administrator General, but the positions were no longer hereditary, and their discharge and appointment were the responsibility of the Governor. Nevertheless, chiefs retained independent authority to appoint a deputy chief for each village. Natives were also required to obey the appointed chiefs in matters of public welfare and peace. Although chiefs had no unilateral power over private property, they and the superintendents did have the authority to adjust property disputes.

The "not wholly dependent" tribes and the "independent" tribes of the Third Charter appear to be two divisions of a similar category. The policy under the Second Charter had been not to extend the activities of the company into new areas without the consent of the aboriginal inhabitants and to "avoid anything which might create in these people suspicion of the intention to violate their independence." This same language is repeated in the Third Charter, along with a specific injunction prohibiting the company from "forcibly extend[ing] the possessions of the Company in regions inhabited by tribes not dependent on the colonial authorities."

The Third Charter also allowed the members of the not wholly dependent tribes to immigrate into areas occupied by the settled tribes and to be treated like members of the settled tribes. However, relations with the "independent" tribes, presumably those dwelling outside areas of Russian activity, were "limited to the exchange, by mutual consent, of European wares for furs and native products."

The 1867 Treaty

Article III of the 1867 Treaty of Cession reduces the elaborate categories and provisions of the Russian charters to two sentences:

> The inhabitants of the ceded territory, according to their choice, reserving their natural allegiance, may return to Russia within three years; but if they should prefer to remain in the ceded territory, they, with the exception of the uncivilized native tribes, shall be admitted to the enjoyment of all the rights, advantages, and immunities of citizens of the United States, and shall be maintained and protected in the free enjoyment of their liberty, property, and religion. The uncivilized tribes will be subject to such laws and regulations as the United States may, from time to time, adopt in regard to the aboriginal tribes of that country.

These two sentences reduce the six categories of the Third Charter to only two—the "uncivilized tribes" and the

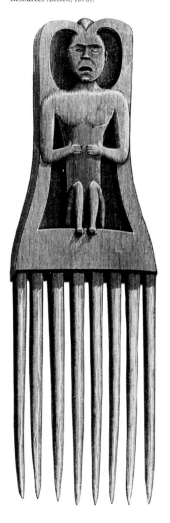

TLINGIT comb.

From William H. Dall's Alaska and Its Resources *(Boston, 1870).*

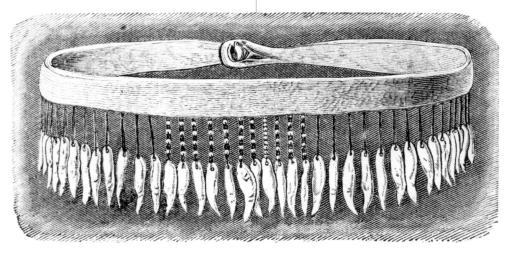

SEAL-TOOTH headdress.

From Rev. Sheldon Jackson's Alaska and Missions on the North Pacific Coast *(New York, ca. 1880).*

other "inhabitants." The latter were entitled to U.S. citizenship if they did not return to Russia. The former were to be treated according to the laws of the United States applicable to "aboriginal tribes," including presumably the settlement of their aboriginal claims. At least one United States court has held that the "inhabitants" entitled to citizenship included Natives of mixed blood ("Creoles" in the terms of the Russian charters) who had abandoned their tribal relationships.[4] The category obviously included the contract employees and colonists also described in the Third Charter.

As to the uncivilized tribes, there seems to be little dispute that this included the "not wholly dependent" and "independent" tribes of the Third Charter. However, some courts have suggested that the "uncivilized tribes" in Article III of the treaty did not include the "settled tribes" of the Third Charter. Carried to its logical conclusion, this suggestion implies that the descendants of the "settled tribes" would not have aboriginal claims to land. On the other hand, in actually settling aboriginal claims in Alaska, the United States has never drawn that distinction.

Moreover, those who actually negotiated the treaty on behalf of Russia and the United States advised their respective governments to the contrary. Secretary William Seward, in a handwritten memorandum almost certainly placed before the President's Cabinet on March 15, 1867, said simply that under the treaty, "The Indians to be on the footing of Indians domiciled in U.S." The Russian minister to the United States, Edouard de Stoeckl, explained Article III in an April 19, 1867, memorandum to his government. There he distinguished only between "Russians" and "savage tribes" and as to the latter noted: "[I]t was impossible for me to stipulate anything in their favor. This would be in a way for us to reserve the right of intervention in the ceded territory."[5]

Conclusion

The Russian categorization of Natives appears to be of only historical interest when it comes to the resolution of Alaska Native aboriginal claims. The tsarist government never attempted any resolution of Native claims, and the United States has never relied on tsarist classifications in resolving those claims. The classifications, with their tsarist emphasis on status, are also somewhat repugnant to American democratic values.

On the other hand, the evolving

An Inventory of the public property in New Archangel (Sitka) delivered to the United States of America, General Lovell H. Rousseau U.S. Commissioner, by his Imperial Majesty Emperor of Russia, Captain Alexis Pestchouroff, Russian Commissioner on the 18th day of October 1867 at New Archangel (Sitka). The letters and numbers on the margin correspond with those on the plan of the city attached to the Protocol of the Transfer and show the situation of the buildings that they refer to.

Letters or numbers on the plan	Description
	Forts
A	Battery No.1. Forward of a timber breastwork and platform situated at the water's edge at the foot of the stairs leading to the Governor House and armed with 5-12lb and 5=18lbs cast-iron guns
B	Battery No 2. Commonly called the Alaskan Battery constructed of timber situated by the Indian Market Place, and armed with six 12lbs cast iron Carronades and one 12lbs cast iron gun
C	Blockhouse No.1. Constructed of timber situated by the Church for the Indians and armed with three 4 lbs cast iron guns and one howitzer
D	Blockhouse No.2. Constructed of timber situated by the Lutheran Cemetery and armed with three six lbs carronades of iron
E	Blockhouse No.3. Constructed of timber situated by the Artificial pond and armed with three cast iron Carronades.
	Buildings
Vnumbers	
3	Subsistence storehouse of timber in two compartments
6	Three storied timber barracks for the Garrison troops
7	Two story timber building for office house
8	Governor's house of timber two stories high with wooden staircase and platforms on the outside etc.
9	wash and bathhouse of timber appertaining to the Government
11.12.13.	Dock yard, consisting of a Ship Slips two workmen's sheds,
14, 15.22.	a shed for boiling pitch, Coal store, sawing shed, two storied
23.	boathouse Smithy and steamKiln all of timber
16	School Building of timber with its appurtenances

classifications show a movement toward more benign treatment, with the notable exception of the forced labor of the settled tribes. Notably, Russian policy guaranteed Natives of mixed blood equal standing with other Russian subjects and allowed Native forms of self-government among the settled tribes some latitude to operate.[6] Russian policy also specifically avoided conflict with tribes outside the immediate areas of Russian occupation and specifically prohibited the Russian-American Company from "forcibly" extending the possessions of the company "in regions inhabited by tribes not dependent on the colonial authorities."

By way of contrast, American policy has seldom hesitated to forcibly extend American possession of Native lands. Similarly, until the civil rights movements of the twentieth century, discrimination against Natives and other people of color has been an all-too-frequent characteristic of American society. It is somewhat peculiar that the tsarist policies of the Russian Empire should in several respects seem more favorable in their treatment of Alaskan Natives than the policies of its democratic successor.

David S. Case is an attorney-at-law in Anchorage.

For Further Reading

Arnold, Robert D. *Alaska Native Land Claims.* Anchorage, Alaska: Alaska Native Foundation, 1978.

Case, David S. *Alaska Natives and American Laws.* Fairbanks, Alaska: University of Alaska Press, 1984.

Davydov, G. L. *Two Voyages to Russian America, 1802-1807.* Kingston, Ontario: Limestone Press, 1977.

Gsovski, Vladimir. *Russian Administration of Alaska and the Status of the Alaskan Natives.* Senate Doc. No. 152. Washington, D.C.: U.S. Government Printing Office, 1950.

Miller, D. H. *The Alaska Treaty.* Kingston, Ontario: Limestone Press, 1981.

Okun, S. B. *The Russian-American Company.* New York: Octagon Books, 1979.

Notes

In the interest of stylistic uniformity, citations to particular sections of the Russian-American Company's charters are normally omitted. Unless otherwise noted, quotations are from the charters.

1. Act of December 18, 1971, P.L. 92-203, 85 Stat. 689, 43 U.S.C. 1601 *et seq.*, as amended.

2. First Charter of the Russian-American Company, Vol. XXV, Complete Laws of the Russian Empire, Law 19030, pp. 699-718 (1799); Second Charter of the Russian-American Company, Vol. XXXVII, Complete Laws of the Russian Empire, Law 28756k, pp. 842-854 (1821); Third Charter of the Russian-American Company, Vol. XIX, part 1, Law 18290, 00612-638 (1844). Excerpted in Gsovski, 43-52. E.g., *In re Minook,* 2 Ak. Rpts. 200 (D. Alas. 1904) and *U.S. v. Berrigan,* 2 Ak. Rpts. 442 (D. Alas. 1904).

3. E.g., *In re Minook,* 219, Russian classification as applied through the 1867 Treaty of Cession entitled a Native of what the Russians called the "settled tribes" to United States citizenship under Article III of the Treaty. Compare *Atkinson v. Haldane,* 569 P.2d 151, 154 (Ak. 1979), "The interactions of the United States government and the Alaska Native peoples as a whole have been much different from those between the government and the tribes in the other states." Citing *In re Minook* and the alleged distinction between "civilized" and "uncivilized" tribes in Article III and the 1867 Alaska Treaty of Cession. E.g., *Tee Hit Ton Band of Indians v. U.S.,* 348 U.S. 272, 285-291 (1955), Alaska Native land claims are claims of aboriginal title and were not affected by the Russian handling of Indian land issues; *Tlingit and Haida Indians of Alaska v. U.S.,* 177 F. Supp. 452, 460, and 464-465 (Ct. Cls. 1959), confirming Tlingit and Haida claims of aboriginal title to virtually all of southeast Alaska and holding that the 1867 Treaty of Cession did not extinguish those claims.

4. *In re Minook,* cited in Note 1.

5. D. H. Hunter, *The Alaska Treaty* (Kingston, Ontario: Limestone Press, 1981), pp. 71, 89; reprinting in translation de Stoeckl's Russian Foreign Office dispatch No. 10. In the memorandum, de Stoeckl uses the terms "savage tribes" and "Indian tribes" interchangeably.

6. The noted Soviet scholar S. B. Okun sets out a less sanguine view of the economic effect of tsarist policies on the Creoles. S. B. Okun, *The Russian-American Company* (New York: Octagon Books, 1979), pp. 213-215.

Russia's Cultural Legacy *in* America: The Orthodox Mission

Barbara Sweetland Smith

C hristian missions have been an integral part of the colonial experience in recent centuries, and Russian America was no exception in this respect. But this was Christianity with a difference—Eastern Orthodoxy, with a Russian stamp. Over the course of the 125 years of Russian activity in Alaska, Orthodoxy made a deep impression on the Native community, and 120 years after the Russians' departure, it is still the largest single religious denomination among Alaska's Natives.

The Orthodox mission officially began in Alaska in 1794, as a frank instrument of "pacification policy." The great leader of Russian Orthodoxy, and himself a priest and bishop in Alaska, Metropolitan Innocent (Veniaminov) noted that in the early days of exploration and exploitation, it was common for Russian *promyshlenniki* to baptize Aleuts indiscriminately. A baptized Aleut was a prize for the entrepreneur, "Since baptized Aleuty [Aleuts] revered their godfathers as their true fathers," and served them willingly and exclusively.[1] Innocent viewed this as unhealthy both in human and spiritual terms. Grigorii Shelikhov felt it destroyed morale and adversely affected the hunt. He successfully importuned Catherine II to send a religious mission to the colonies in order to regularize baptisms and end the unfortunate competition for converts.

In 1794, ten Orthodox monks arrived on Kodiak Island. While they were sent by order of the empress and were under the supervision of an abbot, Ioasaph, they were in a sense employees of the Russian-American Company. Throughout the Russian occupation of Alaska, and even until 1917, clerics were supported by company funds, and after the company left, the imperial treasury. This should not be surprising, as the church in Russia enjoyed state patronage, and monasteries—of which Alaska's mission was an extension—were financed by the state. After Russia sold Alaska, Metropolitan Innocent founded a Missionary Society for the support of schools and orphanages in American Alaska, although the clergy continued to receive a stipend from the Russian government.

Their financial obligation to the Russian State notwithstanding, the missionaries understood their role in the colonies as moral overseers of the Russians, as well as enlighteners of the Aleuts. The company officials obviously wanted the monks to confine themselves to the latter task. Their very different assignments led to frequent clashes between the company and the missionaries. The missionaries strongly objected to the attitudes, style of life, and methods of the company officials, particularly Alexander Baranov's. A major source of tension was the company's treatment of the Aleut population. Several of the first missionaries participated in mutinies against Baranov's rule, and one even went so far as to leave his post without authorization to carry the complaints to St. Petersburg. Both Count Nikolai Rezanov and Naval Lieutenant Vasilii Golovnin visited the mission on their

...Although a foreign implant, Orthodoxy has become identified as "the old way," distinct from American institutions—a powerful appeal in the culturally conservative villages of rural Alaska.

inspection trips in 1805 and 1809, respectively, and drew valuable information from their conversations with the monks. From their findings, important changes were effected in the operations of the company. These were reflected especially in Rezanov's management proposals to Baranov and in Golovnin's proposals for the company's charter renewal in 1821.

The monk most often consulted was German (anglicized as Herman), an elder who had built a dwelling on Spruce Island, near Kodiak. Herman preferred the hermit's life, but his natural sympathy and common sense drew him frequently into society. In addition to advising high Russian officials, he began both a school and an orphanage and started Russian America's first agricultural program. The inspiration of his life and personal qualities left an indelible mark on many, and in 1970, in ceremonies in Kodiak, the worldwide Orthodox communion canonized him as Saint Herman, North America's first Orthodox saint.

Ioann Veniaminov

Another remarkable individual entered the Alaska mission in 1824. Ioann Veniaminov arrived at Unalaska in 1824 as that island's first resident priest; in 1834 he transferred to the capital, Sitka, at the invitation of the company management. Veniaminov left his mark in both places and for posterity by establishing a style of operation that later would be applied to a larger field, when he became Bishop Innocent of Alaska in 1840 and later Metropolitan, head of the church in Imperial Russia. In every position he held, his work was characterized by an attention to literacy, education, and development of local, that is Native, leadership of the mission. He also was a careful observer of the scene about him and has left a seminal ethnography of the Aleuts

as well as valuable observations on Tlingit life and custom. He devised alphabets for the Aleuts and the Tlingits and translated sacred texts and sermons into these languages; he charged priests in his care to do the same. He designed and built the first church at Unalaska and the cathedral in Sitka; his models were used by priests throughout Alaska in building churches in

ICON OF THE Four Saints of Alaska, by Byron Birdsall, 1988. Birdsall is primarily a watercolorist, whose landscapes have included a very popular series of Orthodox churches. Since 1988 the religious art of the icon has inspired this versatile artist, who is not Orthodox. He has produced more than one hundred paintings in the classic iconographic tradition using his own watercolor technique. In 1988 he created an original painting, in watercolor and gold leaf, of Alaska's four Orthodox saints, with the intention of giving it to the Cathedral of St. Innocent in Anchorage for resale to help the building fund. At the presentation, the Bishop of Anchorage blessed the painting and named it an icon, and it now hangs above the altar of the cathedral in Anchorage.

Reproduction courtesy of the artist.

posts as diverse as Russian Mission on the Yukon and St. Nicholas in Juneau. He also was a humane and learned man. He introduced vaccination to the Tlingit people, overcoming their natural fear, and thus saved many lives during the smallpox epidemic of 1836.

As bishop, Innocent also presided over an expansion of the Orthodox mission from four parishes to nine, including a cathedral and thirty-five chapels. From a rather limited parish concept, confined to the areas with the largest concentration of Russians, the mission in twenty-seven years came to embrace vast regions, populated almost exclusively by Natives. The number of clergy assigned to cover all of Russian America south of Norton Sound was thirty-two in 1866, including all priests and their assistants. This compares with four in 1840, at the start of Innocent's episcopacy.

Creole Priests

The Orthodox mission, under Innocent's leadership, emphasized lay leadership, literacy, advocacy on behalf of Native people, and toleration of Native culture and language. The development of local talent was not exclusively a mission policy, but also had been followed by the Russian-American Company. By 1828, a Creole (Aleut-Russian) priest, Iakov Netsvetov, was serving at Atka, having received his training at seminary in Irkutsk; he later went on to open the Orthodox mission on the Yukon River. He was followed at Atka by a succession of Creole priests, and Russian Mission on the Yukon was served for many years by an Aleut priest who trained under Netsvetov.

Native clergy followed Veniaminov at Unalaska, trained in the school he established there and also in the seminary that

ST. HERMAN of Alaska, the first Orthodox saint from North America. The monk Herman was one of the missionaries who arrived at Kodiak from Russia in 1794. He was glorified (Orthodox terminology for naming of a saint) in ceremonies at Kodiak in 1970.

Anchorage Museum of History and Art.

he, as Bishop Innocent, founded at Sitka. Other Native clergy, trained during the Russian time, continued to serve the mission well into the American era. Aside from ordained clergy, the church also promoted local lay leadership, those many individuals who sustain a liturgical church in the absence of a priest.

Education

The Orthodox mission also was active in promoting schools and literacy; it was charged by the imperial government with the major responsibility for education in the colonies. Aside from Bishop Innocent's activity, other missionaries were active in this regard. Father Herman founded a school and a seminary near Kodiak, on Spruce Island. Iakov Netsvetov and his successors on the Yukon and Kuskokwim rivers founded and maintained schools. The schools could not be in constant operation, due to uncertain finances and the seasonal life of the Native clientele, but a consistent effort does appear to have been made well into the twentieth century. It also was official church policy to provide the Natives with sacred writings in their own language. Not only Innocent, but also his protege, Netsvetov, devised alphabets and translated a number of religious works into several dialects of Aleut; the same was accomplished in the Yukon and Kuskokwim area, and in southeastern Alaska.

Tolerant of Native languages from the outset, as noted by Michael Krauss elsewhere in this volume, the Orthodox also displayed a toleration for Native customs uncommon among Christian missions. The clearest enunciation of this policy is found in a set of "Instructions" issued in 1868 by the newly ordained Metropolitan Innocent as a guide to missionaries in Alaska; the instructions reflect Innocent's administration also as Bishop

REV. GERASIM Schmaltz, portrait by Alvin Amason. Father Gerasim was the priest in Kodiak for many years and was godfather to Amason, of Koniag descent. This is one of the first works by the well-known artist, but is atypical of his current work, which focuses on the world of nature.

Kodiak Historical Society.

of Alaska from 1840 to 1858. Among the principles spelled out in great detail are admonitions to administer baptism only after instruction and at the expressed desire of the Native, to be courteous, patient, simple in address, and understanding of both Native culture and tradition and also of all types of spiritual questions. The great bishop also urged toleration in all things, and absence of officiousness regarding fasts and required attendance at ordinary services except the Divine Liturgy. He also advised against overobservance of the forbidden degrees of relationship in marriage (due to "the scantiness of the local population"). Instruction Number 21 also admonishes: "Ancient customs, so long as they are not contrary to Christianity, need not be too abruptly broken up; but it should be explained to converts that they are merely tolerated."[2]

A Bumpy Road

It would be a mistake, however, to suggest that Orthodoxy has had a smooth path since 1867. Quite the contrary. It enjoyed a revival during the early American period, but was at low ebb from 1920 to 1965. In the last twenty years it has experienced an explosive renewal that rivals the early years of Russian occupation. Some statistics will reveal the dimension of recent growth. While there were only nine full-time clergy for all eighty Orthodox communities in 1972, there were thirty-five in 1989. More than half of these are Native—Aleut, Eskimo, and Tlingit.

While Orthodoxy's greatest success in its early years was among the Aleuts, who are still predominantly Orthodox, the new growth has been among the Yup'ik of the Kuskokwim and Yukon deltas, with a majority of the new Native clergy coming from this region. In the period 1967-89, six new parishes were formed, while established communities built thirty-three new structures. The Alaska Diocese supports a seminary dedicated to St. Herman, which has trained 115 students since 1974; almost all are Alaska Natives. The seminary is accredited by the state of Alaska to offer a two-year degree, Associate of Arts in Theological Studies, and a four-year Bachelor of Sacred Theology degree. The underlying causes of this renaissance reveal much about the nature and appeal of Orthodoxy to today's Alaskan.

Protestant Missions

The first flowering of Orthodoxy in the years after 1867 may be explained by Russia's willingness to take up the challenge posed by competition from Protestant missions. Methodist, Moravian, Congregationalist, Episcopalian, Quaker, and Presbyterian missions assumed the responsibility until the turn of the century for bringing American education to Alaskan villages. At first led by Metropolitan Innocent (Veniaminov) in his post as head of the Russian Orthodox church and later by the Russian Foreign Missions Society, the Alaska mission received thousands of dollars from Russia. It spent more on schools in Alaska from 1867 to 1884 than the United States government did.[3] It sponsored several translation and publishing programs that brought both literacy and religious literature to thousands of Alaska Natives.

Following Metropolitan Innocent's "Instructions," Alaska bishops (always Russian) and clergy (Natives, Creoles, and Russians) encouraged local lay leadership by generous dispensation of awards to diligent parishioners. As the Protestant schools and American policy increasingly forbade the use of Native languages in school and removed children from home and community for education, the Orthodox bishops sounded repeated appeals for preservation of language, family, and community. For all that Article III of the Treaty of Sale assured free exercise of religion and protection of property to the Orthodox Church, most of the "new Alaskans"—government and military officials, gold miners, entrepreneurs, adventurers—considered the black-robed, black-capped Orthodox clergy a foreign intrusion. Until 1917, however, the Orthodox were able to more than hold their own, even increasing the number of clergy.

The Russian Revolution brought an end to Imperial Russia and government support of religion. The Alaska Orthodox mission suffered a catastrophic loss in revenue and personnel during the years from 1917 to 1967. Headquartered in New York, the North American diocese, which broke with the Soviet-dominated church in Moscow, struggled to survive and had no resources to expend on its distant northern mission. Clergy in Alaska aged and died and were not replaced. Schools closed for lack of teachers and supplies. Publication aimed at Native Alaskans ceased. Remarkably, it was a devastating fire in 1966 that ignited the revival of Orthodoxy.

St. Michael's Cathedral

In January 1966, St. Michael's Cathedral, as well as much of downtown Sitka, burned to the ground. The loss of the historic structure, built by Bishop Innocent himself, focused attention on the plight of Alaska's Orthodox. In Sitka, citizens of every religious persuasion worked together to raise money to rebuild the cathedral, just as they had saved nearly every sacred object during the fire. Using architectural drawings that the U.S. Historic American Building Survey had made only four years earlier, the citizens' committee was successful. In 1976, a replica of the original Cathedral of the Archangel Michael was consecrated and is today a functioning house of worship, the episcopal see for the Diocese of Sitka and Alaska.

The campaign to raise money for the cathedral was a national one and brought Alaska once again to the attention of Orthodox in the eastern and midwestern United States. Another event brought many of these to Alaska. In Kodiak in 1970, in international ceremonies, Father Herman was canonized as the first Orthodox saint of North America. The presence of St. Herman's relics has made Kodiak a place of pilgrimage for Orthodox worldwide. Some pilgrims stay on to work for a time in the mission or to teach at St. Herman's Seminary. Bishop Gregory (Afonsky) and the diocesan chancellor, Very Reverend Joseph Kreta, established the school in 1974 to train Native Alaskans to serve their own churches. Nearly half of the eighty-eight Orthodox communities now have resident clergy who live and work beside their parishioners, as few communities can afford a full-time priest.

A New Vitality

A new group of Alaskan Orthodox saints have brought the Alaskan mission into additional favor. In 1977 the great bishop of Alaska was canonized as St. Innocent by the Russian church, with the designation "Apostle to America." More recently, the Orthodox have canonized two Alaskan martyrs: Juvenalii, one of the original band of ten who was killed by Natives in 1796, and Peter the Aleut, who died in

California under torture when he refused to renounce Orthodoxy for his Spanish captors.

The current Alaska leadership of the Orthodox church has been able to till a well-prepared soil. The Orthodox faith was planted and nurtured by Russian stewards both before and

THIS LOCK is associated with the first Orthodox Church of the Holy Ascension of Our Lord at Unalaska, founded and built by Rev. Ioann Veniaminov (St. Innocent) in 1825. The present structure is the third church on the site and is a National Historic Landmark.

National Museum of American History, Smithsonian Institution.

after the sale of Alaska. The reasons for Orthodoxy's tenacious hold on the loyalties of its Native Alaskan adherents are the subject of lively debate, reflected in this volume. Scholars who are Orthodox emphasize the affinity of several Native cultures to Orthodox theology and argue that conversion was both welcome and painless. Other scholars hotly dispute this claim, noting that the Aleuts, in particular, were a subject people, forced to conform. What can be agreed is that the rich liturgical life of the Orthodox did have appeal.

Whatever the reasons for the initial conversion, the Church gained long-term loyalty in large measure because of its support of Native language, community-based education, and preservation of many Native customs. Lay leaders, cultivated by Russian government and church policy, maintained the religious community even when a priest was absent for many years. Further, although a foreign implant, Orthodoxy has become identified as "the old way," distinct from American institutions—a powerful appeal in the culturally conservative villages of rural Alaska.

It should not then be surprising that Orthodoxy, given new support at the local level by a vigorous diocesan leadership, would enjoy a revival in present-day Alaska. What is more surprising is the growing public awareness of the important historical and cultural contributions of the Orthodox in Alaska. Only a few years ago, the common view among historians was that Orthodoxy was either already dead or that it would gradually fade away. This theme was taken from the dean of Alaskan historians, Hubert Howe Bancroft, who in 1886 declared:

> *It must be admitted that the Greek [sic] Church was a failure throughout Russian America.... It is nowhere recorded, except by the priests themselves, that with the single exception of Veniaminov, the teaching of the ecclesiastics made much impression on the natives.*[4]

During the last fifteen years, several scholarly studies have focused on the role of the Orthodox church in fostering Native culture, while a number of primary sources have been made available to English readers. A variety of citizens and public agencies have become concerned about the fate of historic church structures, difficult to maintain in the Alaskan climate by residents of the state's poorest villages. In recent years the Alaska Legislature, the Alaska Region of the National Park Service, and a citizens' group, the Icon

Preservation Task Force, have joined forces to identify and restore Orthodox churches and furnishings. As noted by Kathleen Lidfors and Steven Peterson elsewhere in this volume, the churches on the National Register of Historic Places have captured the attention of historians, architects, artists, and public agencies. As a result of these several developments, Alaska's unique Native Orthodox expression, once considered by many Alaskans as foreign and even irrelevant, is now being treated by scholars and the popular media with growing intelligence, affection, and understanding of its historical and cultural importance to Alaska.

In the 120 years since Russia sold Alaska, the Russian cultural legacy has survived, largely fostered by the Orthodox church. The Orthodox faith, expressed here in the rich liturgical practice of the Russians, gained the devotion of Alaska's Native people, particularly the Aleuts and Yup'ik Eskimos. Maintaining churches and chapels through years of financial destitution and without clerical staff, more than eighty Native communities kept the faith alive and thereby preserved for today Russian America's unique contribution to North American culture.

Barbara Sweetland Smith owns Alaska Historical Resources, an Anchorage consulting firm, and is curator of the exhibit, "Russian America: The Forgotten Frontier."

For Further Reading

Afonsky, Gregory, Bishop. *A History of the Orthodox Church in Alaska, 1794-1917.* Kodiak, Alaska: St. Herman's Theological Seminary Press, 1977.

Alaskan Missionary Spirituality. Ed. Michael Oleksa. New York: Paulist Press, 1987.

" 'The Condition of the Orthodox Church in Russian America': Innokentii Veniaminov's History of the Russian Church in Alaska." Ed. and trans. Robert Nichols and Robert Croskey. *Pacific Northwest Quarterly* LXIII, no. 2 (April 1972), pp. 41-54.

Garrett, Paul D. *Saint Innocent, Apostle to America.* Crestwood, New York: St. Vladimir's Seminary Press, 1979.

The Journals of Iakov Netsvetov: The Atka Years, 1828-1844. Trans. Lydia T. Black. *Alaska History Series* 16. Kingston, Ontario: Limestone Press, 1980.

The Journals of Iakov Netsvetov: The Yukon Years, 1845-1863. Ed. Richard A. Pierce, trans. Lydia T. Black. *Alaska History Series* 26. Kingston, Ontario: Limestone Press, 1984.

The Round-the-World Voyage of Hieromonk Gideon, 1803-1809. Ed. Richard A. Pierce, trans. Lydia T. Black. *Alaska History Series* 32. Kingston, Ontario, and Fairbanks, Alaska: Limestone Press, 1989.

The Russian Religious Mission in America, 1794-1837, with Materials Concerning the Life and Works of the Monk German, and Ethnographic Notes by the Hieromonk Gideon. Ed. Richard A. Pierce, trans. Colin Bearne. *Alaska History Series* 11. Kingston, Ontario: Limestone Press, 1978.

Smith, Barbara Sweetland. *Orthodoxy and Native Americans: The Alaska Mission.* Orthodox Historical Society, Occasional Paper No. 1. Crestwood, New York: St. Vladimir's Seminary Press, 1980.

Notes

1. " 'The Condition of the Orthodox Church in Russian America': Innokentii Veniaminov's History of the Russian Church in Alaska," ed. and trans. Robert Nichols and Robert Croskey, *Pacific Northwest Quarterly* LXIII, no. 2 (April 1972), p. 45.

2. Innocent (Veniaminov), Metropolitan of Moscow, "Instructions...to the Missionary of Nushagak, Theophanus, Hieromonk," reprinted in *Russko-amerikanskii pravoslavnyi vestnik [Russian Orthodox American Messenger]* III, pp. 20, 21 (1899), pp. 534-543, 564-574 (Russian and English).

3. In 1884, the U.S. Congress made its first appropriation for education in Alaska, $25,000, which it increased to $40,000 in 1885. In 1887, the governor of the Alaska Territory, A. P. Swineford, reported that the Russian Government made an annual appropriation "for the support of the Greco-Russian Church in Alaska the sum of $40,000; for schools and other extraordinary expenses, $20,000." U.S. Congress: House of Representatives, 50th Congress, 1st session; Executive Document No. 1: Annual Report of the Secretary of Interior, 1887; vol. X, no. 1: Annual Report of the Governor of Alaska, p. 715.

4. H. H. Bancroft, *History of Alaska, 1730-1885* (1886; New York: Antiquarian Press Ltd., 1959), p. 704.

Lenders

Russian America: The Forgotten Frontier," an exhibition organized by the Washington State Historical Society and the Anchorage Museum of History and Art, benefited from the willingness of the following individuals and institutions to lend artifacts or photographs:

Akhiok Village, Kodiak Island

Alaska State Library

Alaska State Museum

American Geographic Society Collection, University of Wisconsin, Milwaukee

Anchorage Municipal Libraries

Anchorage Museum of History and Art

Archives of Foreign Policy of Russia, USSR

Joe Ashby

Baker Library, Harvard University

Bancroft Library, University of California, Berkeley

Beinecke Library, Yale University

Byron Birdsall

Lydia T. Black

The Thomas Burke Memorial Washington State Museum, University of Washington

California State Department of Parks and Recreation

Central Naval Museum, USSR

Denver Art Museum

Virginia Drugg

Fort Nisqually Historic Site

Chester Gordon

Beatrice Halkett

George A. Hall

John H. Hauberg

Henry Art Gallery, University of Washington

Heritage Library-Museum, National Bank of Alaska

Historic American Buildings Survey, National Park Service

Historical Society of Seattle and King County

Honeychurch Antiques

Hudson's Bay Company Archives, Provincial Archives of Manitoba

Henry E. Huntington Art Gallery and Library

Hobart B. Hyatt

Icon Preservation Task Force

Joe Kelly

Kodiak Area Native Association

Kodiak Historical Society

Archpriest Joseph Kreta

Kuskokwim Corporation

William H. Lamme

The Library of Congress

Lowie Museum of Anthropology, University of California, Berkeley

Main Archival Administration of the USSR

Massachusetts Historical Society

The Metropolitan Museum of Art

Archpriest Nicholas Molodyko-Harris

James A. Moody

Museum of Anthropology and Ethnography, Institute of Ethnography, Academy of Sciences, USSR

Museum Palaces and Park of Petrodvorets, USSR

Mutter Museum, College of Physicians of Philadelphia

The National Archives

National Museum of American History, Smithsonian Institution

National Museum of Finland

National Park Service, Alaska Region

Oregon Historical Society

Orthodox Diocese of Sitka and Alaska

Peabody Museum, Salem

Richard A. Pierce

Pratt Museum

Elmer E. Rasmuson Library, University of Alaska, Fairbanks

Royal Ontario Museum

St. Herman's Theological Seminary

San Diego Historical Society

Scalamandré

Scientific-Research Museum, Academy of Arts, USSR

Seattle Art Museum

Security Pacific Bank

Sheldon Jackson Museum

Sitka Historical Society

Sitka Lutheran Church

Sitka National Historical Park

Gregory N. Solak

South Street Seaport Museum

State Historical Museum, USSR

State Russian Museum, USSR

State Unified Museum of Irkutsk, USSR

United States Department of Agriculture, Forest Service

University of Alaska, Anchorage

University of Washington Library, Special Collections

University of Wisconsin, Madison

Douglas W. Veltre

Washington State Historical Society

The Wing Luke Asian Museum

Richard Allen Wood, Alaska Heritage Book Shop